Christ Way, Buddha Way

Jesus as Wisdom Teacher and a Zen Perspective on His Teachings

Also by Tim Langdell from
StillCenter Publications:

Kenosis: Christian Self-Emptying Meditation

Beginner's Mind: An Introduction to Zen

The Practice of the Presence of God by Brother Lawrence with a Christian Meditation Practice Guide by Tim Langdell

A series of books by Evelyn Underhill with Tim Langdell (*Mysticism, Practical Mysticism, The Mystic Way, The Essentials of Mysticism*)

Coming soon by Tim Langdell
from StillCenter Publications:

Now Voyager: The Art of Conscious Living

Mindful Moment: Using Mindfulness to Find Peace in a Stressful World

By Tim Langdell
from Oxbridge Publishing

The Rise of the Angeliti: Book One of the Oxbridge Trilogy

And with Cheri Langdell
from Praeger

Coping with Vision Loss: Understanding the Psychological, Social, and Spiritual Effects

Christ Way, Buddha Way

Jesus as Wisdom Teacher and a Zen Perspective on His Teachings

Tim Langdell

StillCenter Publications
An imprint of Oxbridge Publishing Inc.
Pasadena, California/Oxford, UK

StillCenter Publications
An imprint of Oxbridge Publishing Inc.
Oxford/Pasadena
530 South Lake Avenue, 171
Pasadena, CA 91101
www.oxbridgepublishing.com

Library of Congress Cataloging-in-Publication Data
Langdell, Tim
Christ Way, Buddha Way: Jesus as Wisdom Teacher and a Zen Perspective on His Teachings / Tim Langdell
pages cm
ISBN: 0-9990928-7-1 (pbk)
ISBN-13: 978-0-9990928-7-3 (pbk)
1. Contemplation 2. Mystical Union
3. Zen Buddhism I. Title

Library of Congress Control Number: 2020940401

9 8 7 6 5 4 3 2 1

FIRST EDITION

"I couldn't understand the Christian teaching the way I do if it weren't in the light of Buddhism"

Thomas Merton[1]

Dedicated to my wife, Cheri

---

[11] Aitken & Steindel-Rast, 47; Frank Tuoti, *The Dawn of the Mystical Age,* 1997, 127

Contents

Acknowledgements

It would be impossible for me to acknowledge everyone who has assisted me or influenced me in the writing of this book. The initial idea for this book came to me in June of 1990. I am painfully aware that this book thus took me thirty years to complete. But in a real sense it had to take me this long because there are certain people who came into my life, certain learning experiences I had, only in recent years that enabled its completion.

In part I knew I had to wait until there was greater acceptance in the wider audience to an alternate reading of Christ's teachings and the parallels with Zen. The books by Andrew Harvey, Marcus Borg, John Dominic Crossan and Cynthia Bourgeault helped pave the way as have more recent books by Richard Rohr. A turning point occurred in about 2000 when I read Andrew Harvey's *Son of Man: The Mystical Path to Christ*, around the same time Marcus Borg gave a talk at All Saints Episcopal Church in Pasadena, reading from his book *Reading the Bible Again for the First Time: Taking the Bible Seriously but Not Literally*. And then of course again in 2008 with Cynthia's seminal work, *The Wisdom Jesus* which echoed so closely the writing I had been doing on this book since the early 1990s.

Then more recently we have had the wonderful works by Richard Rohr, *The Naked Now* (2009), *Immortal Diamond: The Search for Our True Self* (2013), *What the Mystics Know* (2015) and *The Universal Christ* (2019). I have been very fortunate to have met with Marcus Borg and Richard Rohr a number of times and am deeply grateful for their teachings.

The earliest influences on me, though, were Douglas Harding (*On Having No Head*) and Alan Watts—literally everything he ever wrote—and Shunryu Suzuki (*Zen Mind, Beginner's Mind*). I was nineteen when I was already deep in my study and practice of Zen and what I and close friends called "mystical Christianity," when I had a *metanoia/ kensho* experience. I had just attended a talk by the incomparable Douglas Harding and shall probably write more about that in a future work. This was also a time I was reading works by such writers as Evelyn Underhill (*Mysticism*) and of course Thomas Merton (*Seven Story Mountain, Zen and the Birds of Appetite, Mystics and Zen Masters).*

Over this early period, I was greatly blessed to have Douglas as my Zen teacher and Archbishop Michael Ramsey and Brother Edward of the UK Franciscan Order as my occasional Christian mentors. There were many others, of course, such as my Psychology Professor at Leicester University, Derek Wright, to whom I am also deeply indebted for helping me wake up. Around this time, too, I had my first meeting in Los Angeles in 1973 with Maezumi Roshi at the Los Angeles Zen Center. That was also probably the first time I met Bernie Glassman.

More recently the influences on me have been my primary Zen teacher, Venerable Wonji Dharma (Paul Lynch), my Christian mentors (Archbishop Emeritus Robert Mary Clement and Archbishop Adrian Ravarour of the ACC and Presiding Bishop Francis Krebs of the ECC) and an array of wonderful people I have been blessed to walk this broad spiritual path with such as the remarkable Yuval Ron.

While this is by no means a full list of those I am grateful to, even this partial list would not be complete without mention of the wonderful support I have had from our cherished daughter, Reverend Melissa Campbell Langdell, and in particular my phenomenal wife, Cheri, without whose support and editing skills this book would never have been completed.

That all said, the contents of this book are my own views and not necessarily shared by any of those I mention above.

PREFACE

First, what this book is not about: it is *not* one of those books that attempts to prove Jesus of Nazareth visited either India or Tibet, or that he was really a Buddhist. What the book *is* about, though, is looking at Christ's teachings again as if for the first time and seeing that in many respects his teachings parallel the teachings of Buddha and his style of teaching resembles that of Zen masters.

This does not mean Jesus was "Buddhist" (although Mahayana Buddhist teachings had reached the Middle East by his time) but rather because what he taught is universal truth, we should not be surprised to find parallels with the Buddha's teachings. That said, as we'll see, it seems certain Christ was aware of Buddhism.

My entire adult life I have identified as both a Christian and as a Zen Buddhist. Indeed, the earliest (very rough) draft of this book was in 1990 when I first started to put my ideas down in writing about both Zen and Christian Mysticism. I am both an ordained Christian Priest as well as an ordained Zen Buddhist Priest and Zen Master Teacher who has received Dharma Transmission. Like many others with this dual religious self-identification (or "dual empowerment" as some rather ostentatiously put it), I have faced perplexity and numerous comments of disbelief such as "But how can you be both a Christian and a Buddhist when Buddhists don't believe in God?" Many of the same people would also comment "Christian Mysticism is a contradiction in terms. You can't be a Christian *and* a mystic."

On the contrary, I found a true home in Zen Buddhist

practice and an equally comfortable home in the teachings of Christ, and in the writings of many so-called Christian mystics, including in particular writers such as Thomas Merton, Evelyn Underhill and Richard Rohr. My Buddhism feeds and nourishes my Christianity, and vice versa. Moreover, when later in adulthood I finally got round to reading the New Testament "properly" for the first time, I was immediately struck by the incredible similarities between the teachings of the Siddhartha Gautama (known by the title "Buddha" meaning the "Awakened One") and the teachings of Jesus of Nazareth (known by the title "Christ" meaning "the anointed one").

The goal of this book is not to convince or persuade you of anything—rather, it is to invite you to consider what is written here and find out *what is true for you*, what you feel comfortable with, right where you are, right now in this moment. The purpose here is not to debate the "truth" or comparative merits of the life and teachings of the historical Jesus ("Christ") and historical Siddhartha ("Buddha"), but rather to present common themes and offer them for your consideration with the prospect that you may see the teachings of Christ, in particular, in a new light.

If you find a point of interest then I invite you to follow it, contemplate it, live with it, savor it. But if anything in this book doesn't "click" for you, skip over it, do not linger on it, but rather perhaps consider returning to it at some later date. Each of our spiritual paths (for want of a better term) is unique to us: no two are the same. The core invitation in this book is to awaken to who you truly are. Your path to this awakening— the "Way" that you personally travel— is absolutely unique to you, and I invite you to follow it with a deep vibrant *passion*.

As a general note, I have endeavored to use "Jesus" when I

am speaking of the historical person, and "Christ" when I speak of Jesus in his role as Wisdom teacher or of the universal Christ. I do not, though, claim to have been entirely consistent with this goal.

1

Jesus: Wisdom Tradition Teacher

This book is in part about the parallels between the teachings of Jesus (known as Christ) and Siddhartha Gautama (known as Buddha). But it is also about re-viewing Jesus' teachings again in a new light, and in large part through the lens of Zen.

There is only *one* Truth as to who you truly are: how that Truth is realized and communicated varies according to the time, place, and culture it manifests in. So, in one instance the Truth is realized and taught through an atheistic lens, whereas in the other it is realized and taught through a theistic lens. I invite you to set aside any preconceptions you may have about what you may believe to be fundamental differences between theistic and atheistic traditions and be open to the commonalities in the teachings.

Let's start with what may be a revelation to some readers: in a sense, both a key that can help us start to unlock Jesus' teachings in the Gospels, and a way to transform our appreciation of what he was teaching. It has been said by leading scholars that quite possibly the single worst translation of any word in the entire Bible is the word *metanoia*. This word is used several places in the Gospels and is most often translated as "repent" or "repentance." Perhaps one of the most well-known instances occurs in the book of Mark (Mk 1:15) *"The time has come," he said, "The Kingdom of God has come near. Repent and believe the good news!"* Or the version in Matthew (Mt 3:2) *"Repent, for the Kingdom of Heaven has come near.*"[1]

Others, building on the mistranslation of the word *metanoia*, even add words not in the original, thus: "*Repent of your sins and turn to God, for the Kingdom of Heaven is near*" (*New Living Bible*). And from this simple mistranslation we get an entire theology of our needing to repent our sins so that after we die, we will go to a place called "Heaven." But that is not what Jesus taught. What he taught was a way to the transformation of consciousness—a fundamental transformation of heart and mind—to a state of being he termed Heaven within, or Heaven on earth. He described this as becoming a Son (or Daughter) of God in the here and now.

Metanoia is made up of two parts: "*meta*" which means above or beyond, and "*noia*" which means mind or thought. Literally, then, what Jesus was teaching was that in order to enter the spiritual state he called "Heaven" (or, "Heaven within you") you must first go beyond thinking or enter into a state of "above" (or "big") mind.[2]

Or put even more simply, in order to enter Heaven—which Jesus makes clear is *here and now* in this moment—you must experience a spiritual awakening. Does this surprise you? Perhaps it should, since this is rarely taught in virtually any main-stream Christian churches, Protestant or Catholic, as the core of Jesus' teaching. Yet that is precisely what it is.

Associated with such mistranslation arose an entire sin-based theology which while generally absent in the synoptic Gospels (Mark, Matthew, Luke) rears its head in the much later written John and in the works of Paul. A theology that includes an emphasis on Original Sin and the idea that God sent his "only begotten son," Jesus, to die for our sins (the so-called substitutionary atonement theology). For many, this idea that we are born sinners is a difficult one to accept since it does not seem to fit with the actions of a loving Creator, the God that Jesus speaks of as *being* Love. And it is even more difficult to accept the idea of the loving God of which Jesus spoke being so cruel as to sacrifice "his (only) son."

It may thus come as somewhat of a relief to learn that this theology—one so heavily based on sin and repentance in order to go to Heaven after you die—was an invention of the Early and Medieval Churches that sadly persists to the modern day. Yes, it is supported by the Gospel of John and the writings of Paul. But it is well to bear in mind how much later John was written (one to two lifetimes after Jesus' death given the average lifespan in the first century Middle East was about 38 years), and that Paul never met Jesus. John is also widely regarded to have the least number of accurate attributions to Jesus or his teachings. In a nutshell, the Gospel of John contains the most words attributed to Jesus, but the fewest words that scholars believe he actually said.

Rather than a focus on Original Sin, then, some authors—notably Matthew Fox[3]—have suggested it is better to talk of Original Blessing (perhaps paralleling the Zen teaching "it's all good"[4]). And rather than a theology of sin and repentance, and a focus on what happens to you after you die, some are finding inspiration in a new appreciation of Christ's teachings as coming from the Jewish Wisdom Tradition of his time, teachings that focus on non-dualistic thought, a focus on the here and now, on unity with all creation and on spiritual awakening.

Most Christians have been taught that to be a Christian involves believing in doctrine that includes such fundamentals as virgin birth, original sin, repentance and the forgiveness of sins in order to go to Heaven after you die, Jesus as the only son of God, and so on. As Marcus Borg has pointed out, much of this doctrine was invented many years after Christ's time, or invented by Saul of Tarsus (Paul) who never met Christ and it runs contrary to Christ's teachings. But what were Christ's *actual* teachings? The simple fact is that the writings we have inherited—the ones we call the canonical Gospels as well as others such as the Gospel of Thomas—are a mixed bag of teachings some of which were likely said by Jesus, some that bear a resemblance to what he said, some that are little more than *at best* in the spirit of what he said, and a remaining sizable portion of which he simply did not say.[5]

Rather, such ideas were introduced many years after the time of Jesus and were codified in so-called "creeds" such as the one arising from the Council of Nicaea (325 CE) from which we get the Nicene Creed. This was followed by six further so-called ecumenical councils: The First Council of Constantinople (381 CE), Council of Ephesus (431 CE), Council of Chalcedon (451 CE), Second Council of Constantinople (553 CE), Third Council of Constantinople (680-681 CE) and the Second Council of Nicaea (787 CE).

Out of these seven councils emerged an *invented* Christian theology that does not reflect what Jesus actually taught, but rather what certain groups of men worked out (to *their* way of thinking) what Christ's teaching meant, what the nature of God, Christ and the Holy Spirit is, why Christ came, what he accomplished, and so forth.

This is not revolutionary or blasphemous thinking about the Gospels, or about the creeds, this is what is taught in many respectable Christian seminaries both in the U.S. and around the world. Why, then, is this so at odds with what priests and other clergy teach on Sundays in Christian churches worldwide? The answer to that is a long and complex one, and ultimately doesn't matter. What matters is that we focus as far as we are able on what Christ actually taught.

When we focus on what Christ taught, we find that his teachings have far more in common with Buddhist teaching that Christians are usually led to believe. It also becomes easier to understand why so many of Christ's parables are also found in Buddhist texts from hundreds of years before the time of Christ, and why Buddha and Christ are unique in their similar use of such stories to convey and enhance their teachings.

This is not to say there are not significant differences in the teachings of Christ and Buddha. To address one elephant in the room, clearly Christ grew up in a theistic culture that was rooted in belief in a Creator God. But what I suggest may be helpful is to consider what Buddha's teachings might have been like if he had been born a Jew in the time and culture of Christ. If he, like Jesus, had become very religious—very spiritual—at a young age, experienced a spiritual awakening and felt a calling to teach, might he perhaps have evolved teachings not unlike those of Christ?

While there is some dispute about the society and culture Buddha was born into, at the time of his birth around 500-600 years before Christ India had a rich religious and philosophical tradition rooted in what are known as the Vedas. There are numerous polytheistic references in these very early Indian writings stretching back to at least 2,000-2,500 B.C.E., but by the time of the Buddha we see the rise of the Upanishads whose core teaching is the realization that you are Atman (soul or true self), which is the same as Brahman (ultimate supreme soul or universal self). While the Indian Atman and Brahman were not seen as Gods—certainly not in the Middle Eastern sense of theism—there was a general trend from polytheism to awareness of a single "True" self which is identical with a Universal Self.

Arguably, this had its parallels in the Jewish tradition Christ was born into in the first century C.E. The Jews too had moved from being essentially polytheistic to coming closer and closer to monotheism (although as one of my professors at seminary taught, James Sanders, its arguable that by the time of Christ the Jewish religion was still not really monotheism since they worshiped Yahweh as the one true God *of the Jews*, not the one true God of Gentiles, too. Indeed, it is arguable that Christianity became the first truly monotheistic religion that taught of a single God for all peoples, Jews and Gentiles alike.

Thus, if we imagine for a moment Buddha being born some 500-600 years later in this Middle Eastern culture, immersed in Jewish tradition and religion, when he had an awakening moment would he have interpreted in terms of his culture as a mystical experience of union with God? Much perhaps as the great Persian poet and Sufi mystic, Rumi, did some 1,200 years later? And if so, how would that have impacted Buddha's teaching, or at least the words he chose to use to teach his realization? Possibly, his teachings would have more closely resembled those of Jesus.

By the time of Christ, the kingly class had ceased, the priestly class no longer ruled Jewish society and they had elevated God to that of a being whose name should never be uttered and who was remote from humankind. It had become central to the Jewish religion that God be known by the tetragrammaton of YHWA or JHVA, all consonants and no vowels so that the name was not designed to be spoken. And along came Jesus and taught not just of a proximal God, and intimate God, but one so close that Jesus referred to him as "abba."

This word is typically translated in the New Testament as "father," but in reality the better translation for the West is "dad" or "papa"—certainly a more familiar and intimate term than "father." That isn't to say Christ's word *abba* meant dad or papa and not father, on the contrary there weren't different words in Aramaic for the familiar and formal forms. But in Western English, "father" can connote a far more formal term than it would have been understood to be in the context of Christ's teachings.

At this distance in time it can be easy to miss just how revolutionary Christ's teachings were, starting with his referring to God in such intimate terms. Of course, this wasn't Christ's only revolutionary gesture: there were many more that we will return to later in this book. For instance, while the powers that be in the established Jewish religion shunned contact with unclean persons, Jesus went out of his way to associate with those on the margins of society such as tax collectors and prostitutes. And in an exceptionally male dominated society (hence God is referred to as male), we learn that wealthy women financed his ministry and women were among his key followers. Jesus also taught some rather revolutionary theology, too, such as the idea that we can forgive each other's sins. In traditional Jewish faith, only God can forgive sins, but Jesus expressly instructed his followers to forgive each other.

In simple terms, Jesus' teachings can be summarized thus: he came to establish what he called "Heaven on earth," and he said this Heaven is "within you" (not a place you go to after you suffer bodily death). He also taught that while we are all children of God—by virtue of being part of God's creation—we can also become a Son (or Daughter) of God, by which he meant we can align our will with God's will and hence enter into unity: into union with God. This unity, or union with God, he taught is a central feature of this Heaven on earth that he also called "God's Kingdom on earth."

What he also taught was a very fundamental equality, one that was very radical: we are all equal in this Heaven on earth, men and women, brother and sister, mother and father, are all equal. When told that his mother and brothers are on the outskirts of a crowd who came to listen to him, he asks those present who are his mother and brothers and responds that all those present are his mothers, brothers, and sisters.[6]

Christ also gave clear instruction on how to enter this Heaven on earth—which he depicted as a state of being, or a state of consciousness. He taught that to enter the Kingdom you need to become like a child again, not being child*ish* but rather child*like*. He also taught that you need to break the ties you have to material things—famously he said that it is easier for a camel to get through the eye of a needle than for a rich man to enter this state of being he called Heaven. I would argue he wasn't saying, "Give up all your wealth and belongings" (although he did advise certain people to do this), since obviously his ministry was being funded in large part by wealthy women. No, his core teaching was about the need to drop attachment to the material world, to material belongings, to status and to money.

As we noted above, key to his teaching—this First Century Wisdom Tradition teaching—was his emphasis on the importance of *metanoia* and hence the need to go beyond thought and enter a state of consciousness which is marked by a unity with God. He also made clear that he found great benefit from seeking a quiet place to pray silently alone, and thus he encouraged his followers to have this kind of silent meditation as part of their daily practice.

We also have Christ's teaching that those who follow him will know eternal life. This is perhaps one of the most difficult teachings Christ gave, and we'll return to it later. Suffice to say at this juncture that in Buddhist terms knowing who you truly are—your True Self—is synonymous with becoming aware that who you truly are is beyond life and death. This has strong parallels with Christ's teaching, but more often than not this is glossed over by Christian theologians (and the church) as being part of his teaching they just do not get. Worse, this and teachings like it are often relegated to being "mysteries" that we are to take on faith and that we are not meant to understand.

All too often it seems, Christian theologians and teachers fall back on "faith" as a way to say we were never meant to understand what Christ taught, and we just have to accept it. But Christ never said this: rather he invited diving deep into this "Way" that he taught, to become fully immersed in it until you embody it fully.

Christ's actual teachings, then, bear a strong resemblance to those of Buddha, and specifically to Mahayana Buddhism which was just coming into being (100 B.C.E. to 100 C.E.) at the exact time that Christ lived and taught. Indeed, Christ could be said to be the very epitome of a Bodhisattva—one who having achieved realization, and then devotes his life to the benefit of others.

How did the early church get so far off course from Christ's original teachings? Put simply, there is copious evidence that many of Christ's core followers did not fully grasp what his teaching was, let alone those who followed and established what we have come to know as the formal Christian or Catholic Church. Indeed, the New Testament is full of examples of Christ's disciples and followers simply not understanding his teachings. Looking at the non-canonical Gospels such as the Gospel of Thomas and the Gospel of Mary, we start to see a pattern of some of Christ's female followers comprehending what he was teaching at a deeper level than his more famous male disciples and apostles. Indeed, as Bart Ehrman reminds us, the apostle Levi said Mary Magdalene had a higher status that the male followers of Jesus.[7]

As I mentioned earlier, Mahayana Buddhism came into being around the time of Christ, starting somewhere in the period 100 B.C.E. to 100 C.E. With the trade routes open for many years between the Middle East and the Far East,[8] it is very likely that these new Mahayana Buddhists made their way to the area where Jesus was exploring his spirituality and where he did his teaching. Whether he actually personally came into contact with such Buddhist teachers we cannot know, but there was some contact, either directly or indirectly, otherwise we cannot explain the strong parallels between Buddha's and Christ's teachings and the use of near-identical parables that we know had Indian origins. There is also a possibility that the apostle Thomas was Christ's connection to India and thus to Buddhism. I'll return to this later.

As this book will explore, there are not only similarities in the teachings of Buddha and Christ, but also in their teaching styles, At the center of Buddhist teaching, especially as realized in the various Zen traditions, is the primary goal of awakening and an acknowledgement that students must achieve this for themselves. That is, nothing either a Christian or Buddhist Teacher can say to a student can cause them in some simple predictable fashion to wake up and realize their true nature.

In the Zen Buddhist traditions, depending on the lineage, there is an emphasis on dharma talks coupled with either just sitting meditation (what Soto Zen practitioners call *shikantaza*) or on working with *koans* (*kong-ans*). In some traditions (Korean traditions like those established by Seung

Sahn, and Japanese ones like Sanbo Kyodan/Harada-Yasutani, for instance) there is a mixing of sitting meditation and *koan* practice. What these approaches have in common is that they present the student with methods through which they can increase the possibility that they will have an awakening experience, or a glimpse of awakening (what Japanese Soto Zen teachers call *kensho*), but they do not guarantee it. Reputedly, Buddha decided to sit under a pipel tree—known as the Bodhi tree—until he achieved awakening. It is said that at the age of 35 years, after sitting in stillness for some 40 days[9] Buddha had a sudden realization of his true nature. Some say it was as the morning star was rising in the East, but as with much written about the Buddha it is hard to differentiate fact from embellishment. Thus, Buddha would be the first to affirm that there is no simple formula or certain steps a teacher can tell a student that will reliably lead to their awakening.

Making the working assumption that Christ, too, had an awakening experience, it seems likely that he also realized that he could not teach others how to have a similar experience by any simple set of instructions. Hence Christ, like Buddha, talked around the topic in the hope the student or follower would wake up. Not surprisingly, then, Christ also adopted the use of parables as a way to help his followers get into the right state of consciousness to become aware of their true nature, their oneness with God. And I believe this is why Christ adopted what I call his "It is like..." method of teaching which points the follower in the direction to achieve realization, knowing that the follower has to have the awakening themselves, the teacher cannot have it for them or invoke it on demand.

There are other parallels in Christ's and Buddha's teaching styles: neither sought to establish a new religion as such ("*Do not think that I have come to abolish the law or the prophets,"* Mt 5: 17). As many have reminded us, Jesus was not a Christian, he was a Jew and a Wisdom teacher. Similarly, Buddha was not a Buddhist. In each case they acquired a group of followers: in Buddha's case he acquired followers who formed a group (or sangha), not unlike the group of followers that Jesus acquired, too. Just as Buddha traveled around expounding the dharma in his talks, so Christ also traveled around giving his oral teachings to groups in various outdoor settings.

There are many other parallels between the life of Christ and that of Buddha, much of which is probably revisionist history and invention by those seeking to pedestalize Christ or Buddha. To note an obvious instance in Christ's case, his name was changed to make it seem that he was unique, not only the "only Son of God," but also the only "Jesus" of history. This isn't true of course. Christ's actual given name was Yeshua a common variant on the name Yehoshua that was in wide usage in Judea the time of Christ. Elsewhere this has commonly been translated as Joshua, but only for Christ is it written and said as Jesus.

Yeshua is both the Hebrew and Aramaic way of writing Christ's name. But the name Jesus was derived from a Latin derivation (*Iesus*) which was a transliteration of the Greek *Iesous,* which was of course derived from the Hebrew *Yeshua.* And Iesous, of course, would be said as "ee-ay-soos" not with a hard "J" sound which isn't present in Greek. It seems that in early English the initial "I" in the Latin and Greek was transposed for a hard "J" from which we get the modern spelling and pronunciation of Jesus.

Thus writing and speaking Christ's name as Jesus, rather than as Joshua as all other persons named Yeshua or Yehoshua were written in English, was a mechanism to pedestalize Christ and to ensure he was perceived in all ways as different from other persons in history. And with this unique translation of what was otherwise an extremely common man's name in First Century Judea, came a general edict to never name oneself or one's child "Jesus" since to do so would be blasphemy to the English-speaking Christian world. As so it remains to this day.

Except of course, the Spanish-speaking world breaks that rule by naming boys Jesus, something few if any in the English-speaking world would dare to do. Of course, many English speaking people try to overlook the Spanish tradition by noting in their case it is "hey-soos" not "geez-us" (although ironically the Spanish pronunciation is far closer to the Greek original, ee-ay-soos). How this tradition of permitting Jesus as a boy's name arose in the Spanish-speaking world is a subject of debate.[10]

Some argue that in the Middle Ages it became a usual practice in Spain to add "de (saints name)" to your regular given name. Thus, people started to call themselves, for instance, names like Teresa de Jesus (St Teresa of Avila). And that over time because it became so common to have "de Jesus" as part of a name, it seemed a natural transition to have first names simply as Jesus. But there is some rather beautiful irony that those early men seeking to pedestalize Christ by giving him a unique name, then have the Spanish speaking world shatter that conceit.

There are numerous other examples of pedestalizing both Buddha and Christ, as well as strong parallels in their life stories: see Appendix 2.

---

[1] Unless otherwise stated, the NIV Bible translation is used in this book.

[2] I am aware of the problem of determining word meaning by looking at the literal meaning of its parts ('butterfly' being an example). But there is

ample evidence that *metanoia* was commonly accepted to refer to a deep spiritual self-transformation.

[3] Matthew Fox, *Original Blessing* Bear & Company, 1983. And, *The Coming of the Cosmic Christ* Harper, 1988

[4] Credit Wonji Dharma

[5] In 1985 Robert Funk, John Dominic Crossan and around 50 other scholars along with 100 laymen formed The "Jesus Seminar." Among other accomplishments, they color coded what Jesus said in the Gospels according to whether he likely really said it (red), probably said it (pink), did not say but is his ideas (grey), and did not say (black). From this work came a number of notable books, such as: Marcus Borg, *Meeting Jesus Again for The First Time*, HarperOne, 1995; John Dominic Crossan, *Jesus:A Revolutionary Biography*, HarperOne, 2009; Robert Funk, *The Five Gospels: What did Jesus Really Say?*, HarperOne, 1996.

[6] Mt 12:46-50

[7] Bart Ehrman, *Lost Scriptures*. Oxford University Press, 2003, 35.

[8] Being British by birth, I am very aware of the kind of 'geographical imperialism' that accompanies such terms as Middle East and Far East—as if the center of the world is based in Greenwich, London. But they are terms still in wide use as of the time of this book's writing and the global clocks are still based on GMT.

[9] Different sources mention a different number of days.

[10] Or, as one wit quipped, "Are you sure Jesus was a Jew? If so why was he given a Spanish first name?"

2

Buddha and Christ

"Christ" is the title given to Jesus of Nazareth, and "Buddha" is the title given to Siddhartha Gautama. Let's take a few moments to consider these titles.

The title "Christ" comes from the Greek Khristos which means "anointed" and is a translation of the Hebrew "Masiah", usually translated into English as "Messiah." The term "Masiah" has been used in various ways in the Judaic tradition, but in the Jewish messianic tradition the term is associated with a leader who is anointed by God to herald the Messianic Age of global peace. In Jesus' case, early Christian writers in referring to him as the Messiah were drawing on prophesy in Isaiah heralding a spiritual savior—a "spiritual king" as it were, in contrast to an earthly ruler of a physical Kingdom.

In the Judaic tradition the Messiah is to come from the House of David, the Jewish King of the Old Testament. It is therefore interesting to see how the writers of the Gospels in the New Testament tried to link Jesus to the Davidic line so that he would be seen as fitting the qualifications of the prophesized Messiah. In fact, two of the four Gospel writers—Mark and John—do not attempt to recite Jesus' lineage at all, and Luke sets out a lineage back to Adam, not David. Matthew was clearly written for a Jewish audience: in the opening of his Gospel he states that Jesus is the "son of David, son of Abraham"—meaning of course that he is of the House of David. Matthew then goes on to give what he means us to read as Jesus' genealogy, starting with Abraham, through King

David, and up to Joseph, husband of Mary, Mother of Jesus Christ.

He then goes on to relate, in common with the Gospel of Luke,[1] that Jesus was born of the virgin Mary who had had no sexual relations with Joseph.

Perhaps you see the problem in what he writer of Matthew was attempting to do. Having made his argument that *Joseph* was of the House of David, he then affirms that Joseph is not Jesus' biological father and thus effectively states that Jesus is not of the House of David. But again, we should not get too wrapped up in what is or what is not historic fact; here, for instance, even in the first century C.E. it would have been impossible for anyone to trace their ancestry back to King David since historic evidence of David's lineage had disappeared long before the time of Christ. Anyone reading what Matthew wrote in the first few years or decades after Jesus' death would have known that it is not possible to trace one's ancestry back to King David. Thus, Matthew's early readers would have understood, perhaps far better than we may now, that what he was trying to convey was more *symbolic* than legalistic, historical, or factual.

In the other Gospels a different picture of Jesus as "Christ" appears, one less based on Messianic prophesy, and more based on Jesus as a spiritual teacher who has achieved a oneness with God, which means he is deserving of the title "Christ." The first suggestion we're going to consider that is at variance with traditional Christian "church teaching" is that it may be more useful in pursuing your spiritual path to think of the term "Christ" as that state of being everyone is seeking to attain—a oneness with God, oneness with everything, oneness with the ground of being, a realization of who you *really* are. Christ's own term for this state of being was to "enter the

Kingdom of Heaven." Thus becoming "Christ" is very similar to the Buddhist concept—particularly Zen Buddhist—of becoming a Buddha,[2] or "realizing your Buddha nature."

This terminology is unfortunate since it arises from a male-centric society—first century Middle Eastern culture—where there was an emphasis on the male. God, while understood as beyond male and female in the Hebrew tradition,[3] was referred to by Christ as "abba"—which translations of the New Testament have for many years translated as "Father." The word Jesus used, though, was the Aramaic for father that was also the word used for the intimate name young children would use to call their fathers. This better translates into English as "papa" or "daddy." Nonetheless, Christ chose to refer to God in the masculine, which in turn lead him to talk of the *King*dom. Today the trend in more liberal churches is to use gender neutral terms since we know that God—the essence of all that is—is neither masculine nor feminine but is simultaneously both and neither. We will return to this later.

Here, then, we will consider the title "Christ" as a gender-neutral term, and the goal of everyone on their spiritual path to become Christ (or, if you prefer, become a Christ). For some of us, the idea of "becoming Christ" may be difficult—it may even sound heretical—so if you find it easier to think in terms of awakening to your "Christ nature." Words should help you on your spiritual journey, not hinder you from moving forward. That said, bear in mind that to have as your goal to become "Christ-like" may be selling yourself short, doing yourself and your spiritual journey a disservice, since in this way of speaking Christ is your true, core nature, not an historic person you are merely emulating the behavior of.

The title "Buddha" means "awakened one." Siddhartha Gautama Buddha is considered by Buddhists to be the

Supreme Buddha, and he is also referred to as "Sakyamuni" (Sage of the Sakyas, the ancient tribe of India). While enlightened Christians have come to accept that there are many Christs and that they, too, potentially may become a Christ[4], in Buddhism it has long been accepted there are many Buddhas and that, indeed, in Zen we teach that everyone is Buddha. And while some sects of Buddhism may raise Gautama Buddha up almost to the status of a deity and talk about there being one and only one Buddha, for most Buddhists—particularly Zen Buddhists—the key goal of their spiritual path is "enlightenment" (entering "*nirvana*"[5]) which they see as being a state of being that is the same as "becoming a Buddha."

In a real sense, then, the titles "Christ" and "Buddha" are very similar: in both cases, it is a title of an ultimate state of being that Christian's on the one hand, and Buddhist's on the other seek to achieve as the ultimate goal of their spiritual path. Indeed, both Christians following Jesus' Wisdom Teaching path, and Buddhists, would say you are already Christ, you are already Buddha. You just need to wake up. For this reason I titled this book "Christ Way, Buddha Way" rather than "Jesus' Way, Gautama's Way" (or even "Jesus' Way, Buddha's Way) to emphasize that we are considering the Way that leads to Christ-hood and the Way that leads to Buddha-hood.

There is another way in which Christ and Buddha would appear to be quite different: generally, Buddhists do not worship the Buddha. He is not considered a God but rather as a regular human being like you or me who had tremendous insight and awakening. But when it comes to Christ, Christianity has elevated Jesus to the status of a deity—far from being merely human like the rest of us. Some have mused that if being a true Christian is simply a matter of emulating Jesus, then a starting point would be to first be born of a virgin, perform some miracles, then develop the ability to not be killed (or, rather, resurrect after 3 days if anyone tries to kill you). In other words, Christianity is a religion seen from this perspective that calls on its followers to perform the impossible task of emulating someone who cannot be emulated. If this sounds blasphemous, ponder it a moment and you will see some truth in it.

Indeed, it seems that Christian theologians are never more tied in knots than when they contemplate the nature of Jesus. Who was he? Well, you may not be aware of this, but there is no universally agreed answer to that question across all versions of Christianity—or even within any given tradition, come to that. Was Jesus fully divine and fully human? Or, as Saul of Tarsus (known as Paul after he had stopped persecuting Christians) suggests, did Jesus give up his divinity in order to become fully human? (Phil. 2:6-7) Did Jesus exist for all time as one with God from the creation of the universe and merely manifest as a human being for 30 or so years in the first century C.E.? Or did Jesus become divine at the point he was chosen by God (the baptism by John the Baptist is often cited as a possible moment)? Or did he become divine when he was born of a virgin? Again, you may be surprised to know that there is no consensus between even the most learned theologians on these questions.[6]

Indeed, perhaps one of the pithiest theological issues is that of the trinity: they are named God, Son, Holy Spirit, but what does this mean? Not for nothing this sermon topic each year is often handed off to a lower priest or wet behind the ears curate, while the established priest beats a hasty retreat from preaching on the topic. Well, some say, it is like the three forms of God. God the Father being the invisible power ("in Heaven"), who became manifest as a man in the form of Jesus, and who acts in the world as the Holy Spirit. The three modes of God as it were. Well, as logical as many might think that is, that is a defined heresy called modalism.[7] So that will not do.

In those early creedal meetings of the early church they sorted this out: what was their solution? Speak of the Trinity as God in three persons. That solves it, right? Well, first you have to understand they didn't mean three people (that would heresy) but rather 'persons' as based on the Greek word *persona*. Three consubstantial persons or *hypostases* as the official version has it. So, what does this mean? Trust me, in the elevated ivory towers of seminaries around the world professors still struggle to enlighten students on this wording. Persona, they may say, is not a person but rather an actor or a role. So, how does that help?

For most people it does not help, since that still sounds like *modalism* and seems to be using a Greek term to try to say we are not saying God as three modes, *really* we are not. What about the other Greek term they rely on, *hypostasis*? This, of course, highlights the influence of Greek thought and philosophy both on Jesus in his day and in the decades and centuries that followed. It has roots in Neoplatonism where there is said to be a hypostasis of the "soul," the "intellect," (*nous*) and "the one" as described by Plotinus. And so hence we ended up with wording "of one substance with the Father" in the Nicene Creed, and I am confident few Christians fully grasp what the framers of the creed precisely intended by that phrase.

Here Christianity has yet again done itself a great disservice. When they elevated Jesus—Christ—to something he never said he was, they made him impossible to emulate,

Jesus' core teachings got set aside and replaced by a form of worship of Jesus as a God. But that is not what Jesus said of himself. As attractive at times the text of the Gospel of John is, with its lovely mystical language, we do well to recall it was written many decades after Jesus' time. The so-called synoptic Gospels[8] (Matthew, Mark and Luke), while perhaps less mystical than John do, I believe, allow us to come closer to the truth of what Jesus actually did teach.

This is a good moment to point out that common wisdom states the earliest writings we have are some of the letters of Paul. They can be dated to about 50 C.E., about 17-20 years after Jesus' death.[9] These are followed by the Gospel of Mark (66-70 C.E.), then Matthew, Luke (around 85-90 C.E.) and finally John (90-110 C.E.). However, while disputed, there is a sizable body of theologians who argue the earliest writings are collections of Christ's sayings.

They talk of a missing text called "Q" (after the German for *quelle*, meaning "source"), a collection of Jesus' *logia* (sayings), which scholars allege both Luke and Mathew drew from in order to explain how similar these two Gospels are. But there are those, and I tend to agree with them, who say that the Gospel of Thomas is based on Q—is thus a version of the earliest writings, pre-dating Paul and his letters. Thus while we can't disregard that what has come down to us as the Gospel of Thomas isn't a substantially altered version of those earliest writings, it has all the hallmarks of being a book of sayings of the kind that would have been written while Jesus was still alive and teaching.

This makes sense: while Jesus was still alive obviously people would not be writing about his death, his resurrection, or even stories about his life or miraculous birth. No, during his lifetime it makes sense that if anything was written down it would have been the records of his sayings and teachings.

But why is it important to remind ourselves that among the oldest writings we have are those of Paul? It is important because we need to remember that the oldest versions we have of even the Gospel of Mark have been heavily edited and amended by the time the versions we have were written down. As a general guideline, the earlier versions no longer available to us (or at least not yet discovered) ended with Jesus' death and did not include the resurrection or any other writing about the post-Easter Jesus. It is also seems likely that the original writings were enhanced at the start of Jesus' life too, by adding stories of his birth to a virgin, and the birth in a stable located by following a star.[10]

If we try to put ourselves in the position of Christ's early followers, it seems clear that many of them—even his main disciples—did not grasp his core teachings. Instead, they heard his message about the coming of a Kingdom of God as being something that would be achieved in Jesus' lifetime. When it appeared that Jesus died with no identifiable Kingdom of God being established, his teachings were retroactively re-interpreted as an eschatological end of times teaching. Rather than an achievement that would take place in Jesus' lifetime, his teachings were reinterpreted as referring to a future time when he would come again to establish the Kingdom he had been talking about. This idea pervades the works of Paul and the embellishments to the Gospels where new text about a resurrection was inserted, along with post-crucifixion sightings of Jesus, etc.

In other words, it was just too terrible to contemplate that Jesus came to establish this wonderful new Kingdom of Heaven on earth but that he had failed in his mission and died before he could attain it. No, that could not be, so instead his followers had to invent a new religion that is expressed in the writings of Paul, the amendments to the synoptic Gospels, and to a large degree in the Gospel of John. And once again, if this is so at odds with what you have been taught about Christianity that you feel it must be blasphemous, then ponder for a moment what Jesus actually taught from what we can discern from those parts of the synoptic Gospels that did survive to our time.

So, what did Christ *actually* teach? That is in large part what this book is designed to address. First, Christ did not present himself as being the son of God or at least not as the only son of God. The synoptic Gospels are full of people trying to pin Christ down on what he would call himself, and he keeps cleverly turning it back on the questioners by saying "Who do you say I am?" Insofar as there is any label put on him, it is that of being Son of Man, which is the standard term in Judaism for being a human being, not being a God or a son of a God. Yes, it was also a term used in the Hebrew Bible for a Messiah who was envisioned to come to save the people of Israel—here the New Testament draws heavily on Isaiah as a source for referring to who his followers believed Christ to be. But this Messiah was always envisioned to be a man, a mere human, albeit a very special one with a status right up there alongside the greatest prophets of ages past.

Rather, what Christ taught was that *you* are a Son of God, and you are a Daughter of God, and you, and you, and you. The idea of Christ being the *only* Son of God, and wording such as you can only come to the Father through the Son, don't appear in the synoptic Gospels, only in John where most of what is attributed to Christ is highly suspect. Indeed, John has the dubious reputation of containing by far the most words supposedly spoken by Christ, and yet the fewest that serious scholars actually believe were words that were ever said by him.[11]

Indeed, Christ could hardly have been clearer in the words that have survived to us from the synoptic Gospels. Not only was he dodging any attempt to label him as a God or as *the* Son of God, or indeed as different or divine or special, some of his more difficult teachings show exactly what he was teaching. In Matthew 12:46-50, Christ is giving a talk to a sizable crowd and someone tells him that his mother and his brothers are at the edge of the crowd trying to get in. His response puzzles many hardline Christians—especially those who elevate his mother Mary to a kind of God-like status, too—since he says, "Who is my mother? Who are my brothers?" And goes on to say that everyone present is his mother, brother and sisters for all are equal, all are one, in the Kingdom of Heaven on earth.

We are hampered by the fact that we have a very incomplete record of Christ's teachings. But there is evidence that he drew a distinction between everyone being a child of God—that is, part of God's creation—and a person achieving what he termed the state of consciousness he called "Son of God." And while we do not have it specifically in his words and noting the heavily male dominated language of his time, we can nonetheless assume he would also have said "Daughter of God." Having generally warned against relying on the Gospel of John as a source of what Christ actually said, I believe this is one exception where what John wrote accurately reflects Christ's teaching. In John Christ clarifies that what he means is that in following his teachings—known as The Way—when your will and God's will become one at that moment you transform from being a child of God to being a Son (Daughter) of God.[12]

If this sounds like just playing with words, it is not, and I do not believe it was not just playing with words for Christ either. Rather it is one of the clearest parallels we have between Buddha's teachings and Christ's teachings, muddied over the years by the incomplete nature of our record of Christ's teachings and the failure of many of even his close followers to fully grasp what he was teaching.

Barabbas *was* Jesus

Last, a quick word about the distinction between the Jewish idea of a Messiah that would come and be the ruler of the Jews, taking them into a new era of peace, and Christ's message of becoming a Son of God. We know more about this and the fact that it was a live topic in the time of Christ, but we often overlook how we know about it. The source is in a place most often missed because scholars, clerics and lay people alike mistake the text as being historical fact rather than metaphor or story.

I refer to the passage in the New Testament where we are told that Jesus is brought before a crowd, and Pilate asks of the crowd "*Whom do you wish that I release to you? Jesus Barabbas, or Jesus known as the Messiah*?"[13]

Were you surprised to see Barabbas written as "Jesus Barabbas"? Depending on which translation of the Bible you've read, this insertion making both men named Jesus was either shocking, or simply something you've come to take for granted. But, if so, perhaps you have not been entirely comfortable with the idea that Barabbas also had the given name of Jesus (Yeshua)?

Well, you are not alone: around 240 C.E. Origen noted in his *Commentary on Matthew*,[14] that in many manuscripts he was studying as sources for the Gospel of Matthew, several stated that Barabbas' given name was Jesus, too. Origen wrestles with this and finally shrugs it off saying that while other names from that time were associated with both good and bad people, Yeshua was only associated with good people. He thus decided not to accept that Barabbas' first name was also Jesus despite numerous otherwise reliable sources stating that it was.

Even to this day, several modern translations of the New Testament call the other person 'Jesus Barabbas' (the *New International Version* and the *Contemporary English Version*, for example) although the majority miss it out. Interestingly, we get a further hint what was really intended by this passage in Matthew from the Aramaic Bible in Plain English which has this version: "Barabba, or Yeshua who is called The Messiah?"

So, what is going on here? The common mistake which many make, and which Origen made too, is to believe the story refers to two people: Jesus Christ and another person—perhaps a thief or crook—whereas the story is talking about the same person. The crowd is not an actual historical crowd, it is symbolic of Christ's followers. The Aramaic version helps us to see this: unlike the other versions which try to create a person's name by adding an "s" to the end of Barabbas, the Aramaic version is clearer when it just states "Barabba." "Bar" means "son of" and "abba" means father. Sound familiar?

So what is actually going on in this passage of Matthew is a fictional gathering at which it is suggested that the local Roman authority asked Christ's followers "Who do you wish me to return to you, Jesus who is known as Son of the Father, or Jesus who is known as The Messiah (King of the Jews)". And, again, the sources that have the first person being called 'Jesus Barabbas' make it clearer that it is the same Jesus that is being referred to—not some other person, or thief or otherwise. This is lost when people start speculating that Barabbas was a thief or that he could not have the given name Jesus since only good people were ever named Jesus/Yeshua. That, by the way, is simply not true since Yeshua was a common first name in First Century Palestine.

As an eleven-year-old boy, I must have been any priest's nightmare to have in a Confirmation Class. In the Anglican/Church of England tradition I was raised in, around eleven years of age you take Confirmation Classes after which you are then permitted to take communion. The parallel is perhaps catechism classes and First Communion for Roman Catholics. In one of these classes I had obviously been reading up on this Christianity thing. Even at that young age I was a fledgling scholar who loved research. Thus, to this day I recall how flustered the Priest became when I said that I did not think Jesus was the actual given name of Christ. The Priest was probably fresh out of seminary and proudly gave a mini lecture on the actual given name likely being Yawehshua, or Yeshua. To which I recall responding, isn't that more usually translated as Joshua? The Priest affirmed that it was, so I asked why was the name translated as Joshua everywhere else in the Bible other than for Jesus where it is translated as Jesus? He responded that I should not worry my little head with such matters and that in time I would eventually be old enough to be able to ask such questions.

But at this early stage I perceived a tendency in the Church to want to elevate Christ to being far more than in any sense mere human. He had to be not just a Son of God, but the *only* begotten Son of God. Others may be called Yeshua, but they would be referred to as Joshua, he alone would be Jesus. And others, like Origen, would even go so far as to say only good people were ever named Yeshua, just to be sure that Jesus is pedestalled as being beyond, above, not like us

Back to the point, though, over the centuries people have been too wedded to the idea of literal reading of the Bible and reading that favors elevating Christ to "other," that they have missed the beauty of the teaching inherent in Matthew 27:17. Indeed, the story is meant to ask Christ's followers who do you follow? It is Jesus Son of the Father who is a great Wisdom Tradition teacher, or is it Jesus the Messiah who has come in accord with prophecy to establish a new earthly Kingdom for the Jews, one based on peace physically led by the Messiah as a king?

This dichotomy runs throughout the scant text we have from the time, and the rare words we have that we believe were actually ever spoken by Christ. Over and again others try to pin him down as the prophesized Messiah come to save the Jewish people from their oppressors, the Romans. And over and again he will not agree to this but rather turns it round on the questioner, asking: "Who do you say I am?" And do make it clearer to them, he further adds "*Render to Caesar that which is Caesar's. Render to God that which is God's*" (Mt 22:21).

Christ is clearly doing his best to make clear that he is not there to establish a new Kingdom of man, one which replaces Roman rule with Jewish self-rule with Christ as king. Rather, he states time and again that he came to establish a Kingdom of God, a Kingdom of Heaven, in contrast to and separate from a Kingdom of man (such as that of the Romans). It seems at times that he struggles to find new ways to say "I've woken up, realized my oneness with God, realized that by aligning my will with God's will, I became a Son of God, but—in a true Bodhisattva tradition—I am staying around to teach until everyone of you has also awoken and entered this Heaven on earth with me." But, sadly, the vast majority of even his closest followers fail to grasp what he is saying.

It is thus ironic that the passage in Matthew has become so distorted over the centuries to become evidence that the "Jews" asked Pilate to put Christ to death. This literal reading of what was only meant to be a form of parable, has people believing people were asked "Do you want me to release this crook and execute Christ, or release Christ and execute this crook?" As if there is any chance whatsoever that Pilate or any local governor of that time would have said or done such a thing. And much of what is reported to have been said and done between Pilate and Christ, or the guards, is not something the writer(s) of Matthew would have witnessed or necessarily have had reported to them. We are to believe that Pilate or the Chief Priest or Elders left that meeting to tell everyone what was said, so it could be recorded? It is just simply not credible, which also goes to show this story is a form of parable that aligns with Jesus teaching "Who do you say I am?" (Son of the Father or The Messiah foretold of old?)

I recall when I first heard this passage as a child in church, I asked myself, who was meant to be in this crowd that Pilate asked the question of? At the time (and repeatedly since) I was told "it was a crowd of Jews" as if they were the 'other' to be despised, not least because they chose Barabbas not Christ, to die. But I recall saying as a child, wasn't Christ a Jew? Weren't his disciples and most of his followers Jews? And what crowd would be likely present at this alleged public question and answer session? Surely, the young version of me said, if anyone was hanging around for news of Jesus, it would surely be his most loyal followers. So why on earth would they vote to release a criminal rather than Christ?[15] It never made sense to me, even as a child. The authors of the Gospels try to explain this away saying the crowd were feeling guilty because they had taken money to turn Christ in. But again, that is not true.

According to the story, one person took money not a large group of people (who then, we are to believe, magically all decided to turn up for this scene).

In short, then, the "crowd" in this scene gave the right answer: they chose Jesus the Son of the Father (Wisdom teacher), over Jesus the Messiah who had been prophesized to come as a new King of the Jews to usher in an era of peace. It is a challenge to more clearly understanding the Gospels that so much was added later which obscures the original messages and meanings.

The earliest versions of the synoptic Gospels had no birth stories and they stopped at the death of Christ on the cross. What followed, in part fueled by the version of Christianity peddled by Saul of Tarsus (which bore scant resemblance to what Christ taught), but a pedestalization of Christ. We can have some sympathy with those early disciples and followers who did not quite grasp his teachings. He spoke of aligning your will with God's will in order to become one with God, which he called the state of Heaven within and of becoming a Son of God. He also taught that God is Love—not that He is a merely a lov*ing* God, but *is* Love, and that this Love is divine love, absolute, selfless and nonjudgmental, just like the love of a father for his only begotten son.

That, in first century Palestine, was the epitome of perfect love—that of a father for an only son—because despite Judaism being a matriarchal lineage tradition, it was still deeply patriarchal with favoritism for men and boys. Today we might say a love so complete it is like that of a mother for their only child, or indeed as we become more and more enlightened in our usage, the love of any parent for their only child.

It is such a short step, then, if you are not quite getting the core point Jesus is trying to teach, to then say that Christ represents the embodiment of this process and that he alone is the Son of the Father. It is a short step from there to the idea that God is Christ's father (and no one else's father). That said, Jesus could hardly have been clearer in his teaching that God—in his language—is *our* father, and that we are *all* the Sons and Daughters of God. Witness the Lord's Prayer and his teaching when his biological mother and brothers are trying to get to the front of the crowd showed this point, too.

He eschewed the idea that his mother was any different from any other person, or that God was his father and his alone, and instead spoke of equality. But from the pedestalization of Christ then came the need to make him as 'different' as possible from us: he had to be born not of a normal mortal mother, but it needed to be a virgin birth. How could Joseph be his real biological father if God was his father? And so, it became necessary to invent birth stories, and ones that aligned themselves with prophecy. It was said that the Messiah (the mythical being Jesus kept denying he was) would be born in Bethlehem of the House of David. Thus, as I mention elsewhere, they had to invent birth lineages back to David (overlooking the fact that only set Joseph up as being of the House, not Christ), and they had to think up a reason why Mary and Joseph would have had to travel to Bethlehem, when all the other records about Christ simply say he was from Nazareth.

The post-Easter Jesus, which was added to the Gospels long after they were first written, grew out this pedestalization of Jesus. Versions of the Gospels up to then had simply said he had died on the cross. End of story. Thus, it became necessary to introduce post crucifixion resurrection stories to once again ensure Christ is pedestalized as no mere human, and thus different from any of us. Which in turn, was the very opposite of the core teachings Christ had given prior to being executed.

While it was unfortunate that so early in the history of Christianity this pedestalization had the impact of obscuring Christ's true teachings, the good news is we are able to uncover them again. This book is part of the movement that calls for a rediscovery of what Christ actually taught. When we do this, the Wisdom Tradition Teaching we uncover is truly marvelous and has the potential to radically transform hearts and minds.

---

[1] Note that the other two Gospels, Mark and John, make no reference to Jesus being born of a virgin.

[2] More accurately, one doesn't *become* a Buddha – it is not a state one attains or becomes. One is already Buddha, just not awake to that fact yet.

[3] God's name was JHWH (the so-called tetragrammaton) without vowels and the name of God was not to be spoken let alone attribute one sex to God and not the other. When fleshed out with vowels, which no devout Jew would do, the name becomes Yahweh, the one God of the Jews. Another God of those times was Salem, after whom Jerusalem was named, as were key people in the Old Testament such as King Solomon, etc.

[4] Or, if you prefer, become Christ-like, or awake to your "Christ nature," or alternatively, perhaps, "merge with the Cosmic Christ" (Matthew Fox) if any of those alternative terminologies works better for you.

[5] Nirvana literally means blowing out or quenching. The ultimate goal of Buddhism.

[6] As we will see, though, Christ would probably have said he was both fully human and fully divine but would have quickly added that so are all of us fully human and fully divine (not just him).

[7] Modalism is the doctrine that the persons of the Trinity represent only three modes or aspects of the divine revelation, not distinct and coexisting persons. Despite this being seen by the established church as heresy, if asked this is how many people interpret the trinity. Some argue, with some merit, that to deny modalism is to pursue the idea of three Gods, not one God with different aspects, which in turn was part of the criticism of Christianity that Islam has, along with their denying any human can be a God or a Son of a God (but in that the Islamic

theologians mean literally rather than metaphorically as in the sense that Christ taught the concept "Son of God")

[8] Synoptic means "seen with one eye" since they resemble each other and seem to have been copied from one another or from a common source document.

[9] There are differing opinions as to whether Jesus died in 30 C.E. or 33 C.E.

[10] It is of course not possible to follow a star to a specific geographic location, and people of that time would have known that, too. Similarly, no other celestial event such as a comet or meteor could lead anyone to a specific geographic location either. Rather, the inclusion of following a star would have indicated to the early reader that this story was intended to be metaphorical, not literal.

[11] Funk, *The Five Gospels*

[12] Jn 1:12 *But as many as received him, to them gave he power to become the Sons of God, even to them that believe on his name* (KJV). Here I make an exception from using the NIV translation since in trying to render a gender neutral version the NIV uses "become children of God" which rather misses the point since we are naturally by birth children of God who, in Jesus' teaching, have the power to become Sons and Daughters of God as a result of the spiritual transformation, the *metanoia*, he speaks of.

[13] Mt. 27:17

[14] Ronald Heine Ed,, *The Commentary of Origen on the Gospel of St. Matthew*, Oxford University Press, 2018.

[15] What the Gospels actually say about Barabbas is a mixed bag. Matthew has him as a "notable" (or "well known") prisoner in custody, Mark states he was a murderer, Luke says he was a murderer and involved in insurrection, and John states he is a robber. Setting aside that someone would not have been called Barabbas (or Barabba as the original text stated), the story seems to have been manipulated to make more sense of it as an actual historical event. It is likely this entire passage in Mt. 27 was far shorter in its original and thus more obviously a parable.

3

The Way

Despite the commonly held view that Christianity and Buddhism could hardly be more different, the similarities between what Siddhartha taught and Christ's teachings are numerous. In Buddhism, we talk of "The Buddha Way" and throughout many Buddhist teachings such as those of Dogen the 12th century founder of Japanese Soto Zen (based on the Caodong School of Chinese Chan Buddhism), the teachings are referred to simply as "the Way":

"To study the Buddha Way is to study the self. To study the self is to forget the self. To forget the self is to be actualized by myriad things. When actualized by myriad things, your body and mind as well as the bodies and minds of others drop away. No trace of enlightenment remains, and this no-trace continues endlessly."[1]

And as Zen Buddhists we vow to attain "the Buddha Way" in our Four Vows:

Sentient beings are numberless; I vow to save them.
Desires are inexhaustible; I vow to end them.
The Dharma Gates are infinite; I vow to enter them all.
The Buddha Way is unattainable; I vow to attain it.

According to the historical record we have of Jesus and his followers, those who followed his teachings referred to themselves as followers of "The Way."[2] Indeed, in the Gospel of John the writer has Jesus describing himself as "*the way, the truth and the life*"[3] and the synoptic Gospels mention "The Way" at least eight times.[4] This raises the question, why were Christ's followers known as those following "The Way" and what was this "Way?" We will return to this later.

Could this be pure coincidence? Possibly. But the version of Buddhism that Christ's teachings bear the closest resemblance to is the Mahayana Buddhist teachings. While we have no firm historic record of when Mahayana Buddhism started, it is generally agreed that it began in the period between 100 B.C.E. and 100 C.E. That is almost exactly during the life of Christ and at a time when the new Mahayana Buddhist teachers were traveling from India to the Middle East on the Silk Road. At this time Buddhist monks from the East were setting up Mahayana Buddhist monasteries in the region where Jesus lived.

Did Christ study with any of these Buddhist teachers? Or were Christ's teachers, or were those he discussed his spiritual path with exposed to this new Mahayana way of thought? We cannot be certain, but we do know the Mahayana Buddhists may have referred to the Siddhartha's teachings as "The Way," and we know from the New Testament that Christ and his teachings were referred to as "The Way," too. We also know that notable among world religious leaders, Christ and Buddha both made use of parables, and that several of Christ's parables have their roots in Buddhist teachings.

While we know nothing about most of Christ's adult life before he started teaching at around the age of 30, it seems very likely that he would have been exploring a wide range of religious and spiritual teachings as he explored his own personal spiritual path and calling. Whether Christ himself ever came into contact with any Buddhists, it seems likely he did: he was immersed in the spiritual trends of his time including the teachings of the Essences, Gnostics, etc., any of whom may themselves have absorbed some of the new Buddhist Mahayana way. Major philosophical thinkers and teachers based in Alexandria, including Buddhists who had settled there from the East or Greeks who had become Buddhists, significantly influenced the region.

The similarities between Mahayana teachings and those of the Gnostics at the time of Christ have been well documented elsewhere by writers like Marcus Borg and Elaine Pagels,[5] so we know there were many sects that had Eastern influences around that time. After his encounter with John the Baptist, Christ then retreats to the desert to fast and prayer in silence for forty days and forty nights. The parallels between Christ and Buddha are striking at times: not only does Jesus go on an extended forty-day retreat at about age thirty, but Buddha reputedly similarly sits quietly for forty days at age thirty-five.[6]

Was this when Christ encountered desert communities with spiritual teachers who had become familiar with Buddhist ways of thought and the term "The Way?" Or did religious thought arising in the Middle East around the last century B.C.E. and first century C.E. find its way back along the Silk Road to India and China to influence the rise of Mahayana Buddhism? We may never know but most important, aside from noting key similarities and parallels, we should not get hung up on this. Again, our key concern here is not historical, factual "truth" but a more fundamental and universal "Truth"—what you find true for you. Ultimately, what you find useful on your spiritual journey or in your meditation, contemplation or centering prayer practice.

Although somewhat of a simplification, in both India at the time of Buddha and in the Middle East at the time of Christ, established religions tended to speak to the rules someone should follow. Religion tended to tell someone what to eat, what to recite, when to recite it, what to believe, what not to believe, and so on. Both Buddha and Christ, by contrast, introduced this alternate option of having a path—a Way—to an ultimate realization or goal, and followers were invited to join this path and travel it with a teacher.

As I mentioned before, Christ's followers were known as followers of The Way. What we are exploring in this book is what it meant to follow The Way, and how we may follow this Way now.

---

[1] *Shobogenzo* by Eihei Dogen

[2] Acts 9:2, 18:24-26, 19:9, 19:23, 24:14, 24:22

[3] Jn 14:16

[4] Mt. 7:13, 7:14, 22:16, Mark 1:3, 12:14, Luke 1:79, 3:4, 20:21

[5] Marcus Borg, *Meeting Jesus Again for the First Time: The Historical Jesus and the Heart of Contemporary Faith*. HarperOne, 1995.

Elaine Pagels, *The Gnostic Gospels*, Random House, 1981

[6] There is a longer summary of the parallels between the life of Christ and the life of the Buddha in Appendix 2.

4

Sayings, Parables and Koans

"It is easier for a camel to get through the eye of a needle than for a rich man to enter the Kingdom of Heaven."[1] Many have commented on the Zen-like flavor of many of Christ's sayings and parables. Of course, no matter how *koan-like* Christ's teachings may sound they are mostly not *koans* as we usually understand them. But his style of teaching and the Zen style known as *koan* introspection (*gong'an* study in Chinese; *gong-an* in Korean; *cong an* in Vietnamese) do have a similar methodology and, I would say, similar goals. That is, in both styles of teaching the teacher is aware that the students or followers must have the realization themselves; the teacher cannot explain what to experience in detail and expect the student to have the experience.

In both cases, whether a saying or *koan*, they act like a finger pointing to the moon. It is up to the student or follower to realize they need to look at the moon, not at the finger. Moreover, only the student can look at the moon themselves, no teacher can look at it for them. Here the "moon" is a deep existential and spiritual truth, that demands personal perception and can never be perceived through another, no matter how good a teacher that other is.

We may be familiar with Christ's sayings like the one above, but what is a *koan*? Perhaps one of the most famous *koans* that has found its way into popular culture is "What is the sound of one hand?" This is often misquoted as "What is the sound of one hand clapping?" which so thoroughly misses the point of the original as to make it just a distraction. Here is the actual *koan* as invented by Hakuin Ekaku (Japanese Rinzai Zen master, 1686-1768):

> *Two hands clap and there is a sound.*
> *What is the sound of one hand?*

The mistake, with this as with any Zen *koan*, is to see it as a riddle to be solved. *Koans* have a simple goal: to help the student wake up and it is the same goal for Zen meditation, too (Zazen). This is an alien concept for many in the West: "What do you mean by 'wake up'? Aren't I already awake?" The simple answer is, no, you are not remotely awake in your day to day life. That is, nearly all people go through life largely in a kind of waking dream seeing what our brain's want us to see, hearing and understanding what our learning, preconceptions and constructs tell us to see, hear and understand. In short, we are not perceiving this moment as it actually is, we perceive it through multiple filters that include a false concept of self largely based on ego and the misconception that we are totally independent beings, separate from others and from all around us.

This is what we call dualistic thinking—thinking that divides the world up into me/you, this/that, object/ground and, yes, me/God. The opposite—nondualism—is at the heart of both Christ's and Buddha's teachings. Non-dual awareness is the transcendence of "I" and "other" where consciousness is spontaneous, unfettered by what we "think" we know. But—and please bear with me here—what Christ and Buddha taught goes one step further than just achieving non-dual awareness, awakening, unity, oneness with God.

Transcending dualism is only half the journey—despite

being a step some may take a lifetime to realize—since completion of the journey is the simultaneous awareness of our separateness *and* non-separateness. Not as an intellectual task, but as direct perception, moment after moment. In Zen terms this is awareness of the *absolute* and the *relative*. In Christian terms we may say it is reflected in being a *child of God* on the one hand (a singular unique part of creation), and a *Son/Daughter of God* on the other hand (at one with all creation, our will aligned with God's will—our eye being single, our entire body filled with light, we see with God's eye not our human eyes[2]).

Let's take a look at the method Christ used, and how he went about teaching non-dualism. In particular, let's look at the saying at the head of this chapter—the proverb on how much harder it is for a camel to pass through the eye of a needle than it is for a rich man to enter the Kingdom of Heaven. This teaching is about attachment and is almost identical to a core teaching by Buddha. It denotes not just attachment to material "things" but attachment to ideas, concepts and constructs, too. In order to enter this state of being that Christ called "Heaven within," you must empty yourself. This self-emptying (referred to in the New Testament by the Greek word *kenosis*), is essential to achieving the non-dual awareness that accompanies entering the Kingdom. What Christ is referring to here is that it is simply not possible to empty yourself in this way if you are attached to possessions, status, prestige, as well as ideas, constructs and concepts. Put simply, you cannot empty yourself in the sense we are talking about here if your concept of your 'self' is inextricably bound up with your wealth, your possessions, your status, and your ideas or so on.

There is another Zen story that has entered popular

culture:

> *There was once a Zen master to whom people came from miles around to receive his wisdom. One day a highly successful professor visited the master and asked him to impart some wisdom to him. The Zen master smiled and said, "OK, but let's have some tea first." The master started to pour tea into the visitor's cup and kept pouring as the tea spilled over on to the table. "Stop! Can't you see the cup is full?!" said the intellectual visitor. "Exactly," said the master, "your mind is like this cup. So full that nothing more can be added. Come back to me when your mind is empty."*

Or, as Zen master Shunryu Suzuki-roshi put it: *In the beginner's mind there are many possibilities, in the expert's there are few.*[3]

To be clear, in speaking of making ourselves "empty" we are not speaking of a negative state of being. This isn't the form of emptiness that some might describe, say, when feeling depressed. On the contrary, it's an emptiness that is absolutely necessary in order to be filled. As a wise Dutch Trappist Monk once told me when I was on retreat at his monastery in Holland in the seventies, "Silence is not an absence, it is a presence."

Whereas the Chinese and Japanese teachings focus on thought, intellect and ideas being a key barrier to a beginner's mind, in Christ's time his focus was on people's obsession with wealth and standing in society—their materialism. As a Bodhisattva, Christ's very being was defined by "How may I help you?", and thus he associated himself with all those on the periphery of society (prostitutes, tax collectors, the poor, those from other cultures) who were shunned by those of high standing in Jewish society. And Christ also focused his teaching on those who were too attached to their possessions and social standing. Or rather, they are attached to their idea of what being "rich" means. Whether you're "too full" because of your intellect or because of your perception of self as defined by possessions or a misguided idea of what it is to be rich, to have everything, the core teaching is about how to empty yourself irrespective of what it is that is "filling" you.

Christ repeats this same core teaching over and again in various forms. In some sayings, he likens the state of mind you will need to adopt to enter Heaven on earth as being like that of a young child.[4] Young children who have not yet lost their wonder of all that is around them and have not yet been sold on the importance of wealth or position to define them. The child's mind is by definition the beginner's mind that Suzuki wrote about: and it is this mind that Christ also recommended to his followers.

> *"Jesus said, "Let the little children come to me, and do not hinder them, for the Kingdom of Heaven belongs to such as these""* (Mt 19:14).

There are times when reading the Gospels that it seems like what Christ actually said got lost in translation. And I don't just mean translation one to the other from Greek, Aramaic or Hebrew or to English, but translation from the spiritual teaching as originally said to what ended up being written down. At times it seems what we ended up with was as the result of playing the "telephone game." If you are unfamiliar with the term, it is when someone whispers a phrase to a person next to them and then they whisper what they believe they heard to the person next to them, and so on down a line. Then, the first person states what she or he said and the last person states what he or she heard. Usually the result is very humorous since by the time the whisper has gone through ten people it ends up bearing little resemblance to what was originally said.

I am not saying this is exactly what is in play here in some of what ended up in the versions of the Gospels as we have them now, but a variation of this effect. The time of Christ was one where the oral tradition was strong, and people were used to memorizing what was said accurately. Rather, what I am speaking of here is the changes that occur when the listener or person doing the transcription can't make sense of the words as they stand, so they change them to make more sense from their perspective.

From what we know of Christ's teachings, he was finding more and more ways to convey what it would take for someone to enter this state of being he called Heaven on earth, Heaven within, or the Kingdom of God. Each time his teachings circle around the core requirements of not being attached to worldly/material things or ideas, being spiritually poor (in the positive sense of being empty and selfless) and adopting a state of mind that is entirely open: the state of mind we discussed earlier known as "beginner's mind," in Zen. This is precisely what children have when born which is lost by their teenage years, let alone adulthood. The sense of wonder of a 3-year-old has a joy about it, clear of many concepts and ideas that they will eventually adopt as they become adult.

Thus, it makes perfect sense that Christ would use children as an example of the kind of state of mind needed to enter the Kingdom. And it is thus in this sense that he most probably meant *"for the Kingdom of Heaven belongs to such as these."* That is, not that it belongs primarily to children—nowhere in his teaching do we find this—but rather to those with a beginner's mind like the one children have prior to societal indoctrination.

Perhaps the most *koan*-like statement attributed to Christ in the New Testament appears in John 8. Early in the exchange "the Jews" are suggesting Christ is possessed by a demon. But Christ rejects this and makes the following seemingly intentionally provocative statement:

"Very truly I tell you, whoever obeys my word will never see death."

They go on to grill him some more, and ask that ever-returning question, "Who do you say you are?" Christ's response is decidedly *koan*-like:

"Before Abraham was born, I am"

Generally, I am hesitant to quote from the Gospel of John as authentic teaching by Christ: it was written long after Jesus' death and is directed to a specific audience with a specific message. This Gospel contains more words attributed to Christ than the other three Gospels combined. The *Jesus Seminar* group who tried to rank the sayings from "probably said" to "likely never said" gave few points at all to any of the speech in John as being authentically the words of Christ.[5] This terminology of "in the beginning was the Word and the Word was with God," etc. (Christ as the *Logos* or Word), appealingly mystical as it is, does not appear in the earlier Gospels written closer to the time of Christ. It thus probably arose out of a movement that incorporated other religious and spiritual traditions, and particularly the writings of Philo, engineered toward the specific audience the author of John was writing for. It was also part of a deliberate pedestalization of Jesus (more about this later in the book).

That said, this Gospel draws more directly on the Jewish

Female Wisdom and Greek Sophia traditions than any of the synoptics, and we now know that Jesus was a Wisdom Teacher in this Jewish/Greek synthesis Wisdom tradition. The opening is pure Philo, with its reference to the Word that is with God since the beginning of creation. This is what is being referred to in the scene in John 8 with the Pharisees: this story, which is written to make a point about who Jesus claimed he is, is intended to clarify that Jesus speaks as one who is in unity with God. As the Wisdom tradition teaches, to enter the Kingdom of Heaven within you, you must first align your will with the will of God. This can also be seen as you becoming aware of your True Self, the self that has always been, is not subject to life and death.

Hence, the reference to those who follow the teachings achieving eternal life, and hence Christ being able to say before Abraham was, I am. And it must be added that the Jewish name for God (YHWH, the "Tetragrammaton" often expanded to Yahweh) means "I am." Clearly, this is an invitation for the reader of John to contemplate what is meant by "eternal life" and what exactly does "I am" mean here? And, to give a hint, Christ is not talking about himself here as Jesus of Nazareth born around 4 B.C.E. This is his True Self he is referring to.

Interestingly, the Book of John is written more as a work in opposition to Judaism rather than as though the audience it is being written for is part of the wider (now largely Gentile) Christian community. But it is still odd that the writer of John has the Pharisees assuming Jesus is a Samaritan possessed by a demon:

"The Jews answered him, "Aren't we right in saying that you are a Samaritan and demon-possessed?"

To which Jesus simply responds:

"I am not possessed by a demon"[6]

But he does not disabuse them of the idea that he is a Samaritan. Indeed, the writer of John seems to support the idea of Christ not being a Jew by referring to the Pharisees as "the Jews" as if Jesus himself were not a Jew. It is likely this tells us a lot about who the intended audience was for this Gospel, which may have been for a group of Christians close to the Jews (geographically and culturally) but not Jews—such as the Samaritans. Indeed, the parable of the Samaritan woman at the well only appears in this Gospel.

Regardless, what is clear from this Gospel is its reliance on Wisdom Tradition teaching, but in lieu of accurate, authentic quotes from Jesus' teaching. Indeed, scholars are still debating if there is any clear evidence that the writer of this Gospel even knew of the synoptic Gospels: Matthew, Mark and Luke. There is only a hint of overlap in sayings of Jesus, his life, the parables, between this Gospel and the synoptics, further suggesting it was written in a vacuum from the core Christian movement that arose after Christ's crucifixion, promoting the idea of a post-Easter Jesus placed on a pedestal as being other, more than human.

There is also considerable dispute about who wrote this Gospel. Indeed, what little is relatively undisputed is that it was not based on the writing or words of John the disciple of Christ, and hence not by "St. John" as tradition falsely claims. Intriguingly, the Gospel claims to be based on the words of the one of Jesus' followers whom it is said he specifically loved. As Bart Ehrman has reminded us, the Apostle Levi confirmed that Jesus favored Mary Magdalene over the other disciples.[7] And it is Mary Magdalene who is referred to in various of the gnostic Gospels as being the disciple Christ loved the most, never (outside of the Gospel of John) is it suggested John is the particular beloved.

Moreover, in the various Gospels it is repeated that only the women were present at the cross. While there is variation on who is present, at least it is consistently stated as Mary the mother of Jesus and Mary Magdalene.[8] Thus when the writer of John states that Jesus looked down from the cross he now says he sees his mother and standing nearby is the disciple whom he loved.[9] This passage has been the source of much contention and debate over the years, since it is consistent across the Gospels that only the women were present at the cross. Thus, it seems odd when the writer of John has just said only the women were present that he should suddenly imply there was a male disciple there, too.

Admittedly it is only conjecture, but given Mary Magdalene is elsewhere identified as the follower that Christ loved more than his other disciples, and since even John talks in terms of there being just women present, then it seems possible the "disciple whom he loved" is in fact Mary Magdalene. What follows in John 19:27 clearly suggests the beloved disciple is a man, but it appears possible the text was changed at a later date rather than suggest that Jesus favored a woman disciple or that he left his mother in the care of a woman.[10]

Ultimately this may be idle speculation, but it does go to the idea that not only was Christ a Wisdom Teacher, but that a wisdom tradition arose in at least some of the communities of his followers that stayed truer to his teaching and also retained mention of the importance of Mary Magdalene as a key disciple. I will return to this topic later since there are other aspects of what we know about Mary Magdalene that speak to Christ's teachings and what came to be known as "the Way."

The Kingdom of Heaven is Like …

Christ's use of his "The Kingdom of Heaven is like…" parables introduce a more *koan*-like flavor to his teachings. Consider the parable of the workers where the employer pays the worker who comes to the vineyard toward the end of the day the same as the worker who showed up for work at the start of the day.[11] Here what Christ is presenting is contrary to what any of his listeners would be used to: if you work part of a day then you get paid for part of a day. Anyone who arrives on time and works a full day is paid for a full day and probably gets credit for being punctual and a hard worker. How then can a great teacher suddenly be saying the lazy later-commers get rewarded just as much as the hard workers? Christ's genius as a teacher lay in large part in his being able to place such conundrums before his followers.

The intellect is invited to respond to the parable: to come up with the conclusion that God is thus like a somewhat crazy, idealistic employer who is so obsessed with treating absolutely everyone equally that he will encourage laziness and at the expense of promptness and hard work. But this is not of course what Christ meant by this story: the invitation is to a realization beyond thought, beyond intellect. Christ's teaching here is about the nature of the "Kingdom of Heaven (within)." What is it like? As it happens, the Kingdom is all about radical inclusiveness, and radical equality, but it is far more than that. This teaching goes to the heart of why it is so hard for a rich man to enter the Kingdom. Here being "rich" does not necessarily mean someone with overt extreme wealth by the measure of society, but those who measure their own self-worth, or self-identity, on the basis of how much they earn.

The Kingdom of Heaven runs on God's time, not human

time. There is no being early or being late to the Kingdom: you enter the timeless, the eternal, and it is entirely irrelevant "when" (in human terms) you entered the Kingdom. The truth is you have always been in the Kingdom, and it is an illusion that you are outside of the Kingdom trying to get in. Similarly, the Kingdom is indeed a place of radical equality: it is not a state of mind where someone is worth more than another nor does it make any sense to speak of being paid in human terms as if a laborer in a vineyard for hours worked.

Putting it around the other way, if you are fixated on the person arriving late getting paid the same amount as you who arrived early, then you are like that "rich" man basing his concept of self on attachments, and thus unable to enter the Kingdom. It is a prerequisite for entry to the Kingdom that you truly empty yourself, even of comparisons or judgments based on measures like hours worked, standing in society, or etc. "*My time is the timeless, my place is the placeless*," as Rumi said.

The beauty of Christ's parables is the various levels they work on. So here the same parable about the workers in the vineyard also shows us not only how the Kingdom of Heaven is radically inclusive and suffused with inherent equality, it is also about the fact that this our True Self, our non-dual consciousness which is one with God, is not of this human time and space. The Kingdom has existed since beginningless time, and as I mentioned above it is only an illusion that we need to 'enter' it since we have always been in it. How can you be late to the vineyard when you were always in the vineyard? You can't.

Others of Christ's parables dealt with similar teachings, such as the parable of the talents and the parable of the prodigal son. We will return to this topic in a later chapter, but it is interesting how Christ changes the concepts in the original

Indian parable about the prodigal son to fit his message, rather than the point being made by the Indian original. And as with most of the parables, and like Zen *koans*, these work so well because they can be understood on many different levels.

Christ's version of the prodigal son parable once again invites the intellect to say "But that's not fair!" The son who is loyal and remains home is taken for granted, but the son who lead a wayward life and then eventually returns is treated like returning royalty. How can that be right? And once again, Christ's parables take on a *koan*-like nature, since they seek to entrap the intellect and provoke a shift to beyond (*meta*) thought (*noia*). One level this works on is like the message we got from the vineyard workers: you will be rewarded no matter when you enter the Kingdom and welcomed like a long-lost son. This reflects the experience many have upon awakening or having an awakening experience (Japanese *kensho*): it can be such a revelation, such an epiphany, that it can be an emotionally overwhelming experience.

What Christ could have added is, do not expect the royal welcome each time you come home (or each time you realize you were always home), don't expect fireworks every time. For some this search for the repeat royal welcome, the initial 'high' of an awakening experience can be what derails their spiritual journey. You may feel like you're on cloud nine as you enter the Kingdom, or have that flash of your True nature, but being in the Kingdom (living the awakened life) isn't about being on cloud nine all the time. That is a fundamental misunderstanding and serious error.

Similarly, the parable of the talents can invoke the intellectual response, "But that's no fair!" too. In the time of Christ, it was thought to be wrong to benefit from others such as by requiring interest on loans. Hence, from a very traditional Jewish perspective of that time, it would be the third servant who did the right thing. Let's remind ourselves of the parable: the owner goes away leaving his estate in the hands of three servants. Each servant is given a number of talents (a unit of currency, a coin) according to his ability. Thus, one servant receives five, another two, and the third receives just one. The first two somehow invest their coins and produce as many more as they received. The owner is happy. The third who only received one decides to bury it and upon the owner's return he hands the same coin back. The owner is angry at him for this, takes the talent from him, gives it to the servant who now has ten, and throws the failing servant out of the household. To a place where there will be "weeping and gnashing of teeth"! (This is a rather fun addition, I think, showing Jesus had quite a sense of humor).

To unpack this, we need to ask some basic questions. Where is the place with weeping and gnashing of teeth? Well, of course it is right here in the material world, full of stress and trauma, where you are not aligning your will with God's will. This is the world of suffering—a key point Buddha constantly made and focused on the need to escape suffering by discovering our true selves. In Christian terms, the regular world we live in is darkness, full of suffering. The Kingdom of Heaven is the place of light and freedom from suffering. Note, not freedom from pain, freedom from suffering. Pain is inevitable, suffering is optional.

So this place the last servant was thrown into was this everyday world where worth is defined by wealth and stature, and where your concept of your self is based on the mistaken idea that you are an individual separate from all other individuals—a living, walking, talking ego among a sea of other living, walking, talking egos. This parable is thus once again about emptying yourself and the need to be empty—to adopt a beginner's mind—in order to enter the Kingdom of Heaven. This is a parable about being who you truly are: living your life to the fullest, using your talents (a play on words that works in modern English) to the full, and truly being all that you can be. To do this you must empty yourself: if you have five then use all five and five will be given to you. If you have two, use all two and two more will be given. But become scared and try to become attached to the one you have such that you hide it, and from you even that one will be taken. That is, your ability to perceive that you are in the Kingdom, and to perceive who you truly are—one with God—will be taken from you.

The question then arises, who does the taking? If you think it is God who takes from you, then revisit this idea. Sit with it, pray with it. It is you and you alone who can realize who you are and that you have always resided in the Kingdom. It is purely an illusion that you perceive things to be otherwise. And if you are also already ranking yourself as a five talent, or two talent or one talent person, then drop that too. Drop it all. You're missing the point if you think this is about ranking.

Let's have a closer look at Christ's other parables and sayings.

~*~

The Parable of the Sower

This parable is present in all three synoptic Gospels (Mt. 13:3-9, Mk 4:1-9, Lk 8:5-8) as well as present in the Gospel of Thomas (Thom. 9). One reason this parable is essential to our discussion is what follows it in each of the synoptic Gospels—namely, Christ's explanation as to why he tells parables.

The wording differs a little Gospel to Gospel, as if perhaps having a single source that lead to variations of the original. But the gist is common to the versions: Christ says he has given the secrets of the Kingdom of Heaven to his followers but to others he has not given the secrets of Heaven and therefore he talks in parables. First, please note the gnostic element that comes in here: the inner group of people who have the knowledge (the *gnosis*) and an outer group who have not yet been inducted into the secrets of the knowledge. Here, perhaps, is a hint that Christ was at least exposed to the gnostic teachings of that time, or perhaps that the writer had been exposed to such terminology even if Christ himself did not actually use it.

Second, this is a point in the Gospels where Christ speaks in a very *koan*-like way:

> *"Whoever has will be given more, and he will have an abundance. Whoever does not have, even what he has will be taken from him. This is why I speak to them in parables: "Though seeing, they do not see; though hearing, they do not hear or understand""*[12]

The abundance portion sits easily with us: if you have something you will be given more. This sounds reasonable (although it invokes what is objectionable about capitalism). But the next portion is where Christ is using his Wisdom Teaching skills to their fullest as he says whoever does not have even that will be taken from them. You can almost hear the wizened old Zen Master who, when the student says, "I have nothing," responds "Show me this nothing that you say you have."

Speaking then as if he has said something simple and intuitively obvious, Christ goes on to say that this is why he speaks to "them" in parables: because they have eyes but do not see, they have ears but do not hear (understand). This is the core of Wisdom Teaching: to understand with the heart not the head would be another way to put it. If you have fully dropped all preconceptions and ideas about what is, then and only then can you see and hear reality as it truly is. Then and only then can you realize your True Self, your oneness with God.

If you have started on this path of self-emptying, then to you will more be added even to abundance. But if you have not, then what is that? It is to have the *idea* that you have not, and this is what stands in your way. That idea that you have not is what needs to be taken away, so as to truly empty yourself. As we see, Christ returns to this fundamental teaching over and again.

Christ then goes on to give us some insight into how he perceived the challenge before him in teaching to those who—like the person whose tea cup is already full—believe they already know and understand, and so with hardened, calloused hearts they cannot see and they cannot hear. He clarifies that many prophets and righteous men have longed to see what his followers see (the secrets of Heaven) but despite looking they could not see, despite listening they could not hear.

This is also one of the few times that Christ goes on to explain what his parable of the sower means. The first seeds sown along the path where the birds quickly eat them up. The version of the explanation that has come down to us it has Christ saying that anyone who hears a teaching but does not understand it, then what is sown in his heart is simply snatched away. And here Christ is at least in part linking his teaching to the prophets and righteous men who are so certain they *already* "know" that they cannot receive new teaching. He is of course also referring to everyone whose heart and mind are closed with certainty, against new ideas, conceptions, and so forth, so that it is simply impossible to penetrate them with new teaching.

The next example, of the seed falling on rocky places, is a very insightful one. At first the person "gets it" and rejoices at the teaching, but because they have no roots—no foundation—to build upon, it takes only a small upset or distraction for it to all be lost again on them. Here we have Christ advocating for training before receiving wisdom, since without training and preparation the impact of the teaching may be short-lived.

So far, it is easy to understand why Christ defends his use of parables. By talking in parables rather than direct attempts to transmit wisdom, those who are receptive will "get it." However, those who are not receptive will simply dismiss the teaching as nonsense or impenetrable. Someone not quite ready for the teaching will get something from it, but if they then lose it again the parable remains to be returned to at a later date to be appreciated again as if for the first time. Teaching in parables has this distinct advantage: readers/listeners can appreciate the parable at various levels depending on where they are at in their personal journey, but they can also return again and again to plumb yet greater depths—hopefully without being scared off by a "too difficult" teaching. Many in the Zen world will immediately appreciate the parallel here with Zen *koan* work.

Christ then goes on to discuss the image of seed falling among thorns: the recipient "gets" the teaching—at least at some level—but his worries about the world or his attachment to material things or status stand in his way rendering the teaching ultimately ineffective. This again is a teaching Christ returns to with his admonitions that a rich man cannot enter the state of being he calls Heaven, or that to enter you must be like a little child.

But the seed that falls on fertile soil results in fruitful teaching and the student hears and understands fully. You may be asking yourself why Christ then says that this person "produces a crop, yielding a hundred, sixty or thirty times what is sown." What is meant here? Why these specific numbers? You may wish to sit with this.

~*~

The Cloth, the Wine, the Lamp and the Builders

These are the first four parables as they appear in the Gospels: *New Cloth Patched to an Old Cloak,*[13] *New Wine in Old Wineskins,*[14] *Lamp on a Stand,*[15] and *Wise and Foolish Builders.*[16] Despite being in a different chronological order, each of these follows naturally after the Parable of the Sower since they deal with many of the same teachings. The challenge facing Christ is palpable: he comes not to replace the Law but to build upon it. But he is also painfully aware that people may be so entrenched in what they believe they already "know" then it is impossible for the person to hear and understand new teachings.

Indeed, as true as it was for Christ in First Century Palestine as he faced those who felt they already "knew" the truth (the prophets and righteous men he refers to above), we face that now with two thousand years of teachings forming a canon that has little to nothing to do with what Christ actually taught. Tempting as it is to "patch" the existing teachings arising from what Saul of Tarsus wrote and the centuries of church misinterpretation, to do so is to (in Christ's words) "make the tear worse." Clarifying the actual teachings and preserving them will take putting new cloth on new garments, new wine in new wineskins.

This goes for the teachings themselves that cannot be a gentle slight reworking of the canonical norms, but it goes for each of us, too. For once again, here Christ is speaking of the need to empty ourselves before we can pour in the new wine since only by emptying ourselves can we convert the old wineskins into new. An unfortunate metaphor, perhaps, given damage alcohol has caused to so many, but keep in mind these are only metaphors. Don't get attached to the words.

The putting the light on a stand rather than hiding it under a bowl goes to the last teaching in the parable of the sower: the teaching having taken root calls on you to respond with "How may I help you?" It does not call on you to retreat to a quiet place where you privately congratulate yourself on how spiritual you now are. The fourth parable, of the wise and foolish builders, parallels the teaching of the sower spreading seed on thin soil. But it also goes to the same teaching of the Lamp: you have been given a teaching in order to put them into practice. In order to respond with joy, saying "How may I help you?" That is both the Christian Way, and the Bodhisattva Way, since they are one in the same.

~*~

The Moneylender

This parable follows a theme that Jesus returned to often. The scene is Jesus visiting the house of a Pharisee named Simon. They are reclining at the table when a local woman enters who is apparently a known local "sinner." She washes

Jesus' feet with her tears and then pours costly perfume on his feet. The Pharisee seems shocked that Jesus would even let this person touch him.

Typical of Jesus' response to such criticism from the established religious elite, he turns the question back on the Pharisee and asks him a question: if a money lender was owed 50 coins by one person, and 200 coins by another, and forgives the debt of both men, which man would love the moneylender more? To which the Pharisee responds that he presumes it would be the man who had the larger debt forgiven. Hearing which Jesus turns it around and says this woman's many sins are all forgiven "because she loved so much." He continues, if one is forgiven little then one loves little.

If this were anyone other than Jesus, I suspect there would be a cry of "non-sequitur!": just because he who is forgiven much loves much in return doesn't necessary mean he who loves much is consequently forgiven more. But we are in the realm of metaphor here, where love and forgiveness are intertwined—two sides of the same coin. Here, then, is the flipside of Korean Zen Master Seung Sahn's teaching regarding dropping ashes on the Buddha.[17] In the Zen teaching someone enters a Zen center and is disrespectful to a statue of Buddha by dropping ashes from his cigarette onto the statue. Here in Jesus' parable we have someone expressly showing proper respect and exhibiting right action, right conduct.

~*~

The Rich Fool

Here in Luke 12:15-21, Christ is once again teaching about the folly of being attached to worldly possessions. The rich man has a particularly good crop and talks about building bigger barns to store it all in for purely selfish reasons of then being able to live in comfort for even longer. The parable has God informing the foolish rich man that he will die that very night, so why store up worldly riches? Seen in one light it's the old cliché "you can't take it with you," But it's more fundamental than that, as Zen teaching has it, who you are is "How may I help you?" not "How can I better improve my own situation?" This all speaks to the cultivation of what we call the Bodhisattva Way—the way Christ spoke of, too, where you focus is on your will being aligned with God's will. Which is no more or less than you being your True Self, and who you truly are is interconnected with everyone. Thus, when you realize your True Self you realize that there is no "helping the other rather than helping yourself" since there is no "other" separate and distinct from your "self."

~*~

Watchfulness

The next parable at Luke 12:35-40 deals with servants waiting for their master to return from a wedding banquet. Ostensibly, it is a teaching on always being prepared. But it is also a teaching on the importance of always being fully awake which in turn means to be fully aware. Again, Buddha means the awakened one, and that is what the core teaching of both Buddha and Christ calls us to do—to wake up and remain awake.

Here we are not talking about being permanently awake as if the teaching means to not sleep—to become an insomniac. No, the wakefulness spoken of here is being completely alive, completely attentive, transparent, without judgment, free from the ties that bind us arising from constructs we have created that we falsely perceive as real, as fact. Rather it is a state of being of perceptual readiness, openness—a state of true presence. As Thomas Keating says,[18] God is present to everything and sees everything just as it is. We, by contrast, are only partially present. What we seek, then, is to become fully present. [19]

~*~

The Faithful and Wise Servant

Next, we have in Luke 12:42-48, a description of a faithful, sensible servant. Yet again, Christ references the relationship as being one of a servant to a master. Our true nature is to live to serve others—indeed who we truly are is a conduit through which the lessening of suffering flows to others. Or to use more Christian terminology, we are the conduit for God's love. It is the core teaching "Not my will but thy will be done" repeated in a new guise. It is also a repeat of the prior lesson: to be always aware, always prepared. Focusing on others ("How may I help you?") rather than our own, closed, narrow egotistical needs is to be focused on non-dualistic perception of reality and no on dualistic perception.

One of the key strengths of Christ's use of parables and sayings to teach was that his words could be interpreted on at least two levels. Here you can take a message of being a "good person" who is not just "good" when s/he knows they are being observed, or being called upon to be good, and the rest of the time acting selfishly. Yet again we are reminded that the word "good" derives from the word "God" so to be good meant in the original context to act in accord with God's will. This was a core teaching Christ kept coming back to: your key goal is to align your will with God's will—let your will and God's will become one and you will become a Son (or Daughter) of God. But this is none other than the same as becoming aware of your True Self: realizing your Christ-nature is the same as realizing your Buddha-nature. It is about becoming fully awake in the moment, moment after moment after moment.

When awake, when wills are aligned and attuned, there is no "me/them," "us/other" and it thus becomes natural as breathing to act in accord with right action, right speech, and right livelihood.

~*~

Seed Sown in Four Types of Ground

This is a seminal parable, often retold (Mt 13:3-23). It is notable for the fact that it is one of the times Christ is asked "Why do you teach in parables?" He replied, "*The knowledge of the secrets of the Kingdom of Heaven has been given to you, but not to them. Whoever has will be given more, and he will have an abundance. Whoever does not have, even what he has will be taken from him. This is why I speak to them in parables: Though seeing, they do not see; though hearing, they do not hear or understand.*"

How wonderfully Zen, and how *koan*-like: "*Whoever does not have, even what he has will be taken from him.*"

Not surprisingly, over the millennia Christian scholars have debated the meaning of this teaching. Indeed, it is often simply labelled as a "difficult saying" with suggestions that perhaps we are not meant to understand what it means. Yet other scholars note that whereas Matthew and Mark (4:25) both have this phrase "even what he has will be taken from him," Luke has a variant, "whoever does not have, even what he thinks he has will be taken from him" (Lk 8:18).

These scholars argue that Mark and Matthew got confused, or simply failed at accurate translations, and that Luke's revised wording is merely a clarification of what Jesus actually said. They base their argument on what they see as the obviously nonsensical nature of the version that appears in both Mark and Matthew: the logic goes, if the earlier two versions don't make sense then Luke was just adding sense where sense was needed. The trouble is, there is no actual evidence for this, nor does it explain why both Mark and Matthew have the same phrase—why, in these scholar's view of things, would Mark and Matthew both make the same "mistake?"

Of course, it's a nice side-step to the teaching to say, "well what Jesus obviously really meant is that to those who have nothing even what he thinks he has will be taken away." After all, now the teaching makes sense, and refocuses the message on people believing they have something when they in fact do not. And because they only thought they had it, therefore of course it is taken away (because they don't actually really have it...), which when we unpack the Luke version like this helps us to realize that this was not what Jesus was teaching. Luke was not merely "clarifying" what Mark and Matthew should have written.

A further blow to these scholars' theory that Luke was clarifying what Jesus really said when he wrote 8:18, the problem for them is that at 19:26 Luke then goes on to put in the mouth of Jesus the following: "*but the one who does not have, even what he has will be taken away from him.*" So much for the simplistic theory Luke was clarifying by adding in "what he thinks he has."

~*~

Ten Servants and Ten Minas

This is the parable (Lk 19:12-27) referred to above. In this teaching, Jesus is responding to his followers appearing to expect the Kingdom of God to appear immediately at that time. He thus told the story of a man of noble birth who went away to a distant country to have himself appointed as king and then to return to take the throne. Before leaving he called ten of his servants and gave them each one mina.

A mina was a coin with a value of between a third and a quarter of the annual wages of an agricultural worker[20] which some have estimated to be around $470 in current day currency.[21] This was thus not an inconsiderable sum to give the servants.

The noble man returns having been made king and sends for the servants he had given the minas to. The first servant reports that he has turned the one mina into ten more, which pleases the king who gives him ten cities to be in charge of. The second reports that he has made five more mina from the one he was given, and again the king is pleased and gives him five cities. Then a third servant comes forward and says that he just kept the one mina safe. The king is furious: "Why," he asks, "did you not at least have the mina make interest while I was away?"

The king then instructs someone standing nearby to take the mina from this servant and "give it to the one who has ten minas." The person addressed exclaims, "Sir, he already has ten!" To which the king responds (echoing the earlier parable), "I tell you that to everyone who has, more will be given, but as for the one who has nothing, even what he has will be taken away."

Now, this doesn't make sense on a couple of levels. First, no servant has ten minas: the one who had his single mina and makes ten more, now presumably has eleven minas. But we can be generous and assume that it was that servant being referred to. Then it isn't true that the servant with nothing had even that taken away from him: he had one mina and it was taken away.

We will never know if this parable was written down inaccurately, or indeed was not a parable actually told by Jesus but rather an invention of the writer—who was less skilled at devising parables than Jesus was. But the fact remains that even Luke who in the prior parable changes "has nothing and even that is taken away" to "has nothing and even what he thinks he has is taken away," here reverts to the enigmatic turn of phrase elsewhere attributed to Jesus: "the one who has nothing, even that will be taken away."

~*~

Three Servants Given Talents

This too is essentially the same teaching—that those who have nothing, even that will be taken away—that appears elsewhere. It seems a very popular theme for Jesus in his parables since it is one theme that is repeated so many times with only minor variations. Here (Mt 25:14-30) once again a man going on a journey calls his servants to entrust his property to them while he is gone. To one he gave five talents. To another two talents and to a third he gave one talent.

The first servant put his five talents to work and earned five more. The second did the same and earned two more. But the third went off, dug a hole in the ground and buried his master's money. When the master returns, he is delighted with the first two servants, but he gets angry with the third accusing him of knowing that he harvests where he has not sown and gathers where he has not scattered seed. And that thus the servant should have at least deposited the talent with bankers to gain the interest.

Now here the master again, as with the prior parable, instructs an unnamed person present to take the one talent from this servant and give it to the one who has ten talents. This is how the master justifies what he has decided: "*Whoever does not have, even what he has will be taken from him. And throw that worthless servant outside, into the darkness, where there will be weeping and gnashing of teeth*."

First, the similarity of the two parables leads one to speculate that the prior parable of the ten minas was possibly a misremembering of this parable. Since here it now makes sense to say take the one coin from the servant with one coin and give it to the servant with ten coins. Supporting this theory of the ten minas parable being a redundant flawed accounting of this same parable, in the ten-mina parable though it calls for ten servants only three servants are addressed in the dialog. I thus believe these are the same parable, the second (of the talents) being likely a more accurate rendition of what Jesus taught than the first (of the minas).

Second, we have the rather astounding statement that the third servant will be thrown outside "into the darkness" where there will be "weeping and gnashing of teeth." Although I didn't mention it earlier, the prior parable of the ten minas also ends with a similarly violent conclusion when the unnamed bystander points out the first servant already had ten minas: "I tell you that to everyone who has, more will be given, but as for the one who has nothing, even what he has will be taken away. But those enemies of mine who did not want me to be king over them—bring them here and kill them in front of me."

Both examples of aggression and violence seem at odds with what we otherwise know about Jesus and his teachings of love and compassion. We shall never know, but it seems likely given Jesus would hardly have spoken such words of aggression, that Luke (or whomever Luke was borrowing from) decided he couldn't just leave that phrase hanging out there: "from he who has nothing even that will be taken." They felt the need to embellish this.

Whereas in the other instance, Luke amends it to be "what he thought he had will be taken." Here he opts for making the consequences of the teaching more violent. Since Jesus is reported several times ending his teaching with the "from he who has nothing even that will be taken," it seems likely that all the additions and amendments arose from Luke trying to make sense of one of Jesus' pithiest teachings.

~*~

One who has nothing, even what he has will be taken away

So, what does this phrase mean? Again, this seems to be one of the most *koan*-like statements Jesus is purported to have said, and he is reported as saying it several times. Some insight into the first century Jewish meaning behind this phrase may be gained from considering Talmud writings. As K.J. Went has observed, the following is a well-known Talmudic writing:

> *"A mortal can put something into an empty vessel but not into a full one, but the Holy One, blessed be He, is not*

> *so, He puts more into a full vessel but not into an empty one.*" (Babylonian Talmud, *Berakôth*, 40*a*; *Sukkah* 46*a*)[22]

The Zen "Cup of Tea" *koan* comes to mind, again:

> *Nan-in, a Japanese master during the Meiji era (1868–1912), received a university professor who came to inquire about Zen. Nan-in served tea. He poured his visitor's cup full, and then kept on pouring. The professor watched the overflow until he no longer could restrain himself. "It is overfull. No more will go in!" "Like this cup," Nan-in said, "you are full of your own opinions and speculations. How can I show you Zen unless you first empty your cup?"*[23]

Here are two different cultures and traditions, two almost opposite metaphorical images. In one we have the image of God giving most to someone whose cup is already overflowing, and in the other a master teacher who cannot teach someone who is already too full of ideas, concepts and preconceptions.

The Jewish way of thinking, though, gives rise to what some have dubbed the "Matthew effect" (otherwise known as the Matthew principle or the Matthew effect of accumulated advantage). Stated simply, the effect says that the rich get richer and the poor get poorer. To those who perform well more tasks and merit are given, to those who underperform, fewer new tasks or rewards are given.

The "Matthew effect" was coined by Robert K. Merton to describe, for instance, how famous researchers get more credit for their work than unknown researchers who do essentially the same work.[24] Seen simplistically, this appears to be what Christ was teaching: if you work actively towards building the Kingdom of God on earth, then God will favor you and reward you, whereas if you are lazy or simply refuse to work toward the Kingdom, then you will fall into God's disfavor and not be rewarded in life.

But the teaching is deeper than that and is ultimately a teaching about dualism versus non-dualism. It is both the joy and the challenge of Christ's parables and sayings that more often than not they can be read on at least two different levels. Here with these several related parables is no exception. At the surface level of understanding, the teachings say that if you work towards establishing the Kingdom of Heaven (on earth) then God will reward you. The harder you work, the more "full" you are of such work, the more you will be rewarded. There is some similarity to a more simplistic view of karma: if you do good then good will happen to you. The more good you do the more you benefit. Again, this is a simplistic view of karma, not an accurate one.

But the deeper teaching goes to Christ's message about dualistic versus non-dualistic thinking and action. Throughout so many of his parables and sayings, Christ keeps coming back to common themes: develop "don't know" mind, the mind of wonder of a child (childlike not childish), align your will with God's will (that is, realize your true self, your Christ nature, your oneness with the ground of being), reject attachment to material things, and so on.

While the two approaches (Zen and Jewish wisdom) may at first seem to be at odds—one teaching your cup must be empty, the other that it must be full—they are in fact both addressing essentially the same teaching. Insight into how this can be is gained from appreciating that a core part of Christ's teaching was the practice of *kenosis*, or "self-emptying."

Kenosis (or rather the verb form *kenóō*) is mentioned five times in the New Testament (Ro.4:14, 1Co.1:17, 9:15, 2Co.9:3,

Phil.2:7) with exponents of Christ's "self-emptying" core practice using the text of Philippians (2:7) which describes Christ emptying himself of his own will and filling himself with God's will. This is Christ's teaching, mentioned elsewhere in here, that a key goal of following Christ's "The Way" was to align your will with God's will, thereby becoming a son (or daughter) of God.

Another way to think of this is that this *kenosis* is an overcoming of ego-based behavior and thought, a transformation from dualistic (ego-based) being to non-dualistic being. An emptying yourself of your "self" (with a small s) and filling yourself with your True "Self" (with a large S). The simple truth is that as you enter into non-dual consciousness then your entire being simultaneously becomes totally empty (of self, ego, dualism), and yet by the very fact of being thus 'empty' is therefore totally full. Non-dual consciousness cannot be partial—it is full to overflowing at all times since it is, after all, awakening.

To evoke a modern parable, it is like the woman who went around with extremely dark glasses on, glasses that turned her world dark and monochromatic, along with blinkers that cut out most of her field of vision. And then one sunny mid-summer day, the woman takes off her glasses and removed the blinkers. In that moment she goes from being full of a dark, limited view of the world to be filled with light, color, expanse of vision.

The spiritual transformation from ego-based, dualistic being to non-dualistic fully awakened being is like this. But it isn't the end of the journey: there is then the integration of the dual and the non-dual. To draw the parallel of a compass, realizing non-dual consciousness is like getting to 180—but our journey doesn't end until we get all the way back round to

360, having fully integrated the dual and non-dual (or in Zen terms, the "absolute" and the "relative"—but more on that later and elsewhere in this and subsequent books).

Let's look again at the core teaching Christ is reported to have used in more than one parable: "*as for the one who has nothing, even what he has will be taken away.*" (Mt 13:12)

In teaching my students as we work on *koan* introspection I caution them to look out for "the hook." Many *koans* have at least one hook, and often there is a core hook. What form this hook takes varies *koan* to *koan*, but in general it is the part of the text that is designed to draw the intellect in. In other cases, it may be just a red herring or a deliberately misleading, or even downright false, statement. But the intellect is drawn to it as if a moth to a flame.

Here in what Christ taught I would suggest the hook is the word "has." Elsewhere in his parables and sayings, Christ focuses on a core part of following "The Way" is to not be attached to material possessions. He speaks of becoming like little children in order to enter the Kingdom of Heaven (within), and of how it is harder for a rich man to achieve this state of consciousness than it is for a camel to pass through the eye of a needle. And elsewhere still he teaches his followers to look at whose face is on a coin: "*Give to Caesar things that are Caesar's and give to God that which is God's.*" (Mt 22:21)

These are all part of Christ's core teaching on attachment, which is also a core part of the Buddha's teaching, too. The teaching goes like this: so long as you think there is a "you" (or "I") that can "have" things, you will not be able to realize your Christ nature/Buddha nature. To believe you "have" things is central to dualist thinking, and a core illusion that keeps us from being awake to who we truly are.

Thus, perhaps credit to the writer of Luke who added in

the nuance of "even what he thinks he has will be taken from him." It's a transformative road we travel that goes from "Oh woe is me, I have nothing" to "How amazing, I have nothing!" As paradoxical as it may seem, it is not until we fully realize our true nature is not to "have things" that we can become empty and thereby have everything. But here the "have" is synonymous with "being:" we realize our oneness with everything (non-dual awareness) means that we are everything. There is no "me" and (separate from) "it," "me" and (separate from) "you."

Yet as I have said before, this realization gets us to 180: when we get there we still have to integrate the reality of being human—of what is meant by form rather than formlessness—and ultimately the realization at 360 that we are both separate and not separate. That the relative and the absolute are not two different "things" or concepts: form is formlessness, and formlessness is form as Zen teachers would have it.

In Christ's teaching, we are both human and divine: we are one with God (a Son or Daughter of God) and thus with the entire universe, but there is still a real sense in which we are individual human beings (children of God). We are God pretending to be human, pretending to be God. And with that, we touch on the whole idea of incarnation which is addressed elsewhere in this book. In us, God plays hide and seek with God.

We will return to this later, but a central theme of these parables and sayings by Christ is *kenosis*: the emptying of the self. Only by emptying ourselves (of the ego, or dualistic thinking), he taught, can we become full of God. Elsewhere Christ refers to this as setting aside our will and aligning ourselves with God's will. This, he teaches, makes one who achieves such alignment a Son (or Daughter) of God. And he contrasts this idea of becoming a "Son of God" with being a child of God—part of God's creation, a unique individual in a universe of unique individuals.

Thus, in Christ's teaching to be a "Son of God" (or Daughter) is the non-dualistic state of being, in contrast to identifying as a "child of God," which is the dualistic state of being. Sadly, this essential, powerful, teaching by Christ gets hidden in the traditional teachings of the established Christian Church. From shortly after his death, it seems there was an immediate push to reinvent Jesus as something "other" and unattainable, a divine being dwelling temporarily in a human body.

From shortly after Jesus' death, starting perhaps with the teachings of Saul of Tarsus (later known as "St. Paul"), writers hurriedly tried to rewrite history in order to elevate—or *pedestalize*—Jesus as a kind of magical being. Hence, only Jesus could be "the" Christ, and only Jesus could be "the" (only) Son of God. By the time the Gospel of John was written, one or two lifetimes after Jesus' death, the audience for such writings had solidly become those who were being taught to believe that Christ was someone *other*, someone beyond a mere mortal, who was and had achieved things that no one else could ever achieve. This was not, however, what Jesus taught during his lifetime.

This is touched on elsewhere in this book, but during his lifetime we have a fairly clear record from the synoptic Gospels (Matthew, Mark and Luke) that whenever any of his followers tried to put Christ on a pedestal and say he was the Son of God, the chosen one, the Messiah, an other-worldly divine being, he replied, "Who do you say I am?" In these early Gospels Christ does not claim to be *the* Son of God or *the* Messiah. This message is clouded, however, by later additions and changes to all three Gospels adding in text well after his death to the effect that Christ admitted he was the Messiah and swore his followers to secrecy that he had admitted this fact (from which follows, if they were sworn to secrecy how could the writer know this? He couldn't, of course).

Here is another useful observation: note how many times in the Gospels—especially Mark and Matthew, the earliest ones—that it is said that something happened in secret or that Christ asked those present not to speak of what was said. This is usually a clue to wording that has been added later to support the post-crucifixion narrative that sought to pedestalize Jesus. Have you ever stopped to ask yourself, in these passages where Jesus is meant to have ordered those present not to say anything, how did it come to be written down? Or if the text indicates something happened in secret, or without a witness, how did that come to be written down?

You can, of course, dismiss such an observation by saying "well, despite his order to say nothing someone must have said something." But this is not likely. Although tradition has the four Gospels named after disciples, there is wide agreement that none of them were written by any of Christ's followers. Nor do we believe that any of Christ's disciples contributed directly to the writing of any of the Gospels. The earliest Gospel writings seem to date from around 66 C.E., or at least 33 years after the crucifixion.

This was just a brief exploration of how Christ's parables can be viewed in a different light—as being far closer to Buddhist teachings than usually acknowledged. A comprehensive "re-viewing" of all his sayings and parables through the lens of Zen will be the topic of a subsequent book since a full commentary on and discussion of all of the parables and sayings would fill an entire separate volume.

[1] Mt. 10:25
[2] Mt. 6:22
[3] Shunryu Suzuki, *Zen Mind, Beginner's Mind,* Weatherhill, 2006
[4] Mt. 19:14
[5] Funk, W. Robert (1996) *The Five Gospels: What Did Jesus Really Say? The Search for the Authentic Words of Jesus.* HarperOne: San Francisco.
[6] Jn 8:48
[7] Ehrman, Bart D (2003). *Lost Scriptures.* New York: Oxford University Press. p. 35.
[8] Jn 19:25
[9] Jn 19:26
[10] Not wishing to belabor this point, but we do know that Jesus' brother, James, survived him and would presumably have looked after Mary. There is thus some evidence that the writer of John was anti-James and anti-Thomas (as discussed elsewhere in this book) and thus deliberately didn't mention James. This point clearly bears further reflection and research.
[11] Mt. 20:1-16
[12] Mt. 13:12-13
[13] Mt. 9:16
[14] Mt. 9:17
[15] Mt. 5:14-15
[16] Lk 6:46-49
[17] *Dropping Ashes on the Buddha: The Teachings of Zen Master Seung Sahn,* Grove Press, Reissue Edn, 1994.
[18] Thomas Keating, *Intimacy with God,* Crossroads Publishing, 1994.
[19] The goal of a chaplain is to become a non-anxious, non-judgmental presence and indeed ideally to be fully present to their patient or client. This is one reason why chaplaincy is an ideal career choice for those traveling on The Way.
[20] The value of 3-4 months wages is widely stated in Bible commentary.
[21] This value is arrived at by noting that according to *Pseudolus* written by the ancient Roman playwright Plautus (191 B.C.E.) the price of a slave was 20 mina which was estimated to be worth $18.05 in the currency of 1912 when it was first calculated. By using standard US inflation calculators that would make a mina worth around $470 today.
[22] https://www.studylight.org/language-studies/difficult-sayings.html
[23] Paul Reps, *Zen Flesh, Zen Bones,* Tuttle, 1957
[24] Merton, Robert K. (1968). *The Matthew Effect in Science.* Science, 159 (3810): 56–63.

5

The Gospel of Thomas

The Gospel of Thomas is critical to any thorough consideration of Christ as a First Century Wisdom Teacher. I've discussed above that the common consensus among theological scholars is that the earliest writings we have regarding Christ are some of the Letters of Saul of Tarsus from around 50 C.E. These are then followed by the Gospels: Mark, Matthew Luke and John, most likely in that order, dating from around 66 C.E. to 110 C.E.

Dating the Gospels and other New Testament writings proves to be a very complex, imprecise area of scholarship. General scholarly consensus on the dates would put Mark around 66-70 C.E., with Matthew and Luke (who both draw upon Mark) around 80-85 C.E., with John following anywhere from 90-110 C.E. But to give an idea of the complexities here, some argue that the synoptic Gospels must have been written before 66 C.E. since none of them mention the fall of the Jewish Temple in 70 C.E. when the Romans sacked Jerusalem. Still others, looking at the same evidence, say the opposite: the synoptic Gospels have Jesus predicting the fall of the Temple and, they argue, since no one can actually predict the future therefore they were all written after 70 C.E.

The arguments for and against given date estimates are often deeply flawed. Indeed, most articles about dating the synoptic Gospels miss a key point that is elsewhere well-documented. That is, they speak as if the synoptic Gospels were each written as complete works that had no drafts, no variants and no later amendments. To say that any Gospel must have been written after 70 C.E. because it does or does not mention a certain event misses the point that it could have been written in earliest form far earlier than 70 C.E. and then later amended well after 70 C.E.. We know, for instance, that the early version of Mark did not have Jesus' birth story in it, and that it originally ended with Jesus dying on the cross. These later additions are in a different hand and style.

Similarly, saying that a Gospel had to have been written before 70 C.E. because it has Jesus predicting the fall of the Temple, yet doesn't boast about a prediction being fulfilled is missing the point that the fall of the Temple would have been so well-known in the period after 70 C.E. that there would have been no need to point out to the reader that Jesus' prediction was accurate.

What seems much more likely is that the earliest draft of Mark was fairly early—say around 50-55 C.E.—and then the earliest versions of Matthew and Luke (since they drew on Mark) followed some years later (to give time for Mark to be distributed and become known). But, most importantly, that all the Gospels underwent amendments, additions and revisions as a result of Paul's writings and the movement that he inspired.

Some scholars have even suggested that the writer of Mark must have known Paul since they have similar style and theology. But what these scholars miss is that it is far more likely that Paul and his followers edited the earlier versions of Mark to text to make Mark's message more like that of Paul, and to add in theology that Paul favored.

What this leads us to is the hypothesis that the early versions of Mark may have pre-dated the writings of Paul and thus been before 50 C.E., which in turn could place the earliest drafts of Matthew and Luke earlier than previously thought, too. Indeed, scholars speculate about the assumed "missing" manuscript of sayings known at Q[1] that it seems clear that what Matthew and Luke both drew upon was written before 50 C.E. And this in turn leads us to consider the Gospel of Thomas in this light.

Intuitively, it seems likely that if anything was written down during Christ's life then it would have been his oral teachings, sayings and parables. Then, sometime after his death the writings were expanded to include details of his life and works but at this stage (prior to 50 C.E. to around 55 C.E. or so) there is no added detail such as birth or resurrection narratives. Then as Paul becomes active writing in the early 50s through to his death (likely around 64 C.E.) the early Gospels are edited and added to in order to better fit the narrative Paul and his followers are putting forth. These additions focus on pedestalizing Christ to make him more than human and thus separate and distinct from we 'mere' human beings.

Where the idea of a very early text prior to 50 C.E. known as Q comes from is that there are sayings in Matthew and Luke that are not included in Mark, and which thus point to both the writers of Matthew and Luke as having access to this earlier book of sayings (*logia*). The Gospel of Thomas is just such a book of sayings. It was discovered near Nag Hammadi in Egypt in 1945 among some scrolls that had been buried there in the distant past.

The assumed missing work Q has several things in common with the Gospel of Thomas: it is a book of sayings with no historical or even pseudo-historical events. Missing from both are birth stories or the passion narrative culminating in the accounts of resurrection. It is fascinating to see scholars along with so-called church fathers, instantly dismiss the Gospel of Thomas as later heretical gnostic writing because it lacks any reference to birth stories or the passion narrative. These same scholars then have great difficulty with the presumed early text Q, since it too would appear to have lacked any such birth stories or passion narrative. It's one thing to dismiss a text you wish to argue was written somewhere in the region of 150-250 C.E. as heretical, but it is an entirely different thing to try to also dismiss Q which is believed to be the oldest writing of all—dating from well before 50 C.E. when Paul started writing.

By some analysis, Matthew and Luke have around 230 verses in common. They are not identical, but there are substantial portions that are identical. Of course, while the theological scholars are seemingly wedded to the idea that if an earlier text "Q" exists, then it is a singular text, the reality is that there were likely numerous early texts that both Matthew and Luke drew upon. Indeed, the early sources they drew on other than Mark may have been both oral and written, all of which goes to explain why there would be as many as 230 similar passages not found in Mark, that are also not identical as if copied from a single common source document.

Setting such academic considerations to one side, we come back to the sizable revelation that there is strong evidence that the earliest writings, predating Paul and perhaps written around the time of Christ, were focused on sayings and teachings, with no birth or passion narratives.

Thus, when we come to consider the Gospel of Thomas, which purports to be the secret sayings of Jesus, we cannot simply reject it as a heretical work by a later gnostic group in the mid-second to mid-third century. I think we can go further and say that we have good reason to believe that at least in part Thomas has its roots in an earlier text that either was Q or was part of a family of Q-like texts of Jesus' sayings and teachings.

All of which is by way of arguing that we need to consider the Gospel of Thomas as likely being a more authentic insight into what Christ actually said and taught. Indeed, we have reason to believe that much of the Gospel of Thomas rather than being a later heretical invention instead has much in common with the very earliest authentic writings about Christ and his teachings, writings that pre-date those of Saul of Tarsus and the version of Christianity he created.

It is worth noting that some who dismiss Thomas as heretical try to assert that it is so different from the Jesus we meet and hear from in the synoptic Gospels. But this simply isn't true. Indeed, as we saw in considering the Parable of the Sower, the synoptic Gospels have Christ telling his followers that he has imparted secret teachings to them, whereas he chooses to teach the masses in the form of parables instead. Also, the core themes that go through Thomas (Heaven is within, become like a child to enter Heaven within, etc.) are all there in the non-contested synoptics as being central to Christ's accepted teachings.

Here, then, is a public domain translation of the Gospel of Thomas based on that by Mark M. Mattison followed by a discussion. Notice as you read through these 114 sayings the similarities to the accepted teachings of Christ in the synoptic Gospels, and the overlap with the 230 sections of Matthew and Luke that are attributed by scholars to the missing Q book of sayings (*logia*). This may not be Q, but there is surely significant overlap.

The Gospel of Thomas

Prologue

These are the hidden sayings that the living Jesus spoke and Didymos[2] Judas Thomas[3] wrote down.

Saying 1: True Meaning

And he said, "Whoever discovers the meaning of these sayings won't taste death."

Saying 2: Seek and Find

Jesus said, "Whoever seeks shouldn't stop until they find. When they find, they'll be disturbed. When they're disturbed, they'll be [...] amazed, and reign over the All."

Saying 3: Seeking Within

Jesus said, "If your leaders tell you, 'Look, the Kingdom is in Heaven,' then the birds of Heaven will precede you. If they tell you, 'It's in the sea,' then the fish will precede you. Rather, the Kingdom is within you [and outside of you].

"When you know yourselves, then you'll be known, and you'll realize that you're the children of the living Father. But if you don't know yourselves, then you live in poverty, and you are the poverty."

Saying 4: First and Last

Jesus said, "The older person won't hesitate to ask a little seven-day-old child about the place of life, and they'll live, because many who are first will be last, and they'll become one."

Saying 5: Hidden and Revealed

Jesus said, "Know what's in front of your face, and what's hidden from you will be revealed to you, because there's nothing hidden that won't be revealed."

Saying 6: Public Ritual

His disciples said to him, "Do you want us to fast? And how should we pray? Should we make donations? And what food should we avoid?"

Jesus said, "Don't lie, and don't do what you hate, because everything is revealed in the sight of Heaven; for there's nothing hidden that won't be revealed, and nothing covered up that will stay secret."

Saying 7: The Lion and the Human

Jesus said, "Blessed is the lion that's eaten by a human and then becomes human, but how awful for the human who's eaten by a lion, and the lion becomes human."

Saying 8: The Parable of the Fish

He said, "The human being is like a wise fisherman who cast a net into the sea and drew it up from the sea full of little fish. Among them the wise fisher found a fine large fish and cast all the little fish back down into the sea, easily choosing the large fish. Anyone who has ears to hear should hear!"

Saying 9: The Parable of the Sower

Jesus said, "Look, a sower went out, took a handful of seeds, and scattered them. Some fell on the roadside; the birds came and gathered them. Others fell on the rock; they didn't take root in the soil and ears of grain didn't rise toward Heaven. Yet others fell on thorns; they choked the seeds and worms ate them. Finally, others fell on good soil; it produced fruit up toward Heaven, some sixty times as much and some a hundred and twenty."

Saying 10: Jesus and Fire

Jesus said, "I've cast fire on the world, and look, I'm watching over it until it blazes."

Saying 11: Those Who Are Living Won't Die

Jesus said, "This Heaven will disappear, and the one above it will disappear too. Those who are dead aren't alive, and those who are living won't die. In the days when you ate what was dead, you made it alive. When you're in the light, what will you do? On the day when you were one, you became divided. But when you become divided, what will you do?"

Saying 12: James the Just

The disciples said to Jesus, "We know you're going to leave us. Who will lead us then?"

Jesus said to them, "Wherever you are, you'll go to James the Just, for whom Heaven and earth came into being."

Saying 13: Thomas' Confession

Jesus said to his disciples, "If you were to compare me to someone, who would you say I'm like?"

Simon Peter said to him, "You're like a just angel."

Matthew said to him, "You're like a wise philosopher."

Thomas said to him, "Teacher, I'm completely unable to say whom you're like."

Jesus said, "I'm not your teacher. Because you've drunk, you've become intoxicated by the bubbling spring I've measured out."

He took him aside and told him three things. When Thomas returned to his companions, they asked, "What did Jesus say to you?"

Thomas said to them, "If I tell you one of the things he said to me, you'll pick up stones and cast them at me, and fire will come out of the stones and burn you up."

Saying 14: Public Ministry

Jesus said to them, "If you fast, you'll bring guilt upon yourselves; and if you pray, you'll be condemned; and if you make donations, you'll harm your spirits.

"If they welcome you when you enter any land and go around in the countryside, heal those who are sick among them and eat whatever they give you, because it's not what goes into your mouth that will defile you. What comes out of your mouth is what will defile you."

Saying 15: Worship

Jesus said, "When you see the one who wasn't born of a woman, fall down on your face and worship that person. That's your Father."

Saying 16: Not Peace, but War

Jesus said, "Maybe people think that I've come to cast peace on the world, and they don't know that I've come to cast divisions on the earth: fire, sword, and war. Where there are five in a house, there'll be three against two and two against three, father against and son and son against father. They'll stand up and be one."

Saying 17: Divine Gift

Jesus said, "I'll give you what no eye has ever seen, no ear has ever heard, no hand has ever touched, and no human mind has ever thought."

Saying 18: Beginning and End

The disciples said to Jesus, "Tell us about our end. How will it come?"

Jesus said, "Have you discovered the beginning so that you can look for the end? Because the end will be where the beginning is. Blessed is the one who will stand up in the beginning. They'll know the end and won't taste death."

Saying 19: Five Trees in Paradise

Jesus said, "Blessed is the one who came into being before coming into being. If you become my disciples and listen to my message, these stones will become your servants; because there are five trees in paradise which don't change in summer or winter, and their leaves don't fall. Whoever knows them won't taste death."

Saying 20: The Parable of the Mustard Seed

The disciples asked Jesus, "Tell us, what can the Kingdom of Heaven be compared to?"

He said to them, "It can be compared to a mustard seed. Though it's the smallest of all the seeds, when it falls on tilled soil it makes a plant so large that it shelters the birds of Heaven."

Saying 21: The Parables of the Field, the Bandits, and the Reaper

Mary said to Jesus, "Whom are your disciples like?"

He said, "They're like little children living in a field which isn't theirs. When the owners of the field come, they'll say, 'Give our field back to us.' They'll strip naked in front of them to let them have it and give them their field.

"So I say that if the owner of the house realizes the bandit is coming, they'll watch out beforehand and won't let the bandit break into the house of their domain and steal their possessions. You, then, watch out for the world! Prepare to defend yourself so that the bandits don't attack you, because what you're expecting will come. May there be a wise person among you!

"When the fruit ripened, the reaper came quickly, sickle in hand, and harvested it. Anyone who has ears to hear should hear!"

Saying 22: Making the Two into One

Jesus saw some little children nursing. He said to his disciples, "These nursing children can be compared to those who enter the Kingdom."

They said to him, "Then we'll enter the Kingdom as little children?"

Jesus said to them, "When you make the two into one, and make the inner like the outer and the outer like the inner, and the upper like the lower, and so make the male and the female a single one so that the male won't be male nor the female female; when you make eyes in the place of an eye, a hand in the place of a hand, a foot in the place of a foot, and an image in the place of an image; then you'll enter [the Kingdom]."

Saying 23: Those Who are Chosen

Jesus said, "I'll choose you, one out of a thousand and two out of ten thousand, and they'll stand as a single one."

Saying 24: Light

His disciples said, "Show us the place where you are, because we need to look for it."

He said to them, "Anyone who has ears to hear should hear! Light exists within a person of light, and they light up the whole world. If they don't shine, there's darkness."

Saying 25: Love and Protect

Jesus said, "Love your brother as your own soul. Protect them like the pupil of your eye."

Saying 26: Speck and Beam

Jesus said, "You see the speck that's in your brother's eye, but you don't see the beam in your own eye. When you get the beam out of your own eye, then you'll be able to see clearly to get the speck out of your brother's eye."

Saying 27: Fasting and Sabbath

"If you don't fast from the world, you won't find the Kingdom. If you don't make the Sabbath into a Sabbath, you won't see the Father."

Saying 28: The World is Drunk

Jesus said, "I stood in the middle of the world and appeared to them in the flesh. I found them all drunk; I didn't find any of them thirsty. My soul ached for the children of humanity because they were blind in their hearts and couldn't see. They came into the world empty and plan on leaving the world empty. Meanwhile, they're drunk. When they shake off their wine, then they'll change."

Saying 29: Spirit and Body

Jesus said, "If the flesh came into existence because of spirit, that's amazing. If spirit came into existence because of the body, that's really amazing! But I'm amazed at how [such] great wealth has been placed in this poverty."

Saying 30: Divine Presence

Jesus said, "Where there are three deities, they're divine. Where there are two or one, *I am* is with them."

Saying 31: Prophet and Doctor

Jesus said, "No prophet is welcome in their own village. No doctor heals those who knows them."

Saying 32: The Parable of the Fortified City

Jesus said, "A city built and fortified on a high mountain can't fall, nor can it be hidden."

Saying 33: The Parable of the Lamp

Jesus said, "What you hear with one ear, listen to with both, then proclaim from your rooftops. No one lights a lamp and puts it under a basket or in a hidden place. Rather, they put it on the stand so that everyone who comes and goes can see its light."

Saying 34: The Parable of Those Who Can't See

Jesus said, "If someone who's blind leads someone else who's blind, both of them fall into a pit."

Saying 35: The Parable of Binding the Strong

Jesus said, "No one can break into the house of the strong and take it by force without tying the hands of the strong. Then they can loot the house."

Saying 36: Anxiety

Jesus said, "Don't be anxious from morning to evening or from evening to morning about what you'll wear."

Saying 37: Seeing Jesus

His disciples said, "When will you appear to us? When will we see you?"

Jesus said, "When you strip naked without being ashamed, and throw your clothes on the ground and stomp on them as little children would, then [you'll] see the Son of the Living One and won't be afraid."

Saying 38: Finding Jesus

Jesus said, "Often you've wanted to hear this message that I'm telling you, and you don't have anyone else from whom to hear it. There will be days when you'll look for me, but you won't be able to find me."

Saying 39: The Keys of Knowledge

Jesus said, "The Pharisees and the scholars have taken the keys of knowledge and hidden them. They haven't entered and haven't let others enter who wanted to. So be wise as serpents and innocent as doves."

Saying 40: A Grapevine

Jesus said, "A grapevine has been planted outside of the Father. Since it's malnourished, it'll be pulled up by its root and destroyed."

Saying 41: More and Less

Jesus said, "Whoever has something in hand will be given more, but whoever doesn't have anything will lose even what little they do have."

Saying 42: Passing By

Jesus said, "Become one who passes by."

Saying 43: The Tree and the Fruit

His disciples said to him, "Who are you to say these things to us?"

"You don't realize who I am from what I say to you, but you've become like those Judeans who either love the tree but hate its fruit or love the fruit but hate the tree."

Saying 44: Blasphemy

Jesus said, "Whoever blasphemes the Father will be forgiven, and whoever blasphemes the Son will be forgiven, but whoever blasphemes the Holy Spirit will not be forgiven, neither on earth nor in Heaven."

Saying 45: Good and Evil

Jesus said, "Grapes aren't harvested from thorns, nor are figs gathered from thistles, because they don't produce fruit. [A person who's good] brings good things out of their treasure, and a person who's [evil] brings evil things out of their evil treasure. They say evil things because their heart is full of evil."

Saying 46: Greater than John the Baptizer

Jesus said, "From Adam to John the Baptizer, no one's been born who's so much greater than John the Baptizer that they shouldn't avert their eyes. But I say that whoever among you will become a little child will know the Kingdom and become greater than John."

Saying 47: The Parables of Divided Loyalties, New Wine in Old Wineskins, and New Patch on Old Cloth

Jesus said, "It's not possible for anyone to mount two horses or stretch two bows, and it's not possible for a servant to follow two leaders, because they'll respect one and despise the other.

"No one drinks old wine and immediately wants to drink new wine. And new wine isn't put in old wineskins, because they'd burst. Nor is old wine put in new wineskins, because it'd spoil.

"A new patch of cloth isn't sewn onto an old coat, because it'd tear apart."

Saying 48: Unity

Jesus said, "If two make peace with each other in a single house, they'll say to the mountain, 'Go away,' and it will."

Saying 49: Those Who Are Chosen

Jesus said, "Blessed are those who are one – those who are chosen, because you'll find the Kingdom. You've come from there and will return there."

Saying 50: Our Origin and Identity

Jesus said, "If they ask you, 'Where do you come from?' tell them, 'We've come from the light, the place where light came into being by itself, [established] itself, and appeared in their image.'

"If they ask you, 'Is it you?' then say, 'We are its children, and we're chosen by our living Father.'

"If they ask you, 'What's the sign of your Father in you?' then say, 'It's movement and rest.'"

Saying 51: The New World

His disciples said to him, "When will the dead have rest, and when will the new world come?"

He said to them, "What you're looking for has already come, but you don't know it."

Saying 52: Twenty-Four Prophets

His disciples said to him, "Twenty-four prophets have spoken in Israel, and they all spoke of you."

He said to them, "You've ignored the Living One right in front of you, and you've talked about those who are dead."

Saying 53: True Circumcision

His disciples said to him, "Is circumcision useful, or not?"

He said to them, "If it were useful, parents would have children who are born circumcised. But the true circumcision in spirit has become profitable in every way."

Saying 54: Those Who Are Poor

Jesus said, "Blessed are those who are poor, for yours is the Kingdom of Heaven."

Saying 55: Discipleship

Jesus said, "Whoever doesn't hate their father and mother can't become my disciple, and whoever doesn't hate their brothers and sisters and take up their cross like I do isn't worthy of me."

Saying 56: The World is a Corpse

Jesus said, "Whoever has known the world has found a corpse. Whoever has found a corpse, of them the world isn't worthy."

Saying 57: The Parable of the Weeds

Jesus said, "My Father's Kingdom can be compared to someone who had [good] seed. Their enemy came by night and sowed weeds among the good seed. The person didn't let anyone pull out the weeds, 'so that you don't pull out the wheat along with the weeds,' they said to them. 'On the day of the harvest, the weeds will be obvious. Then they'll be pulled out and burned.'"

Saying 58: Finding Life

Jesus said, "Blessed is the person who's gone to a lot of trouble. They've found life."

Saying 59: The Living One

Jesus said, "Look for the Living One while you're still alive. If you die and then try to look for him, you won't be able to."

Saying 60: Don't Become a Corpse

They saw a Samaritan carrying a lamb to Judea. He said to his disciples, "What do you think he's going to do with that lamb?"

They said to him, "He's going to kill it and eat it."

He said to them, "While it's living, he won't eat it, but only after he kills it and it becomes a corpse."

They said, "He can't do it any other way."

He said to them, "You, too, look for a resting place, so that you won't become a corpse and be eaten."

Saying 61: Jesus and Salome

Jesus said, "Two will rest on a couch. One will die, the other will live."

Salome said, "Who are you, Sir, to climb onto my couch and eat off my table as if you're from someone?"

Jesus said to her, "I'm the one who exists in equality. Some of what belongs to my Father was given to me."

"I'm your disciple."

"So, I'm telling you, if someone is single, they'll be full of light; but if they're divided, they'll be full of darkness."

Saying 62: Mysteries

Jesus said, "I tell my mysteries to [those who are worthy of my] mysteries. Don't let your left hand know what your right hand is doing."

Saying 63: The Parable of the Rich Fool

Jesus said, "There was a rich man who had much money. He said, 'I'll use my money to sow, reap, plant, and fill my barns with fruit, so that I won't need anything.' That's what he was thinking to himself, but he died that very night. Anyone who has ears to hear should hear!"

Saying 64: The Parable of the Dinner Party

Jesus said, "Someone was planning on having guests. When dinner was ready, they sent their servant to call the visitors.

"The servant went to the first and said, 'My master invites you.'

"They said, 'Some merchants owe me money. They're coming tonight. I need to go and give them instructions. Excuse me from the dinner.'

"The servant went to another one and said, 'My master invites you.'

"They said, "I've just bought a house and am needed for the day. I won't have time.'

"The servant went to another one and said, 'My master invites you.'

"They said, 'My friend is getting married, and I'm going to make dinner. I can't come. Excuse me from the dinner.'

"The servant went to another one and said, 'My master invites you.'

"They said, "I've just bought a farm and am going to collect the rent. I can't come. Excuse me.'

"The servant went back and told the master, 'The ones you've invited to the dinner have excused themselves.'

"The master said to their servant, 'Go out to the roads and bring whomever you find so that they can have dinner.'

"Buyers and merchants won't [enter] the places of my Father."

Saying 65: The Parable of the Sharecroppers

He said, "A [creditor] owned a vineyard. He leased it out to some sharecroppers to work it so he could collect its fruit.

"He sent his servant so that the sharecroppers could give him the fruit of the vineyard. They seized his servant, beat him, and nearly killed him.

"The servant went back and told his master. His master said, 'Maybe he just didn't know them.' He sent another servant, but the tenants beat that one too.

"Then the master sent his son, thinking, 'Maybe they'll show some respect to my son.'

"Because they knew that he was the heir of the vineyard, the sharecroppers seized and killed him. Anyone who has ears to hear should hear!"

Saying 66: The Rejected Cornerstone

Jesus said, "Show me the stone the builders rejected; that's the cornerstone."

Saying 67: Knowing Isn't Everything

Jesus said, "Whoever knows everything, but is personally lacking, lacks everything."

Saying 68: Persecution

Jesus said, "Blessed are you when you're hated and persecuted, and no place will be found where you've been persecuted."

Saying 69: Those Who Are Persecuted

Jesus said, "Blessed are those who've been persecuted in their own hearts. They've truly known the Father. Blessed are those who are hungry, so that their stomachs may be filled."

Saying 70: Salvation is Within

Jesus said, "If you give birth to what's within you, what you have within you will save you. If you don't have that within [you], what you don't have within you [will] kill you."

Saying 71: Destroying the Temple

Jesus said, "I'll destroy [this] house, and no one will be able to build it [...]"

Saying 72: Not a Divider

[Someone said to him], "Tell my brothers to divide our inheritance with me."

He said to him, "Who made me a divider?"

He turned to his disciples and said to them, "Am I really a divider?"

Saying 73: Workers for the Harvest

Jesus said, "The harvest really is plentiful, but the workers are few. So pray that the Lord will send workers to the harvest."

Saying 74: The Empty Well

He said, "Lord, many are gathered around the well, but there's nothing to drink."

Saying 75: The Bridal Chamber

Jesus said, "Many are waiting at the door, but those who are one will enter the bridal chamber."

Saying 76: The Parable of the Pearl

Jesus said, "The Father's Kingdom can be compared to a merchant with merchandise who found a pearl. The merchant was wise; they sold their merchandise and bought that single pearl for themselves.

"You, too, look for the treasure that doesn't perish but endures, where no moths come to eat and no worms destroy."

Saying 77: Jesus is the All

Jesus said, "I'm the light that's over all. I am the All. The All has come from me and unfolds toward me.

"Split a log; I'm there. Lift the stone, and you'll find me there."

Saying 78: Into the Desert

Jesus said, "What did you go out into the desert to see? A reed shaken by the wind? A [person] wearing fancy clothes, [like your] rulers and powerful people? They (wear) fancy [clothes] but can't know the truth."

Saying 79: Listening to the Message

A woman in the crowd said to him, "Blessed is the womb that bore you, and the breasts that nourished you."

He said to [her], "Blessed are those who have listened to the message of the Father and kept it, because there will be days when you'll say, 'Blessed is the womb that didn't conceive and the breasts that haven't given milk.'"

Saying 80: The World is a Body

Jesus said, "Whoever has known the world has found the body; but whoever has found the body, of them the world isn't worthy."

Saying 81: Riches and Renunciation

Jesus said, "Whoever has become rich should become a ruler, and whoever has power should renounce it."

Saying 82: Jesus and Fire

Jesus said, "Whoever is near me is near the fire, and whoever is far from me is far from the Kingdom."

Saying 83: Light and Images

Jesus said, "Images are revealed to people, but the light within them is hidden in the image of the Father's light. He'll be revealed, but his image will be hidden by his light."

Saying 84: Our Previous Images

Jesus said, "When you see your likeness, you rejoice. But when you see your image that came into being before you did – which doesn't die and isn't revealed – how much you'll have to bear!"

Saying 85: Adam Wasn't Worthy

Jesus said, "Adam came into being from a great power and great wealth, but he didn't become worthy of you. If he had been worthy, [he wouldn't have tasted] death."

Saying 86: Foxes and Birds

Jesus said, "[The foxes have dens] and the birds have nests, but the Son of Adam has nowhere to lay his head and rest."

Saying 87: Body and Soul

Jesus said, "How miserable is the body that depends on a body, and how miserable is the soul that depends on both."

Saying 88: Angels and Prophets

Jesus said, "The angels and the prophets will come to you and give you what belongs to you. You'll give them what you have and ask yourselves, 'When will they come and take what is theirs?'"

Saying 89: Inside and Outside

Jesus said, "Why do you wash the outside of the cup? Don't you know that whoever created the inside created the outside too?"

Saying 90: Jesus' Yoke is Easy

Jesus said, "Come to me because my yoke is easy, and my requirements are light. You'll be refreshed."

Saying 91: Reading the Signs

They said to him, "Tell us who you are so that we may trust you."

He said to them, "You read the face of the sky and the earth, but you don't know the one right in front of you, and you don't know how to read the present moment."

Saying 92: Look and Find

Jesus said, "Look and you'll find. I didn't answer your questions before. Now I want to give you answers, but you aren't looking for them."

Saying 93: Don't Throw Pearls to Pigs

"Don't give what's holy to the dogs, or else it might be thrown on the manure pile. Don't throw pearls to the pigs, or else they might [...]"

Saying 94: Knock and It Will Be Opened

Jesus [said], "Whoever looks will find, [and whoever knocks], it will be opened for them."

Saying 95: Giving Money

[Jesus said], "If you have money, don't lend it at interest. Instead, give [it to] someone from whom you won't get it back."

Saying 96: The Parable of the Yeast

Jesus [said], "The Father's Kingdom can be compared to a woman who took a little yeast and [hid] it in flour. She made it into large loaves of bread. Anyone who has ears to hear should hear!"

Saying 97: The Parable of the Jar of Flour

Jesus said, "The Father's Kingdom can be compared to a woman carrying a jar of flour. While she was walking down [a] long road, the jar's handle broke and the flour spilled out behind her on the road. She didn't know it and didn't realize there was a problem until she got home, put down the jar, and found it empty."

Saying 98: The Parable of the Assassin

Jesus said, "The Father's Kingdom can be compared to a man who wanted to kill someone powerful. He drew his sword in his house and drove it into the wall to figure out whether his hand was strong enough. Then he killed the powerful one."

Saying 99: Jesus' True Family

The disciples said to him, "Your brothers and mother are standing outside."

He said to them, "The people here who do the will of my Father are my brothers and mother; they're the ones who will enter my Father's Kingdom."

Saying 100: Give to Caesar What Belongs to Caesar

They showed Jesus a gold coin and said to him, "Those who belong to Caesar demand tribute from us."

He said to them, "Give to Caesar what belongs to Caesar, give to God what belongs to God, [and give to me what belongs to me]."

Saying 101: Discipleship

"Whoever doesn't hate their [father] and mother as I do can't become my [disciple], and whoever [doesn't] love their [father] and mother as I do can't become my [disciple]. For my mother [...], but [my] true [Mother] gave me Life."

Saying 102: The Dog in the Feeding Trough

Jesus said, "How awful for the Pharisees who are like a dog sleeping in a feeding trough for cattle, because the dog doesn't eat, and [doesn't let] the cattle eat either."

Saying 103: The Parable of the Bandits

Jesus said, "Blessed is the one who knows where the bandits are going to enter. [They can] get up to assemble their defenses and be prepared to defend themselves before they arrive."

Saying 104: Prayer and Fasting

They said to [Jesus], "Come, let's pray and fast today."

Jesus said, "What have I done wrong? Have I failed?

"Rather, when the groom leaves the bridal chamber, then people should fast and pray."

Saying 105: Knowing Father and Mother

Jesus said, "Whoever knows their father and mother will be called a bastard."

Saying 106: Unity

Jesus said, "When you make the two into one, you'll become Children of God, and if you say 'Mountain, go away!', it'll go."

Saying 107: The Parable of the Lost Sheep

Jesus said, "The Kingdom can be compared to a shepherd who had a hundred sheep. The largest one strayed. He left the ninety-nine and looked for that one until he found it. Having gone through the trouble, he said to the sheep: 'I love you more than the ninety-nine.'"

Saying 108: Becoming Like Jesus

Jesus said, "Whoever drinks from my mouth will become like me, and I myself will become like them; then, what's hidden will be revealed to them."

Saying 109: The Parable of the Hidden Treasure

Jesus said, "The Kingdom can be compared to someone who had a treasure [hidden] in their field. [They] didn't know about it. After they died, they left it to their son. The son didn't know it either. He took the field and sold it.

"The buyer plowed the field, [found] the treasure, and began to loan money at interest to whomever they wanted."

Saying 110: Riches and Renunciation

Jesus said, "Whoever has found the world and become rich should renounce the world."

Saying 111: Those Who are Living Won't Die

Jesus said, "The Heavens and the earth will roll up in front of you, and whoever lives from the Living One won't see death."

Doesn't Jesus say, "Whoever finds themselves, of them the world isn't worthy"?

Saying 112: Flesh and Soul

Jesus said, "How awful for the flesh that depends on the soul. How awful for the soul that depends on the flesh."

Saying 113: The Kingdom is Already Present

His disciples said to him, "When will the Kingdom come?"

"It won't come by looking for it. They won't say, 'Look over here!' or 'Look over there!' Rather, the Father's Kingdom is already spread out over the earth, and people don't see it."

Saying 114: Peter and Mary

Simon Peter said to them, "Mary should leave us because women aren't worthy of life."

Jesus said, "Look, am I to make her a man? So that she may become a living spirit too, she's equal to you men, because every woman who makes herself manly will enter the Kingdom of Heaven."

~ENDS~

Reflecting on Thomas

While there is unfounded speculation that Jesus spent part of his adult life in India, in contrast it is well-known and universally accepted that following the crucifixion Thomas did go to India for the remainder of his life. We will return to this fact later.

Considering the Gospel of Thomas and what we know about Thomas, several key points emerge that we will explore: first, that the Gospel of Thomas may be a version of the earliest Christian text we have; second, that Thomas may have been at least part of Christ's connection to Buddhism; and third, that Thomas along with Jesus' brother James may have been the core group that tried to continue Christ's teachings after he died. We'll start by looking at the Gospel of Thomas, including a deep dive into what we know that may help us date the origins of the text.

Certainly, the sayings in the translation above are a mixed bag. It is likely that it suffers from being repeatedly translated from one language to another (translated at least four or more times before we get to this particular English translation of the Coptic original found in Egypt in 1945). The scroll found was dated to be from about 340 C.E. but references to a Thomas Gospel are found in writings of Origen of Alexandria (c 233) and Hippolytus of Rome (c 222-235), which in turn seem to be referring to a work that had been known for a long time. Some scholars place the original as early as before 50 C.E. whereas others believe it is the product of a gnostic Christian sect, perhaps Syrian, from around 150-250 C.E. given that Thomasine texts were popular in Syria in that period.[4]

We can glean further clues to the dating of this Gospel from a closer reading of its contents. Saying 12, for instance, has the disciples asking Jesus who will lead them after he leaves, and Jesus responds saying James the Just. Of course, we know this is true since it is recorded that after the crucifixion the church in Jerusalem was headed by James, known as the brother of Christ.[5] There are two, and I believe only two, ways we can interpret this. Either this is a genuine statement made by Jesus that was carried down through oral and written tradition to this Gospel, or these were words attributed to Jesus at a later date given that James did become head of the church. But either way, these interpretations suggest that Saying 12 dates either from before Jesus' death or very soon afterwards—perhaps at a time the writer of Thomas was trying to convince Christians to be loyal to James' church in Jerusalem rather than to some other alternative. Since James is reported to have been martyred in either 62 or 69 C.E., this strongly suggests that the original Thomas text predates James' death. If James was already dead when the earliest version of Thomas was written, why suggest that after Jesus leaves, people should follow James?

Those who would argue the Gospel of Thomas is an invention from much later (150-250 C.E.) which borrowed from the known synoptic Gospels, cannot account for why the writer(s) of Thomas would see it as necessary to mention James the Just succeeding Jesus as head of the early church. By even 150 C.E. that would have felt like ancient history, being many lifetimes after the time of Christ. By 150 C.E. it was some 90 years after we believe James was killed, equivalent to almost three lifetimes given the average life expectancy of that time was 38 years. And by 220-250 C.E., when some argue this Gospel was written, James had been dead 190 years, or six lifetimes.

Rather, it makes far more sense that the mention of James in Saying 12 shows that at least this part of the text must date from around 33-60 C.E. (or 30-60 C.E.), being the period when it would have been relevant to direct any reader to James being the new leader of the early movement. Of course, we know that somewhat more than half of this Gospel dates from at least 50-70 C.E. since it mirrors what is written in the synoptic Gospels. The question is whether it precedes the synoptic Gospels or postdates them. But we have some further support for the remainder of the Gospel—or at least a sizable portion of it—also dating from this earliest period.

Many of us may instantly associate Thomas with the phrase "doubting Thomas." But this story of Thomas *only* appears in the Gospel of John, a late text probably written around 90-110 C.E. This story, unique to John, singles out Thomas as the only disciple who needed proof of the resurrection. Could this be a coincidence that the Gospel of Thomas, like the presumed source text Q, is a book solely of sayings with no mention of the birth story or the passion narrative and resurrection? No, I do not think it's a coincidence at all. Rather, by the time John was written the early church had split into those who still spoke of Jesus as a teacher ("rabbi"[6]) and had links to James' church in Jerusalem, and those who proclaimed him as not merely a sage and teacher, but as one with superhuman abilities who had died and had been resurrected three days later.

While the details of this early era are sketchy, there is evidence that the former branch—consisting of the likes of James and Thomas—did not speak of the post-Easter Jesus, but rather focused on Christ's wisdom teachings just as Jesus had done during his lifetime. This group was less focused on an apocalyptic view in which it is supposed Jesus failed to establish the Kingdom of God but instead will come again to judge the living and the dead. Rather, as Jesus himself taught, they continued to teach that the Kingdom of Heaven (Heaven *within*) is here and now, already arrived, eternal, and has existed since beginningless time. This group seemed to be the focus of those still ministering to the Jews, based out of James' first church in Jerusalem, or (in the case of Thomas) ministering in the East in places like India.

The second group, including those like Saul of Tarsus (Paul), together with the writer of John and those who made all the later additions to the synoptic Gospels, were instead focused on the apocalyptic message of the Second Coming, and that Jesus was more than mortal having died and been resurrected. Thus, by the time of John there were tensions between the group that focused on continuing Christ's teachings, and those ministering primarily to Gentiles who focused on the passion narrative, the resurrection, and all that then flowed from that theologically.

Thus, it makes sense that the writer of John was targeting the Thomasine movement with his story about "doubting Thomas," trying to persuade his audience that Thomas, his Gospel, and that group were wrong to avoid mention of the resurrection. Hence the writer of John depicts Thomas as the one apostle who doubts that Jesus was really resurrected, reflecting the fact that the Gospel of Thomas makes no mention of the post-Easter Jesus; this in turn strongly suggests that the Gospel of Thomas, or a book of solely sayings that was associated with Thomas, was well known to the writer of John by 90-110 C.E. when he was writing the work.

Circumstantial, certainly, but perhaps further evidence that this Gospel was known well before 90 C.E. and probably well before 50 C.E., which would make it (or at least a substantial part of it) earlier than the writings of Paul. It may also indicate that all the synoptic Gospels may have drawn on this Gospel of Thomas, and that a version of it may have been Q, or a variant of it, and that those who conclude Thomas merely copied from the synoptics may have understood it exactly backwards.

Who was Thomas?

The answer is not as simple as you might first think. Traditionally, he is one of the twelve apostles and is usually listed as Thomas Didymus. The problem with that is Thomas Didymus are two words that both mean "twin" in Hebrew (or Aramaic) and Greek and they are not his actual name. There is substantial tradition (primarily Syriac, most closely associated with Aramaic) that his given name was Judas, and this is why the Gospel of Thomas starts by stating his name is Didymos Judas Thomas (where Didymos is a variant on Didymus). Of these three words, only Judas is a given name.

As to what the name (or rather, nickname) "twin" meant, there are references to his being the twin of Jesus. Scholars then differ as to whether this was meant to be taken literally, or to suggest that he had a similar physical appearance to Jesus. Or perhaps it suggests he and Jesus were twins in the sense of having similar spirituality. It certainly doesn't seem to suggest any familial relationship. This becomes more complex when we consider that the Gospel of Thomas makes a very notable reference to James the Just—who is widely confirmed to be the "brother" of Jesus, known as the Christ.[7] James of course was the head of the Church in Jerusalem after Jesus' death, and Thomas assisted James with that church and, eventually, its outreach to India.

Thomas' loyalties thus lay with James and his followers in Jerusalem, but that fact and the history of that first church doesn't help us discern whether his given name really was Judas (or Jude). Certainly, all the others named Judas are accounted for, and distinguished as not being the person called Thomas. And nowhere in the Gospels is there any mention of Thomas having another given name, whether Judas or otherwise. This seems to be limited to certain Syriac traditions, and of course to the surviving copies of the Gospel of Thomas.

Nonetheless, it is most intriguing that he alone of all the characters in the New Testament should be known solely by his nickname "(the) Twin." And this is a fact we tend to easily overlook because the name Thomas has entered popular culture as a male name, we now think nothing of. It seems highly unlikely that Thomas was literally the twin brother of Jesus, since that would have been mentioned in the synoptic Gospels. More feasible is that Thomas was a twin to Jesus in a spiritual sense. And there is another reason this may be the correct interpretation. Sophia was known to the Gnostics as the *syzygy* (or twin) of Christ, the term used in Gnosticism for male and female pairings known as *Aeons* that emanate from God, the One, the Monad. Thus, perhaps Thomas was said to be the twin of Christ in the same sense that Sophia (Wisdom) was said to be the twin (*syzygy*) of Christ. Thus, the theory that "twin" meant Thomas was a spiritual twin of Jesus seems to have most credibility given this widely known use of the term twin at that time, and the clear influence of Hellenistic thought on Christ's teachings. Buddhism also had an influence on Christ, and it is possible Thomas is at least part of Christ's link to Buddhism.

There is one other possibility, and granted it is speculation. But it is possible Thomas was called "the twin" because he shadowed Jesus in the sense of being assigned to memorize what Christ said, or even perhaps wrote down what he said. This would explain why the sole document we have that bears a resemblance to what we believe "Q" to be is "The Gospel of *Thomas*." The designated scribe? The *Hafiz* (memorizer) to use the Islamic term? This fits better than the alternatives.

One of the deep mysteries of Christ's teachings is that he so clearly was exposed to Buddhist teachings, and to Buddhist parables in particular, but we don't know how Christ became familiar with Buddhism. We know from historical research that with the Silk Road and the free flow of merchants between the East and the Middle East, that it seems certain that Mahayana Buddhist communities had settled in or near Judea by the time of Christ. But there is another possibility for how Christ became aware of Indian teachings, a possibility until now seemingly overlooked.

While there is no credible evidence that Jesus himself ever went to India, whereas it is recorded that after the crucifixion and establishment of James' church in Jerusalem, Thomas did go to India. Indeed, from all reports he spent the rest of his life there, opening churches and baptizing people. What is surprising, perhaps, is that scholars often mention that Thomas went to India and converted many people there to Christianity, and indeed, reputedly mainly wealthy, upper caste, intellectual people, without stopping to acknowledge what this means.

Put simply, a relatively uneducated man from Judea in the First Century could not likely go to India and have success there in such a short time unless he already knew the local language and culture. Indeed, unless he was already familiar both with and *to* the people of that region. That is, Thomas didn't simply just go to India, he went *back* to India.

Eusebius quoting from Origen[8] tells us that after the crucifixion the apostles drew lots as to who would go where to spread the Word. And in this telling, Thomas drew Parthia, whereas Andrew drew Scythia and John drew Asia. However, the apocryphal text *Acts of Thomas* states that Thomas drew the lot for India, and this is why he went there. Realizing that Parthia and India were intimately connected—the Indo-Parthian Empire ran from 19 C.E. to 224 C.E.—helps us understand that there is likely no conflict between what Eusebius (Origen) wrote and what is in the apocryphal text. There is thus a fascinating interconnection here between the spread of Buddhism to the Middle East at the time of Christ, the rise of Mahayana Buddhism at this time, and the fact Mahayana had its source in Northern India. If Thomas had strong ties to Northern India, he may thus have introduced Christ to Buddhism. We will look at this in the next chapter on Buddhism in the Greco-Roman world of the first century.

---

1 From the German *Quelle*, meaning 'source'

2 Meaning "twin"; variant of Didymus

3 Also meaning "twin"

4 In the interest of transparency, the author is himself a member of a Thomasine Order.

5 See for instance Flavius Josephus *Antiquities of the Jews* (94-95 C.E.): "...the brother of Jesus, who was called Christ, whose name was James...". Hegesippus (c 110-180 C.E.), in his fifth book of Commentaries, refers to James as the bishop of Jerusalem. Clement of Alexandria (late 2nd C.) also refers to James being made head of the first church in Jerusalem following Jesus' death.

6 Mark 9:5, Mark 14:45

7 Josephus *ibid*

8 See the *Apology of Origen* (written by Pamphilius, assisted by Eusebius), and Eusebius' *Church History* (*Ecclesiastical History*). Also see Harold Attridge, Ed., *Eusebius, Christianity, and Judaism,* Wayne State University Press, 1992, 177.

6

Buddhism in the Greco-Roman World

There appears to be a misconception that in the First Century C.E., Judaism and Christianity were in the Middle East, and Buddhism was completely separate somewhere far much farther East in India, China, Tibet and elsewhere. This misunderstanding led to wild speculation that Jesus must have travelled to somewhere in the Far East in order to explain the similarities between his teachings and those of the Buddha.

It may thus come as a surprise to many readers to learn that Buddhism was well established in the Greco-Roman world at the time of Christ. There would have been no need for Christ to travel outside of Palestine or even outside of Galilee to come into contact with Buddhist teachings.

The famous Indian Emperor of the Mauyra Dynasty, Ashoka the Great, ruled most of India from about 268 B.C.E. to 232 B.C.E. Ashoka's fame derives in part from his legendary brilliance as a leader, and from his promotion of Buddhism over most of the then civilized world—including Greece. He was known as *Devanampriya* (Beloved of the Gods) and *Priyadarsin* (One Who Regards Everyone With Affection).

Sri Lankan writings of the time by the monk Moggaliputta-Tissa reveal that Ashoka was his patron and that he sent out at least nine missions to promote Buddhism far and wide in around 250 B.C.E. Thus, in around the eighteenth year of Ashoka's reign, one of these missions is sent to what they referred to as "the Greek country."

From other writings of that time, known as the "Edicts of Ashoka," we know that Ashoka actively encouraged the transmission of Buddhism to the Hellenistic world, and that he converted many Greeks in his Kingdoms to Buddhism. In the Rock Edict, a section of the Edicts of Ashoka, we read:

> *Now it is conquest by Dhamma that Beloved-of-the-Gods considers to be the best conquest. And it (conquest by Dhamma) has been won here, on the borders, even six hundred yojanas away, where the Greek king Antiochos rules, beyond there where the four kings named Ptolemy, Antigonos, Magas and Alexander rule, likewise in the south among the Cholas, the Pandyas, and as far as Tamraparni.*

A yojana was about 8 miles so the writer is speaking of Ashoka's transmission of the dharma (or dhamma, both of which mean Buddha's teachings) having travelled as much as around 500 miles. In fact, it seems Ashoka's reach was further than that since evidence shows that his missionaries got as far as Alexandria in Egypt.

When Ashoka's reign was over, Buddhism continued to flourish in Greek Culture. The fall of the Mauryan empire led to the establishment of the Greco-Bactrian Kingdom (250-125 B.C.E.), which was followed by the Indo-Greek Kingdom in Northern India (180 B.C.E. - 10 C.E.) and eventually to the Kushan Empire (from the 1st to 3rd centuries C.E.).

During the hundred years prior to Christ's birth, a tremendous amount of trade occurred between the East (China, India) and the Middle East, creating what is known as the "Silk Road." This major east-west travel route was named the Silk Road after the Roman Empire's intense passion for silk.

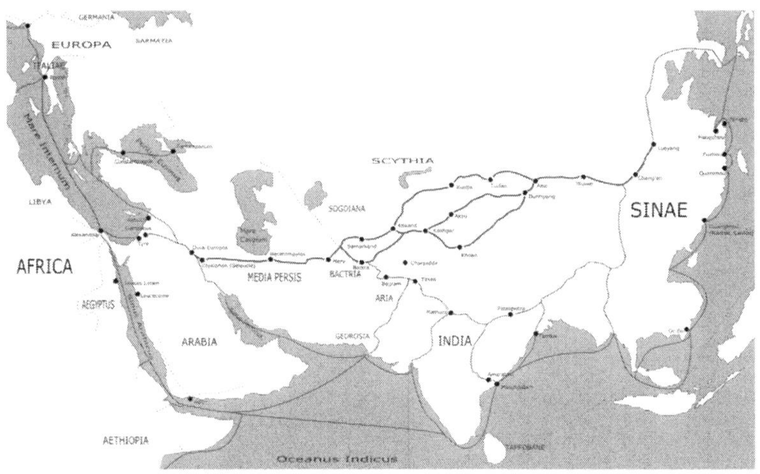

1stC trade routes, including the Silk Road

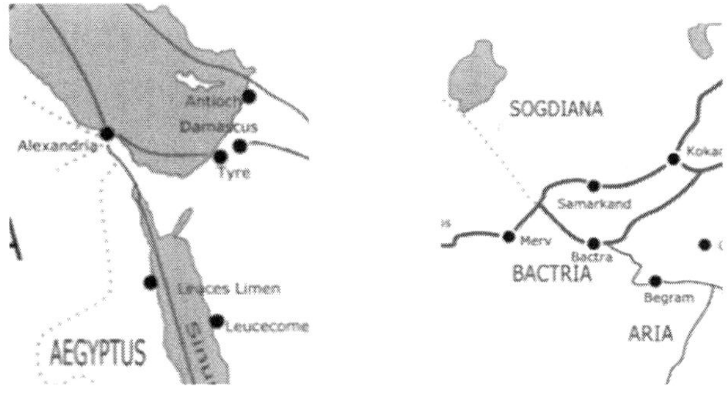

And the portions of interest here

The Silk Road ran from the Far East to Europe, and in particular passed right through Bactria and on to Tyre, a few miles north of Palestine. While traditional depictions of the Silk Road show a maritime connection from Tyre to Alexandria, it is certain that traders and other travelers continued south from Tyre and took the land route to Alexandria.

This land route, which was in real terms part of the Silk Road, went right through Galilee. Indeed, it went right through Magdala (home of Mary Magdalene) and Nazareth where Christ lived. It is here that the Silk Road connected with the ancient *Via Maris* and the ancient *Kings Highway*, routes through the Middle East that had existed in Bronze Age times.

Thus, despite what has been widely believed regarding the absence of Buddhism in the Middle East at the time of Christ, we have solid evidence that Buddhism was well known in the Holy Land at that time. The apparent mystery as to how Jesus could have become so familiar with Buddhism as to quote from Buddhist parables is solved in at least two possible ways (and probably both): the spread of Buddhism to that region and Thomas' connection to Northern India where the then new Mahayana Buddhism (that Christ's teachings most closely resembles) was birthed at that time.

Let us now look more closely at the geography of the Middle East at that time. As we will see, the important trade routes ran right through the region Jesus was born into and in which he taught. While it is circumstantial, there is also some indication Mahayana Buddhist communities were established in this region around the time of Christ.

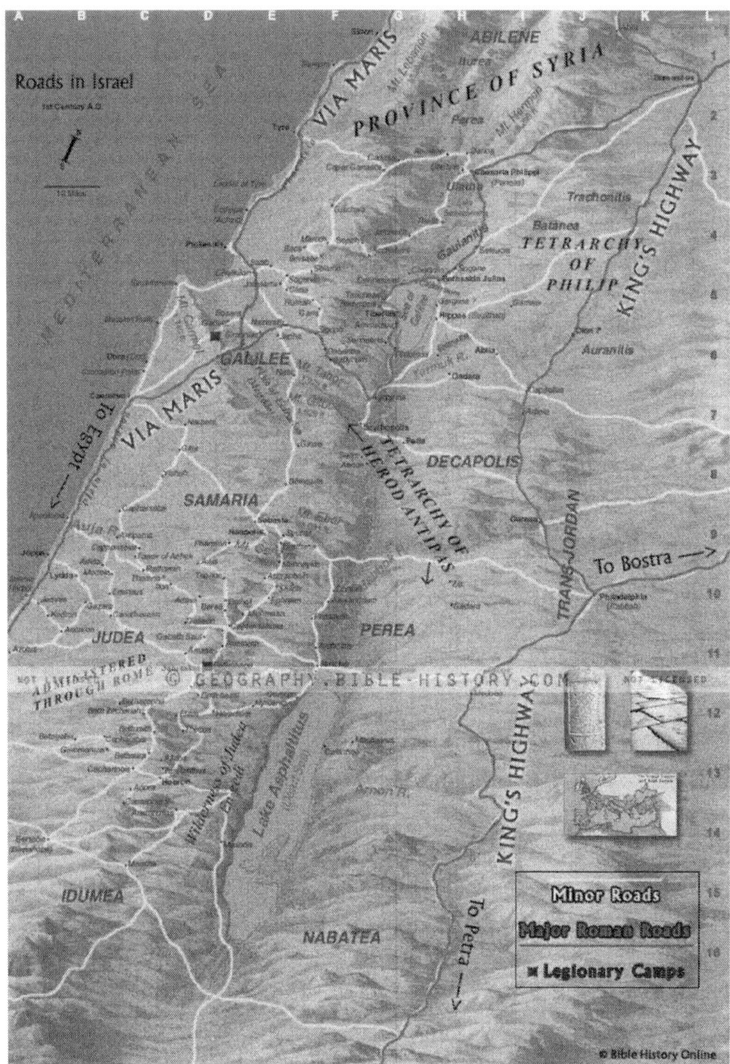

The Silk Road: Via Maris and The King's Road at the time of Christ

And the section of particular interest here:

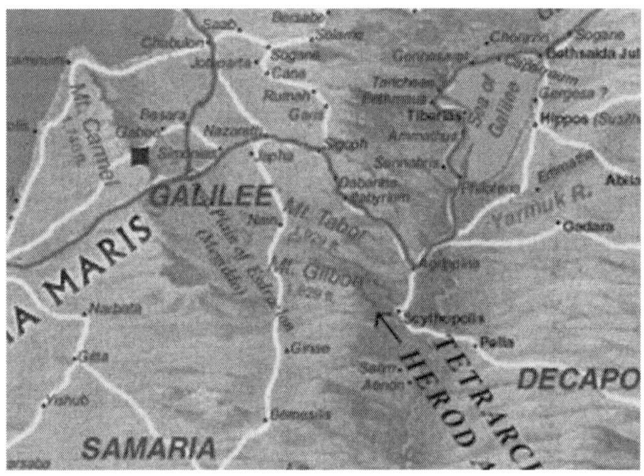

Magdala was just north of Tiberias, and Capernaum was just north of that

The major trade route of that time coming from the Far East thus went around the Sea of Galilee, right through Capernaum and Magdala, on through Nazareth and south eventually to Alexandria. Greek monks known as the Alexandria Buddhists, who we know were flourishing in Bactria at that time, would have passed through Galilee as they traveled back and forth between Alexandria in Egypt and Alexandria in the Caucasus in Bactria.

We also know that the Greek Buddhist monks played a key role in the spread of Buddhism under Ashoka around 260 B.C.E. and later under King Menander (around 165-130 B.C.E.) because this is written about in the *Mahavamsa*. The Mahavamsa—or "Great Chronicle"—is a 6th century document written in Sri Lanka in Pali (the sacred language of Theravada Buddhism). This document reviewed the history of Buddhism from the 6th century B.C.E. to the 4th century C.E. Tradition has it that it was written in the 6th century C.E. by a Theravada

Buddhist monk named Mahanama.

The *Mahavamsa* itself is said to have relied heavily on the *Dipavamsa* ("Island Chronicle") written five centuries earlier. From these and from the Ashoka Edicts we learn that Ashoka sent elders in the Buddhist tradition from northern India as far away as Alexandria to spread the Buddhist dharma. Not only that, but some of these elders were already Greek monks. The Greeks were known as "Yona" ("Ionians") in the classical world, and in the Edicts we learn that Ashoka sent a Yona named Dhammarakkhita to spread the dharma to Aparantaka. And that Ashoka sent another elder named Mahyantika, who we believe was also Greek, to teach Buddhism in Kashmir and Gandhara.

The Indo-Greek king Menander I was in power from 160-135 B.C.E. and had his capital in what today is Punjab. He was described as a great Greek leader, even greater than Alexander. It is during this time of king Menandar's rule that the Greek monk (Ionian elder) Mahadhammarakkhita came from "Alesandra" (Alexandria of the Caucasus) along with 30,000 Greek Buddhist monks. Together they attended the foundation ceremony of the Maha Thupa, or the "Great Stupa" at Anuradhapura in Sri Lanka during the 2nd century B.C.E.

This bears repeating: in the second century B.C.E. the Buddhist community in Alexandria of the Caucasus, near Bactria in Northern India, was so well-established that an elder along with 30,000 monks traveled to Sri Lanka. Yet these were Greek monks, with strong ties to the Greek civilization to the West. Certainly, many of these monks would have traveled to Alexandria in Egypt, and to other destinations to the western edge of the Hellenistic world.

Those traveling Greek Buddhist monks almost certainly would have passed right through Galilee. By the time of Christ, then, there had been at least 200 years of familiarity with Buddhism in the region, and specifically with these Greek Buddhist monks traveling right through Galilee on what may well have been a regular basis.

There were also strong connections between Buddhists and leaders of the Roman world at the time of Christ. Various historical Roman texts speak of an emissary sent by the Indian King Porus to Caesar Augustus sometime between about 22 B.C.E. to around 13 C.E. Because this emissary was related to the monk who had immolated himself in Athens as part of his Buddhist faith, Nicolaus of Damascus recorded these facts for perpetuity. That said, there are fewer confirmations of Buddhist connections to the Roman Empire than there are to the Hellenistic world.

The other indication we have that Buddhism may have influenced Greek thought is the emergence of Neoplatonism in the 1st and 2nd century C.E. The creation of Neoplatonism is ascribed to Plotinus (204-270 C.E.) and his teacher Ammonius Saccas (175-242 C.E.), who taught Plotinus from 232 C.E. to 243 C.E. Both Plotinus and his teacher spoke of the fundamental ideas as being ancient stemming from many generations before.

Plotinus' philosophy is outlined in the collection of his works known as the *Enneads*, compiled by his student Porphyry. This included three main principles of "the One," "the Intellect," and "the Soul." These ideas—explored further in the work of the Cappadocian Fathers, Pseudo-Dionysius the Areopagite and, famously, Augustine of Hippo—went on to influence Christian and Muslim theologians and teachers for generations to come.

Plotinus' writings are often compared to Christian theology, not surprisingly given the impact Neoplatonism had on early Christian thought. However, Neoplatonism arguably owes more to Buddhism than to Christianity or to its roots in traditional Jewish theology. On its surface, Neoplatonism's focus on the One, the Intellect and the Soul evokes a parallel to Christian Trinity. Yet, when we look at what Plotinus meant by "the One" it takes on characteristics more in common with Buddhism than with Jewish tradition.

The One, or the "Source" or the "Monad," in Neoplatonic terms, is completely transcendent undivided and not susceptible to splitting into being and non-being: it is beyond all categorization. What the Monad is *not* is some kind of God, or Creator Being, or indeed a self-aware being or entity of any kind. The Monad is also not just a simplistic statement of the totality of all things but is (to quote Plotinus) "prior to all existents."

His philosophy sees this One as encompassing mind or thinking and object or construct (form) since the moment there is a thinker or self-aware intelligence (known as the "*noesis*" or the "*nous*") then there is already duality and no longer the One. Sound familiar? Neoplatonism cries out for comparison with Buddhist teachings of emptiness is form, and form is emptiness, as well as with the idea of "dependent origination" or "dependent arising" (*pratityasamutpada* in Sanskrit). The latter is a key doctrine in Buddhism which teaches us that all dharmas are dependent on all other dharmas. Thus, in Buddhism we talk of "if this exists then that exists," and "if this ceases to exist that also ceases to exist."

In Neoplatonism Plotinus writes that everything emanates from the One, the Monad. His idea of emanation is in contrast to the Christian idea that God created everything out of nothing, although nowhere in his writings does he ever refer to Christianity. Rather, he likens this emanation is being like a sun that shines light, but it is not diminished by that shining (in fact, in modern day science, we know that isn't technically true). Another parallel he draws is that of a reflection not taking anything away from that which is reflected.

In his philosophy, the first emanation of the One is the *nous*—the reason, thought, order, the "*Logos*." From the *nous* emanates the *World Soul*. From this *World Soul* human souls emerge and then at the lowest level *matter* emerges. Immediately, we see parallels to dualistic and non-dualistic thought in Buddhist teachings, and to the idea of the Self (the true self, the One or the absolute) and self (the relative, or the material world of form including ego, the illusion of separateness, our human mind generated concepts of individual 'things' and so on).

Where Plotinus' ideas most clearly evoke both Buddhist and Sufi teaching is the contemplative and practice-based nature of his work that envisaged the ultimate goal as being ecstatic union with the One, or the Monad, through meditation—having much in common with Buddhist enlightenment as well as the mystical union goals of both the Islamic Sufi tradition and Christian Mysticism. This union with the One is what he termed *henosis*.

Henosis, then, is Plotinus's ultimate goal of becoming one, or entering into unity with, the Monad or Source of everything. The goal of the practice he proposed was to reach the state of emptiness he referred to as *tabula rasa* or empty mind that has merged with the Source. Interestingly, Plotinus saw the way this state of unity would be achieved is through meditation (or, as it is often named in Christianity in the West, contemplation). He thus saw meditation as enabling a person to essentially reverse the "thinking" of the world, to reverse the duality that the *nous* (or mind) had created in order to reconnect with the "prior to existents" reality of the One.

Anyone familiar with Buddhist teaching will immediately perceive someone who, in Plotinus and his teacher, learned about Buddhist teaching and sought to integrate it with classical Platonic philosophy. Indeed, Plotinus and Ammonius made no secret that Neoplatonism was based on ancient ideas and teachings. They just never named Buddhism, just as Plotinos also steered clear of referring to Christianity even while evoking his core trinity concept.

This has to be speculation, of course, since so far we have not uncovered writings that clarify what the foundations of Plotinus's philosophy were. But we do know that by 250 B.C.E. Buddhism had been introduced to the Greek world, and indeed to Alexandria in Egpyt, where Plotinus was born. We know that Greek Buddhism was flourishing by the 1st and 2nd century C.E. and thus was likely infused into Greek discourse and thinking.

Why this is of particular interest is not only because of the link to Buddhist teachings, but because this is the world Christ was born into: one in which he was surrounded by Jewish and Buddhist teachings as well as immersed in the world of Greek philosophy and culture. Inherent in Plotinus's ideas is the concept that in a real sense a person is both human and divine. The One, or Monad, can be in unity (divine nature) or duality (human nature)—thus paralleling the idea that Christ was both human and divine. But with the key difference—that all human beings are both divine and human in this sense since they are both integral to and separate from (in *appearance* or by *illusion*) the One.

Neoplatonism, then, did not arise out of a vacuum in the late 1st and 2nd century C.E. Rather, it emerged from a smorgasbord of philosophical ideas and teachings present in the Middle East in that period that arose in the decades prior to the birth of Christ. This feast of ideas comprised of not just Jewish theology and Greek thinking but also various teachings and traditions such as Buddhism, Wisdom teaching (the Sophia) and various Gnostic and Pre-Gnostic traditions, together with the writings of the Hellenistic Jew Philo.

Wisdom traditions and a variety of Wisdom teachings were prevalent in the first century C.E. Wisdom (Greek: *Sophia*, Sanskrit: *prajna*) was central to Christ's teachings and undoubtedly to the training and teaching he received prior to starting his mission known as "the Way." Sophia is a central concept in Jewish tradition, Christian theology, Greek religion and philosophy (Platonism), and Gnosticism. Indeed, Plato's term "philosophy" literally means love of wisdom.

The idea of Sophia underwent a transformation in the 3rd and 4th centuries B.C.E. where Plato introduced his term philosopher as one who loves wisdom (that is literally what the word *philosopher* means). Here the Sophia referred to is a higher intellect or knowledge having the connotation that the person possessing this wisdom is particularly skillful. While historic records indicate that King Ashoka sent emissaries (variously referred to in the literature of the time as "monks," *bhikkhus*, *sramanas*, or "elders") to Greece and Alexandria in Egypt to spread Buddhism in around 250 B.C.E., Buddhist teaching could well have permeated Hellenistic civilization well before that time since it is unclear whether the emissaries sent by King Ashoka were the first to spread it the Hellenistic world.

The Buddhist term *prajna* (Sanskrit, *panna* in Pali) also literally means a higher knowledge, understanding or consciousness. *Prajna* evokes a kind of higher wisdom that is spontaneous, supreme and emerging from deep understanding beyond thoughts and words. The revision, then, of Sophia in ancient Greece may well have been influenced by the Buddhist concept of *prajna* finding its way into Greek thought and philosophy in the 4th and 3rd centuries B.C.E.

In Gnosticism, the concept of Sophia is represented as female who combines attributes of the human soul with those of the feminine aspect of the divine. To Gnostics Sophia was the female twin divine *Aeon* of Christ. Sophia was known to the Gnostics as the *syzygy* (or 'twin') of Christ, the term used in Gnosticism for male and female pairings known as *Aeons* that emanate from God, the One, the Monad. In this tradition, the Holy Spirit is seen as having the qualities of Sophia and as being feminine.

As an aside here, this may relate to why the disciple Thomas was known by that name—that is, "the twin." What this may refer to is Thomas' wisdom, or his grasp of Christ's teachings, was viewed as on a par with Christ's own wisdom. Hence, like Sophia, Thomas was seen as a twin in the sense derived from Hellenistic ideas of Jesus and Thomas both being emanations of God, of the One, 'twined' in their parallel wisdom. However, this may not mean at all that Thomas' naming suggested an identify with Jesus or that he was at the same level as Jesus, but rather that it may have been an honorific reflecting how wise Thomas was. That said, the alternative proposed here for the first time, that Thomas was the assigned "twin" of Christ in the sense of being the designated scribe or memorizer, may be an even better fit.

As we have observed elsewhere here, Thomas clearly had a connection with the Indian subcontinent and hence, perhaps, with Buddhism. It is recorded that after Jesus' death, Thomas is sent to India to establish a branch of Christianity there. But it is also recorded that he almost immediately found favor in the highest echelons of the local Indian culture and established at least seven churches. It is unlikely that he acquired the necessary extensive grasp of both language and culture in the brief time he spent in India after Jesus died, and its thus more likely that Thomas had spent time in India before becoming Christ's disciple.

While it can only be informed speculation, it is possible that Thomas himself is one link Christ had to Buddhism: not only was Christ likely exposed to Buddhism through Greek Buddhists passing through his region, and indeed living there, but he was informed about Buddhism by Thomas who had perhaps even been born in a Jewish settlement in India, or at least spent time there. This is not unlikely given there were numerous Jewish settlements in India in the period 100 B.C.E. to 100 C.E. as well as an extensive presence of Greek Buddhists in Northern India since before 250 B.C.E.

Sophia is referenced in the *Nag Hammadi*—the collection of early Gnostic and Christian scrolls found in the northern Egyptian town of Nag Hammadi in 1945. And of course, one of the most famous works written in Coptic that make up these scrolls is the Gospel of Thomas. While the specific Gospel of Thomas texts found in 1945 appear to date from the fourth century C.E., there is wide acceptance that the text is based on far earlier sources.

As we saw above, the similarity of the Gospel of Thomas to the hypothetical missing text "Q" suggests that Thomas is based on the very earliest Gospel of Christ from before 50 C.E. which contained primarily sayings and teachings of Christ. Logically, what was written down during the time Christ was teaching, and immediately following his death, is most likely to have been what Christ taught, what he said. This is supported by the much later dating of added text supplementing the

Gospels of Mark, Matthew and Luke where historic detail about Jesus is affirmed to be a later addition.

If Thomas was called the twin because he was assigned to record the words of Christ—to be Christ's shadow or twin in the Gnostic sense—this may explain why the main text we have of Christ's sayings is called the *Gospel of Thomas*.

7

The Trinity and the Three Treasures[1]

It has been said that Christ presented the first true monotheism to come out of the Middle East. That is, prior to the time of Christ, we see a gradual change in the Jewish concept of God from a polytheistic beginning, to a phase when there are many Gods in the pantheon but Yahweh is the head God. Next it moved to a phase around the time of Christ where there is just one God, but that God is the God of the Jews, not of the Gentiles. Then Jesus enters the scene and his teaching spreads to Jews and Gentiles alike, preaching about one single God—one so intimate you should call him "papa" or "daddy"—that is the one God for *all* people. But that then, in some people's view, after Christ's death there was a transformation of his teachings that created three Gods from the one—Father, Son and Holy Spirit.

As discussed in an earlier chapter, this concept of the Trinity—God as three in one—has burdened Christianity since its earliest days and led to seasoned priests handing the Trinity Sunday sermon off on to fledgling curates. The problem is that Christ never taught that he was divine in any other sense than we are all divine. Or rather we all have our divine nature (the True Self, with our will aligned with God's) and our human nature (the lesser self, the ego, living in a dualistic world: me and you, us and them). Similarly, Christ never referred to himself as the *only* son of God, or even implied he was a God, or even of one substance with God. At least this does not appear in the synoptic Gospels, and instead Christ rebuffs such questions, turning them around in the form "Who do *you* say I am?"

Certainly, nowhere in Christ's core teachings is there anything that speaks of a Trinity of Father, Son and Holy Spirit: his teachings are focused on unity of all, and radical inclusiveness where we are all brother, sister, mother, father, fully equal in the Kingdom. That is not the language of a Trinity of superior beings above us, and we ordinary human beings somewhere way down below the pedestals we have placed the superior beings on.

But there may be another way to look at the Trinity which draws on the Three Treasures of Buddhism. The Three Treasures of Buddhism are Buddha, Dharma and Sangha. I would argue we can see a parallel here with the Trinity. These three translate into the Way, the Truth and the Life: Buddha nature/Christ nature, Truth (Teaching) and life (Community). In this way of looking at the Trinity, God is who we truly are, the essential nature of all. The Son is the teaching, the Word. And thus, the Holy Spirit is God in community, it is us being in community, with the goal of living together in the Kingdom.

Since we are all Sons and Daughters of God when we realize our True Selves, enter the Kingdom, and align our will with God's will, it doesn't make sense to single out one Son—here to single out Jesus—not least since he didn't do that himself. Rather the "Son" in the Trinity becomes what Jesus was to us: a teacher and embodiment of the Word. Similarly, we are all interconnected, we are all one. Indeed, we enter the Kingdom not as individuals (we've covered that pretty thoroughly above) but rather it is by virtue of the fact we are all interconnected that we are (and have always been) in the Kingdom as a single community. This is the Spirit. It is us in community, in the Kingdom, aware of our true selves and equally aware in the moment of our individuality. Aware of being a child of God as well as a Son or Daughter of God. Simultaneously aware of both the absolute and the relative.

But there's yet another way to look at the Trinity by considering what Christ taught about how we can enter the Kingdom. How do we achieve this state of *metanoia*, of going beyond thought? Jesus teaches that to enter the Kingdom you will need to be born again. Depending on the translation and source, this is variously "born again of water and spirit" or simply born again. What is invoked here is a clear, simple message by Christ and whereas our biological birth is by our biological parents, similarly our spiritual (re)birth is through our as it were spiritual parents: that is, you become a Son (or Daughter) of God by being reborn of the Father (God) and the Mother (Holy Spirit, depicted as the feminine aspect of the ground of our being).

This is not idle speculation, drawing a connection between Spirit and the feminine. Rather, scholarly research reveals that in the time of Christ, what was referred to as "Spirit" was linked to Sophic thought and Wisdom (Sophia, wisdom teaching). Since we now accept Jesus was a First Century Wisdom Tradition teacher, it is hardly surprising that he drew on these ideas of wisdom being feminine and related to 'spirit.'

Further support for this also comes from Christ's teaching that to enter the Kingdom, to find Heaven within, you need to be born again. There can be little doubt that by this he meant a spiritual rebirth, and rebirth where the 'parents' are God (the Father) and the Holy Spirit (Wisdom, Sophia, the feminine divine aspect: "Mother"). And once reborn of your spiritual 'parents' you become a Son of God (or Daughter of God). It is unclear whether Christ himself would have supported the idea of a Trinity, but I suspect this version of it likely came closest to his teachings.

---

[1] This chapter is the working title of a separate book currently in development. This chapter is some initial thoughts on the topic.

8

Parallel Parables

Some of the most compelling proof that Jesus had knowledge of Buddhist teachings are the striking parallels between his teachings and sayings and those attributed to the Buddha. Note I say *attributed* to the Buddha: the fact is we have little to no real evidence of what he actually said and did—not too dissimilar to our lack of clarity as to exactly what Christ did and said.

The similarities between the stories and sayings in both traditions is clear. So much so that it is quite likely that Jesus did get at least some of his stories and sayings from the Buddhist tradition. Still, we cannot know if it was directly from Buddhists or from Jesus' teachers and mentors who themselves were familiar with the Buddhist sources. On the one hand we have the possibility that Thomas introduced Jesus to such teachings, and on the other hand it is possible that Buddhist teachers in Galilee either spoke with Jesus directly or that such teachers influenced local Jewish Wisdom Teachers that in turn then taught Jesus.

Parables from the pre-Christian era Buddhist tradition include many that will sound familiar to anyone who knows the Christian Gospels. Here are just a few of the B.C.E. Buddhist parables: The Prodigal Son, The Widows Mite, The Man Born Blind, The Woman at the Well, The Mustard Seed, The Sower, and Walking on Water. Again, these are all *Buddhist* parables that predate the time of Christ.

One of the clearest examples of Christ borrowing from the

Buddhist tradition is the Parable of the Prodigal Son. While Christ's version is shorter than the Buddhist version, the similarities are obvious. So much so that it is not credible that Christ's version was not based on the original Indian version.

The Christian version is found in the Gospel of Luke (15:11-32):

The Parable of the Lost Son

[11] Jesus continued: "There was a man who had two sons. [12] The younger one said to his father, 'Father, give me my share of the estate.' So he divided his property between them.

[13] "Not long after that, the younger son got together all he had, set off for a distant country and there squandered his wealth in wild living. [14] After he had spent everything, there was a severe famine in that whole country, and he began to be in need. [15] So he went and hired himself out to a citizen of that country, who sent him to his fields to feed pigs. [16] He longed to fill his stomach with the pods that the pigs were eating, but no one gave him anything.

[17] "When he came to his senses, he said, 'How many of my father's hired servants have food to spare, and here I am starving to death! [18] I will set out and go back to my father and say to him: Father, I have sinned against Heaven and against you. [19] I am no longer worthy to be called your son; make me like one of your hired servants.' [20] So he got up and went to his father.

"But while he was still a long way off, his father saw him and was filled with compassion for him; he ran to his son, threw his arms around him and kissed him.

21 *“The son said to him, ‘Father, I have sinned against*
Heaven and against you. I am no longer worthy to be called
your son.’

22 *“But the father said to his servants, ‘Quick! Bring the*
best robe and put it on him. Put a ring on his finger and
sandals on his feet. 23 *Bring the fattened calf and kill it. Let’s*
have a feast and celebrate. 24 *For this son of mine was dead*
and is alive again; he was lost and is found.’ So they began
to celebrate.

25 *“Meanwhile, the older son was in the field. When he*
came near the house, he heard music and dancing. 26 *So he*
called one of the servants and asked him what was going
on. 27 *‘Your brother has come,’ he replied, ‘and your father*
has killed the fattened calf because he has him back safe
and sound.’

28 *“The older brother became angry and refused to go in.*
So his father went out and pleaded with him. 29 *But he*
answered his father, ‘Look! All these years I’ve been slaving
for you and never disobeyed your orders. Yet you never gave
me even a young goat so I could celebrate with my
friends. 30 *But when this son of yours who has squandered*
your property with prostitutes comes home, you kill the
fattened calf for him!’

31 *“‘My son,’ the father said, ‘you are always with me,*
and everything I have is yours. 32 *But we had to celebrate*
and be glad, because this brother of yours was dead and is
alive again; he was lost and is found.’”

The original Buddhist version is considerably longer and is found in the *Saddharma Pundarika Sutra* 4 (also known as the *Lotus Sutra* or, literally, *Sutra on the White Lotus of the Sublime Dharma*), created in first century B.C.E and thus predates the time of Christ:

The Generous Father and the Spendthrift Son

A young man left his father and ran away. For a long long time he dwelt in other countries: he had lost track of time but it had been perhaps fifty years. The older he grew, the more needy he became. Wandering in all directions to seek clothing and food, he without intending to do so, he approached his native country. The father had searched for his son all those years in vain and meanwhile had settled in a certain city. The father had become exceedingly rich, his home very grand and his goods and treasures were fabulous.

At this time the poor son, wandering through village after village and passing through countries and cities, at last reached the city where his father had settled. The father had always been thinking of his son, yet, although he had been parted from him over fifty years, he had never spoken of the matter to anyone. He only pondered within himself and harbored regret in his heart, saying, "Old and worn out I am. Although I own much wealth - gold, silver, and jewels, granaries and treasuries overflowing - I have no son. Someday my end will come, and my wealth will be scattered and lost, for I have no heir. If I could only get back my son back and commit my wealth to him, how contented and happy would I be, with no further anxiety!"

Meanwhile the poor son, hired for wages here and there, by sheer chance found himself at his father's house completely unaware of who lived there. Standing by the gate, he saw from a distance his father seated on a lion-couch, his feet on a jeweled footstool, and with expensive strings of pearls adorning his body, revered and surrounded by priests, warriors, and citizens, attendants and young slaves waiting upon him right and left. The poor son, seeing his father having such great power, was seized with fear, regretting that he had come to this place. He reflected, "This must be a king, or someone of royal rank, it is impossible for me to be hired here. I had better go to some poor village in search of a job, where food and clothing are easier to get. If I stay here long, I may suffer oppression." Reflecting thus, he rushed away.

Meanwhile the rich elder on his lion-seat had recognized his son at first glance, and with great joy in his heart reflected, "Now I have someone to whom I may pass on my wealth. I have always been thinking of my son, with no means of seeing him, but suddenly he himself has come and my longing is satisfied. Though worn with years, I yearn for him." Instantly he sent off his attendants to pursue the son quickly and fetch him back. Immediately the messengers hasten forth to seize him. The poor son, surprised and scared, loudly cried out, "I have committed no offense against you, why should I be arrested?"

Hearing this the messengers were even more determined to secure the son and bring him back. The poor son feared that that although he was innocent he would be imprisoned, and that now he would surely die. He became more terrified, fainted and fell on the ground. The father, seeing this from a distance, sent word to the messengers, "I am not asking you to detain this man for wrongdoing. Do not bring him by force. Sprinkle cold water on his face to restore him to consciousness and do not speak to him any further." Why did the father say this? The father, knowing that his son's disposition was inferior, knowing that his own lordly position had caused distress to his son, yet convinced that he was his son, tactfully did not say to others, "This is my son."

A messenger said to the son, "I set you free, go wherever you will." The poor son was delighted, gaining the unexpected release. He arose from the ground and went to a nearby village in search of food and clothing. Then the Father, wishing to attract his son, set up a device. Secretly he sent two men, sorrowful and poor in appearance, saying, "Go and visit that place and gently say to the poor man, 'There is a place for you to work here. We will hire you for scavenging, and we both also will work along with you.'" Then the two messengers went in search of the poor son and, having found him, presented him with the proposal. The poor son, having received his wages in advance, joined them in his first task of removing a refuse heap.

His father, beholding the son, was struck with compassion for him. One day he saw at a distance, through the window, his son's figure, haggard and drawn, lean and sorrowful, filthy with dirt and dust. He took off his strings of jewels, his soft attire, and put on a coarse, torn and dirty garment, smeared his body with dust, took a basket in his right hand, and with an appearance fear-inspiring said to the laborers, "Get on with your work, don't be lazy."

By such means he got near to his son, to whom he afterwards said, "Ay, my man, you stay and work here, do not leave again. I will increase your wages, give whatever you need, bowls, rice, wheat-flour, salt, vinegar, and so on. Have no hesitation; besides there is an old servant whom you can get if you need him. Be at ease in your mind; I will be like a father to you; do not be worried again. Why? I am old and advanced in years, but you are young and vigorous; all the time you have been working you have never been deceitful, lazy, angry or grumbling. I have never seen you, like the other laborers, with such vices as these. From this time forth you will be as my own begotten son."

The elder gave him a new name and called him a son. But the poor son, although he rejoiced at this happening, still thought of himself as a humble hireling. For this reason, for twenty years he continued to be employed in scavenging. After this period, there grew mutual confidence between the father and the son. He went in and out and at his ease, though his abode was still in a small hut.

Then the father became ill and, knowing that he would die soon, said to the poor son, "Now I possess an abundance of gold, silver, and precious things, and my granaries and treasuries are full to overflowing. I want you to understand in detail the quantities of these things, and the amounts that should be received and given. This is my wish, and you must agree to it. Why? Because now we are of the same mind. Be increasingly careful so that there be no waste." The poor son accepted his instruction and commands and became acquainted with all the goods. However, he still had no expectation of inheriting anything, his abode was still the original small hut and he was still unable to abandon his sense of inferiority.

After a short time had again passed, the father noticed that his son's ideas had gradually been enlarged, his aspirations developed, and that he despised his previous state of mind. Seeing that his own end was approaching, he commanded his son to come, and gathered all his relatives, the kings, priests, warriors, and citizens. When they were all assembled, he addressed them saying, "Now, gentlemen, this is my son, begotten by me. It is over fifty years since, from a certain city, he left me and ran away to endure loneliness and misery. His former name was so-and-so and my name was so-and-so. At that time in that city I sought him sorrowfully. Suddenly I met him in this place and regained him. This is really my son and I am really his father. Now all the wealth which I possess belongs entirely to my son, and all my previous disbursements and receipts now belong to this, my son." When the poor son heard these words of his father, great was his joy at such unexpected news, and thus he thought, "Without any mind for, or effort on my part, these treasures now come to me."

World-Honored One! The very rich elder is the Tathagata, and we are all as the Buddha's sons. The Buddha has always declared that we are his sons. But because of the three sufferings, in the midst of births-and-deaths we have borne all kinds of torments, being deluded and ignorant and enjoying our attachment to things of no value. Today the World-honored One has caused us to ponder and remove the dirt of all diverting discussions of inferior things. In these we have hitherto been diligent to make progress and have got, as it were, a day's pay for our effort to reach Nirvana. Obtaining this, we greatly rejoiced and were contented, saying to ourselves, "For our diligence and progress in the Dharma what we have received is ample". The Buddha, knowing that our minds delighted in inferior things, by his tactfulness taught according to our capacity, but still we did not perceive that we are really Buddha's sons. Therefore we say that though we had no mind to hope or expect it, yet now the Great Treasure of the King of the Law has of itself come to us, and such things that Buddha-sons should obtain, we have all obtained.

A couple of observations may help us appreciate the parallels here: first, the "Tathagata" is an honorific term for the

Buddha. So, toward the end of the Buddhist version of the story it is revealed that the Father (the rich man) is actually the Buddha in what is clearly meant to be a metaphorical story not a literal one. Christ uses the same story in an almost identical way, where the Father in his parable is clearly God. In both stories, the male centered cultures of both 500 B.C.E.-50 B.C.E. India and first century Palestine means that in one case we are all identified as being (lost) sons of Buddha, and in the other all (lost) sons of God. Clearly, since these stories are symbolic and not intended to be literal, if we are female, we can substitute the son in each case for a daughter—daughter of Buddha, daughter of God.

In each case the essentially identical story is shaped to fit the core teaching of the two traditions. In Christ's version he returns to his familiar teaching that if you return to God, then God will welcome you as if a long-lost son. You will be received with Love like that of a father for his only son. Again, this was a patriarchal culture. Christ repeats his teaching here that if you turn toward God, shape your will to God's will, abandoning your selfish ego-centric frame of mind, God will come running toward you with open arms. The core message is, as a true son (or daughter), everything God has is yours—you only need to realize this is your true self.

With the Buddhist version, the focus is slightly different. It underscores the fact that sometimes the Buddha's teachings can be overwhelming. It can be easy to fall into the trap of saying to yourself, "I am not worthy; I will never be enlightened." This version of the story helps us to realize that the dharma—Buddha's teachings—will come to you in various forms. In Zen terms, we say there are countless dharma gates to pass through, but realization comes when we see that they are all gateless gates.

It may be in the form of teachers or mentors who will work alongside us for many years, or they may take other forms. But at the moment of realization we see that all the time you were the true sons and daughters of Buddha: you were Buddha, that was always your true nature, your *Buddha nature*. There never was anything to attain.

The consensus of religious scholars is that the Buddhist version of this parable predates Christ by at least some decades, and is probably far earlier.[1] The Lotus Sutra is a mainstay of the Mahayana Buddhist movement which came into being between 100 B.C.E. and 100 C.E. and it is, of course, from the Mahayana tradition that Zen Buddhism derives. Once again, then, we see this interchange—or should we say interplay?—between the emergence of the Mahayana Bodhisattva branch of Buddhism and the Christian branch of Judaism which also emphasized the ideal of self-sacrifice. Christ was the embodiment of the Bodhisattva ideal.

The Widow's Mite

Here again we have such strong similarities that it seems certain that Christ got the story from a Buddhist source. Here is the version from the Gospel of Mark (12:41-44):

> 41 *Jesus sat down opposite the place where the offerings were put and watched the crowd putting their money into the temple treasury. Many rich people threw in large amounts.*
> 42 *But a poor widow came and put in two very small copper coins, worth only a few cents.*
>
> 43 *Calling his disciples to him, Jesus said, "Truly I tell you, this poor widow has put more into the treasury than all the others.*
> 44 *They all gave out of their wealth; but she, out of her poverty, put in everything—all she had to live on."*

The Buddhist version is found in several sources: Kumaralata's *Kalpanamanditika*, Asvaghosa's *Sutralamkara*, and the *Jakata* stories that date from as early as 300 B.C.E. It has been reviewed in numerous works such as *The Widow's Two Mites* by the author of the *Open Court Monthly Magazine*, XVII, 353-354. This author relates that the original story must date before 62 C.E. when the Buddhists books including those translated by Asvaghosha were imported into China and the Chinese translations became available. Since Christianity did not become well known in India or China until at least the 3rd Century C.E., hence the Indian version of the parable predates the time of Christ. There is thus no real possibility that the Christian version of this parable came first. The parable is also related in *Buddha*: *The Gospel of Buddha Compiled from Ancient Records* by Paul Carus 1894/1915. Here is the Buddhist version:[2]

> *There was once a lone widow who was very destitute and having travelled to a nearby mountain, she came across some hermits holding a religious assembly. On seeing this sight, the woman was filled with joy, and uttering praises, said, "It is well, holy priests! But while others give precious things such as the ocean caves produce, I have nothing to offer."*
>
> *Having said this the woman sought in vain for something to give, and she recalled that some time before she had found in a dung-heap two coppers, so taking these she offered them as a charitable gift to the priests.*
>
> *The head priest, a wise man who could read people's hearts, disregarding the rich gifts of others and beholding the deep faith dwelling in the heart of this poor widow, and*

wishing the priests present to notice the religious merit of her gift, raised his hand and exclaimed, "Reverend priests take notice!" He went on, "The poor coppers of this widow are worth more than all the treasures of the oceans and the wealth of the broad earth. As an act of pure devotion, she has done a pious deed; She has attained salvation, being free from selfish greed."

Hearing this the woman was emboldened, and said, "It is even as the Teacher says: what I have done is as much as if a rich man were to give up all his wealth."

As you can see, these are essentially the same underlying story, and as was the case with the Prodigal Son, the Buddhist version substantially predates the one attributed to Christ by at least some decades: perhaps by some centuries. Christ goes on to expand on and explore this them with parables and sayings such as that it is harder for a rich man to get into Heaven than for a camel to get through the eye of a needle. Or, blessed are the meek for theirs is the Kingdom of God; the last shall be first and the first shall be last, and so on.

The Man Born Blind

In the Gospels we have two stories of Jesus healing a blind man: one in Mark and the other in John. First the story in Mark (8:22-26):

22 They came to Bethsaida, and some people brought a blind man and begged Jesus to touch him. 23 He took the blind man by the hand and led him outside the village. When he had spit on the man's eyes and put his hands on him, Jesus asked, "Do you see anything?"

24 He looked up and said, "I see people; they look like
trees walking around."
25 Once more Jesus put his hands on the man's eyes.
Then his eyes were opened, his sight was restored, and he
saw everything clearly. 26 Jesus sent him home,
saying, "Don't even go into the village."

And now the version in John (9:1-12):

1 As he went along, he saw a man blind from birth. 2 His
disciples asked him, "Rabbi, who sinned, this man or his
parents, that he was born blind?"
3 "Neither this man nor his parents sinned," said
Jesus, "but this happened so that the works of God might be
displayed in him. 4 As long as it is day, we must do the works
of him who sent me. Night is coming, when no one can
work. 5 While I am in the world, I am the light of the world."
6 After saying this, he spit on the ground, made some
mud with the saliva, and put it on the man's eyes. 7 "Go," he
told him, "wash in the Pool of Siloam" (this word means
"Sent"). So the man went and washed, and came home
seeing.
8 His neighbors and those who had formerly seen him
begging asked, "Isn't this the same man who used to sit and
beg?" 9 Some claimed that he was.
Others said, "No, he only looks like him."
But he himself insisted, "I am the man."
10 "How then were your eyes opened?" they asked.
11 He replied, "The man they call Jesus made some mud
and put it on my eyes. He told me to go to Siloam and wash.
So I went and washed, and then I could see."
12 "Where is this man?" they asked him.

"I don't know," he said.

Now compare this to the Buddhist version[3] that predates the Christian era and we find that Christ once again borrowed from the Buddhist teaching:

> *There was a man born blind, and he said: "I do not believe in the world of light and appearance. There are no colors, bright or somber. There is no sun, no moon, no stars. No one has witnessed these things."*
>
> *His friends remonstrated with him, but he clung to his opinion: "What you say that you see," he objected, "are illusions. If colors existed, I should be able to touch them. They have no substance and are not real. Everything real has weight, but I feel no weight where you see colors."*
>
> *A physician was called to see the blind man. He mixed four healing poultices, and when he applied them to the eyes of the blind man the film on them melted, and his eyes could see. The Tathagatha is the physician, the cataract is the illusion... and the four poultices are the four noble truths.*

Once again, the parables seem almost identical between the Indian originals and the Christian variations. But the differences are telling: the earlier Buddhist version makes clear at the end that the parable is a metaphorical story not meant to be taken literally. There is no suggestion that the Buddha, or any other person *actually* cured anyone of blindness. Rather, the blindness is clearly a *spiritual blindness* that is 'cured' by 'application' of four poultices that are made clear to be the core four truths of Buddha's teachings.

When the parable reappears attributed to Christ the clarification that it is meant to be taken metaphorically has disappeared. Was it ever there? We will never know, since the earliest writings we have relate the parables as they are without any suggestion they are not to be taken literally. While this may not be a popular observation in some Christian circles, the high likelihood is that Christ was repurposing the Buddhist parable for his teaching purposes. That is, for Christ too the parable was clearly meant to be seen as metaphorical and to refer to spiritual blindness, not actual physical blindness.

For some, though, it will come as some relief that Jesus absolutely would have realized these stories were intended to be used as teaching metaphors and those listening to Jesus at the time would have realized he didn't mean for them to be taken literally. It has been a challenge for some that while it is possible to aspire to be Christ-like, to align ones will with God will and become a "Son of God" (or Daughter) as Christ taught, one of the things that seems impossible to achieve is Jesus' ability to cure the blind, raise the dead back to life and so on.

Realizing that Christ was teaching in a hybrid Greek-Jewish Wisdom Tradition that favored metaphor, and drawing on the Buddhist tradition that also expressly relied on metaphor, we can now appreciate Christ's teachings in a new light: the light of generations of Jewish tradition of telling stories meant to be understood as metaphor and not taken literally.

The alternative seems unlikely: that Christ came to know the Buddhist parables (here, the healing of the blind man), which it was well known were metaphorical teaching tools, and he just happened to *actually* do what the metaphor spoke of. It is far more likely that Christ learned the method of teaching in metaphor, and that his followers were not confused by this. The confusion thus seems to have come when later scribes wrote down what Christ taught and what he said.

What is the metaphor, then, in Christ's version(s) of this Buddhist parable? Note that in both versions what comes through is that the healing was a two-step process. In the first version, Jesus spits on the man's eyes and then places his hands on them. The man reports he can now see, but not perfectly. Christ places his hands on his eyes again and the man reports he can now see perfectly.

In the second version, in the Gospel of John, again we have two stages: the first stage is Jesus spitting on the earth to create some mud he places on the man's eyes. The second step is that the man is asked to wash his eyes off in the Pool of Siloam. When he does so, he can now see perfectly. What was Christ teaching here? At this distance from the original words, undoubtedly conveyed inaccurately to us, we can only speculate.

We do know that the Buddhist original parable that Jesus was drawing upon had four steps to cure the 'blindness.' Thankfully, the Buddhist version clarifies the four poultices are not really healing pastes applied to heal physical blindness, but the Four Nobel Truths the Buddha taught would lead to liberation—Enlightenment.

So, what did Christ teach that comes in twos? One key focus of his teaching was that in order to enter the Kingdom of Heaven (realize your true self, your Christ nature, through *metanoia*), you need to first be born again of water and the spirit (John 3:5). The first version of this re-worked Buddhist parable seems to be changed to present Christ's key teaching rather than the Buddha's Four Truths: the first step in removing spiritual blindness is to apply water (he spits in the man's eyes in the metaphor). The second step is that Christ simply holds his hands over the man's eyes again: metaphorical of the Spirit.

The second version has parallels, too. The first step has the water (spit on earth, making mud that is applied). The second step is washing in the Pool of Siloam. This is where some further research is needed: current research reveals that at the time of Christ it was a tradition for Jews to make three pilgrimages to Jerusalem each year, and pilgrims were required to wash in this pool's purifying waters. The pool was on the outskirts of the city before the stone path leading to the Temple. So here, then, washing in the pool becomes symbolic of purification of the Spirit.

The challenge, though, with John is the distortion of message and corruption of the text in this Gospel. There is good reason why this Gospel is not considered one of the synoptic Gospels, since it differs so significantly from them. One of its questionable claims to fame is that John contains the most words supposedly spoken by Christ, while at the same time having the fewest words spoken by Christ that scholars believe he actually spoke.[4] We are thus always having to question how authentic John is, which in turn can make interpretation of, or reliance on, the text problematic.

John was written with a Jewish audience in mind, while the author focused on differentiating itself from Judaism. Indeed, as we know, Christianity post-John did separate and become a religion of a wider Gentile community. But this process the writer of John was in the midst of, may have caused him (or her) to use the Pool of Siloam symbolically in the second part of this parable, being a symbol well-known to the original Jewish audience.

There is thus the possibility that the version in John is a transformation of the original version in Mark, re-worked and re-worked again for the different audience the author was writing for. That said, it is tempting to speculate that neither version in Mark or John is true to the original teaching Christ gave since it is likely he would have made his metaphors clearer than either of these versions show. Either that, or the symbolism of what each version speaks about has been lost on us over the millennia.

The Woman at the Well

The parallels between the earlier Buddhist version of this parable and the one that appears in the Gospel of John are striking. It could be a coincidence, but that seems very unlikely. However, the only version that survives from the time of Christ is that from John which has the tell-tale signs of being re-written to convey the theology the writer is keen to convey, to the differing audience of this later time period.

Here is the version we find in John (4:4-42):

4 Now he had to go through Samaria. 5 So he came to a town in Samaria called Sychar, near the plot of ground Jacob had given to his son Joseph. 6 Jacob's well was there, and Jesus, tired as he was from the journey, sat down by the well. It was about noon.

7 When a Samaritan woman came to draw water, Jesus said to her, "Will you give me a drink?" 8 (His disciples had gone into the town to buy food.)

9 The Samaritan woman said to him, "You are a Jew and I am a Samaritan woman. How can you ask me for a drink?" (For Jews do not associate with Samaritans.)

10 Jesus answered her, "If you knew the gift of God and who it is that asks you for a drink, you would have asked him and he would have given you living water."

11 "Sir," the woman said, "you have nothing to draw with and the well is deep. Where can you get this living water? 12 Are you greater than our father Jacob, who gave us the well and drank from it himself, as did also his sons and his livestock?"

13 Jesus answered, "Everyone who drinks this water will be thirsty again, 14 but whoever drinks the water I give them will never thirst. Indeed, the water I give them will become in them a spring of water welling up to eternal life."

15 The woman said to him, "Sir, give me this water so that I won't get thirsty and have to keep coming here to draw water."

16 He told her, "Go, call your husband and come back."

17 "I have no husband," she replied.

Jesus said to her, "You are right when you say you have no husband. 18 The fact is, you have had five husbands, and the man you now have is not your husband. What you have just said is quite true."

19 "Sir," the woman said, "I can see that you are a prophet. 20 Our ancestors worshiped on this mountain, but you Jews claim that the place where we must worship is in Jerusalem."

21 "Woman," Jesus replied, "believe me, a time is coming when you will worship the Father neither on this mountain nor in Jerusalem. 22 You Samaritans worship what you do not know; we worship what we do know, for salvation is from the Jews. 23 Yet a time is coming and has now come when the true worshipers will worship the Father in the Spirit and in truth, for they are the kind of worshipers the Father seeks. 24 God is spirit, and his worshipers must worship in the Spirit and in truth."

25 The woman said, "I know that Messiah" (called Christ) "is coming. When he comes, he will explain everything to us."

26 Then Jesus declared, "I, the one speaking to you—I am he."

And here is the Buddhist version that predates the time of Christ:[5]

Ananda, the favorite disciple of the Buddha, having been sent by the Time Honored One[6] on a mission, passed by a well near a village, and seeing Pakati, a girl of the Matanga caste, he asked her for water to drink. Pakati said: "Brahman, I am too humble and mean to give you water to drink, do not ask any service of me lest your holiness be contaminated, for I am of low caste." And Ananda replied: "I ask not for caste but for water"; and the Matanga girl's heart leaped joyfully and she gave Ananda to drink.

Ananda thanked her and went away; but she followed him at a distance. Having heard that Ananda was a disciple of Gautama Sakyamuni[7], the girl approach the Blessed One[8] and cried: "Lord help me, and let me live in the place where Ananda your disciple dwells, so that I may see him and minister to him, for I love Ananda." The Blessed One understood the emotions of her heart and he said: "Pakati, your heart is full of love, but you don't understand your own sentiments. It is not Ananda that you love, but his kindness. Accept, then, the kindness you have seen him practice to you, and in the humility of your station practice it to others. Verily there is great merit in the generosity of a king when he is kind to a slave; but there is a greater merit in the slave when he ignores the wrongs which he suffers and cherishes kindness and good-will to all mankind. He will cease to hate his oppressors, and even when powerless to resist their usurpation will with compassion pity their arrogance and supercilious demeanor.

"Blessed are you, Pakati, for though you are a Matanga you will be a model for noblemen and noble women. You are of low caste, but Brahmans may learn a lesson from you. Swerve not from the path of justice and righteousness and you will outshine the royal glory of queens on the throne."

Again, it does not seem credible that the version in John is not based on the Buddhist original, however many re-writes and modifications later it might be. The stories are essentially identical. Moreover, for once the version attributed to Christ does not pretend to be a story to be taken literally, but rather a teaching about living water quenching a spiritual thirst, and about how Gentiles would follow God. Here we have a repetition of the water and spirit symbolism this time more clearly stated that God is spirit: the story stresses the importance of following the Spirit (here, God) and "the truth."

As to its ending where Jesus proclaims himself to be the Christ, to be the Messiah, this is at significant odds with the teaching of Christ in the synoptic Gospels. There, Jesus is careful never to say that he is the Messiah (he dodges the topic) and never refers to himself as the Son of God, let alone as the only Son of God as John has him saying.

I do not wish to belabor this point, but it is also noteworthy that the woman at the well is not a Jew. Since she is not a Jew, it is hardly likely that she would talk about a coming Messiah, which is a quintessentially Jewish idea not shared by the Samaritans. That said, such a detailed analysis of the Buddhist and Christian versions of the story is beside the point: the metaphorical meaning is the purpose of these parables, and the meaning is similar in each. It is not difficult to see how, exposed to the Buddhist original, Christ saw a way to repurpose the Buddhist story in a first century Palestinian context as a tool to assist in his teaching.

That said, since this parable only appears in the Gospel of John, which dates from a time substantially after Jesus' death, it is not necessarily a reliable source of what Christ actually taught. Clearly, the writer of John had a specific audience and was familiar with Greek ideas like the '*Logos*' which the writer draws directly from Philo and Platonism. We also know that the Greeks were very familiar with Buddhism several hundred years before the time of Christ, and thus this story may have been repurposed by the writer of John from his Greek sources. It may not have been something that Christ taught. That acknowledged, it would fit with a general trend found in the synoptic Gospels that Christ did borrow heavily from Buddhist sources.

The Marriage Feast (Canna/Loaves and Fishes)

The next connection is more speculative but does show that general themes in Buddhist parables were reflected in the parables Christ taught, even when the exact story is not replicated. Here is the Buddhist Parable of the Marriage Feast that predates the Christian era:[9]

> *There was a man in Jambunada who was to be married the next day, and he thought, "Would that the Buddha, the Blessed One, might be present at the wedding." And the Blessed One passed by his house and met him, and when he read the silent wish in the heart of the bridegroom, he consented to enter. When the Holy One appeared with the retinue of his many bhikkhus, the host, whose means were*

limited, received them as best he could, saying: "Eat, my Lord, and all your congregation, according to your desire."

While the holy men ate, the meats and drinks remained undiminished, and the host thought to himself: "How wondrous is this! I should have had plenty for all my relatives and friends. Would that I had invited them all."

When this thought was in the host's mind, all his relatives and friends entered the house; and although the hall in the house was small there was room in it for all of them. They sat down at the table and ate, and there was more than enough for all of them. The Blessed One was pleased to see so many guests full of good cheer and he quickened them and gladdened them with words of truth, proclaiming the bliss of righteousness:

"The greatest happiness which a mortal man can imagine is the bond of marriage that ties together two loving hearts. But there is a greater happiness still: it is the embrace of truth. Death will separate husband and wife, but death will never affect him who has espoused the truth. Therefore, be married to the truth and live with the truth in holy wedlock. The husband who loves his wife and desires for a union that shall be everlasting must be faithful to her so as to be like truth itself, and she will rely on him and revere him and minister to him. And the wife who loves her husband and desires a union that shall be everlasting must be faithful to him so as to be like truth itself; and he will place his trust in her, he will provide for her. Verily, I say to you, their children will become like their parents and will bear witness to their happiness. Let no man be single, let everyone be wedded in holy love to the truth. And when Mara, the destroyer, comes to separate the visible forms of your being,

you will continue to live in the truth, and will partake of the life everlasting, for the truth is immortal."

There was no one among the guests but was strengthened in his, spiritual life, and recognized the sweetness of a life of righteousness; and they took refuge in the Buddha, the Dharma, and the Sangha.

Immediately we are reminded of two parables attributed to Christ—the Wedding in Cana (John 2:1-12) and the Loaves and Fishes (Mark 6:30-44, Matt 14:13-21, John 6:1-14):

Jesus Changes Water into Wine

On the third day a wedding took place at Cana in Galilee. Jesus' mother was there, [2] and Jesus and his disciples had also been invited to the wedding. [3] When the wine was gone, Jesus' mother said to him, "They have no more wine."

[4] "Woman, why do you involve me?" Jesus replied. "My hour has not yet come."

[5] His mother said to the servants, "Do whatever he tells you."

[6] Nearby stood six stone water jars, the kind used by the Jews for ceremonial washing, each holding from twenty to thirty gallons.

[7] Jesus said to the servants, "Fill the jars with water"; so they filled them to the brim.

[8] Then he told them, "Now draw some out and take it to the master of the banquet."

They did so, [9] and the master of the banquet tasted the water that had been turned into wine. He did not realize where it had come from, though the servants who had drawn the water knew. Then he called the bridegroom aside [10] and said, "Everyone brings out the choice wine first and then the cheaper wine after the guests have had too much to drink; but you have saved the best till now."

[11] *What Jesus did here in Cana of Galilee was the first of the signs through which he revealed his glory; and his disciples believed in him.*

[12] *After this he went down to Capernaum with his mother and brothers and his disciples. There they stayed for a few days.*

Jesus Feeds the Five Thousand (Mark's version)

[30] *The apostles gathered around Jesus and reported to him all they had done and taught.* [31] *Then, because so many people were coming and going that they did not even have a chance to eat, he said to them, "Come with me by yourselves to a quiet place and get some rest."*

[32] *So they went away by themselves in a boat to a solitary place.* [33] *But many who saw them leaving recognized them and ran on foot from all the towns and got there ahead of them.* [34] *When Jesus landed and saw a large crowd, he had compassion on them, because they were like sheep without a shepherd. So he began teaching them many things.*

[35] *By this time it was late in the day, so his disciples came to him. "This is a remote place," they said, "and it's already very late.* [36] *Send the people away so that they can go to the surrounding countryside and villages and buy themselves something to eat."*

[37] *But he answered, "You give them something to eat."*

They said to him, "That would take more than half a year's wages! Are we to go and spend that much on bread and give it to them to eat?"

38 *"How many loaves do you have?" he asked. "Go and*
see."
When they found out, they said, "Five—and two fish."
39 *Then Jesus directed them to have all the people sit*
down in groups on the green grass. 40 *So they sat down in*
groups of hundreds and fifties. 41 *Taking the five loaves and*
the two fish and looking up to Heaven, he gave thanks and
broke the loaves. Then he gave them to his disciples to
distribute to the people. He also divided the two fish among
them all. 42 *They all ate and were satisfied,* 43 *and the*
disciples picked up twelve basketfuls of broken pieces of
bread and fish. 44 *The number of the men who had eaten*
was five thousand.

We note again that the marriage parable only appears in John, which gives pause as to how much we can rely on this being part of what Christ actually said or taught. But reviewing the Buddhist original that it is likely Christ and the writers of all four Gospels had access to, it seems likely the two parables in the New Testament may have been drawn at least in part from the Buddhist sources.

The key difference, though, is that once again the Buddhist original parable makes clear it is not attributing magical powers to the Buddha, and that the story is obviously meant to be metaphorical. As a result, the Buddha is not usually thought of either as someone who regularly did magical acts that you and I cannot do. On the contrary, its core to Buddhism that we are all Buddha: our *Buddha-nature* is identical to Buddha's *Buddha-nature*; he was not somehow "above us" or "better than us."

In the parables attributed to Christ, though, they have come down to us as if they were supernatural acts that Christ actually did. We know, as with the other previous parables, that Christ was drawing on earlier parables that were clearly intended as metaphorical instruction. In using these stories to illustrate his teachings, Christ undoubtedly intended the listener (it was originally an oral tradition) to know that the story was metaphorical.

However, it is difficult to discern at this distance whether the Gospel writers simply assumed—as was common at the time—that such fantastical tales were always understood to be metaphorical, or whether they intentionally wrote as if Christ had actually done the deeds, thus using wording that deliberately distracted readers from a metaphorical interpretation.

Elsewhere we have discussed the pedestalization of Christ: the clear trend after his death to elevate Christ to a super-human, deific status by editing and adding to the synoptic Gospels, and in the creation of John which takes this trend to its highest level.

Walking on Water

The story of Jesus walking on water appears in Mark (6:45-56), Matthew (14:22-36) and in John (6:16-24). Interestingly, the versions in Mark and John are fairly similar. In these two versions the disciples are on a boat on a lake and Jesus walks on the water toward them while the wind is blowing. In both, Christ's message is that the disciples should not be afraid.

What is significant is that Matthew's version is longer and is the strongest parallel to the Buddhist version of the parable that appreciably predates the time of Christ. In both Matthew's version and the original Buddhist version, it is a disciple or student who walks on the water and is praised for their strong faith.

Here is the version from Matthew (Mt 14:22):

[22] Immediately Jesus made the disciples get into the boat and go on ahead of him to the other side, while he dismissed the crowd. [23] After he had dismissed them, he went up on a mountainside by himself to pray. Later that night, he was there alone, [24] and the boat was already a considerable distance from land, buffeted by the waves because the wind was against it.

[25] Shortly before dawn Jesus went out to them, walking on the lake. [26] When the disciples saw him walking on the lake, they were terrified. "It's a ghost," they said, and cried out in fear.

[27] But Jesus immediately said to them: "Take courage! It is I. Don't be afraid."

[28] "Lord, if it's you," Peter replied, "tell me to come to you on the water."

[29] "Come," he said.

Then Peter got down out of the boat, walked on the water and came toward Jesus. [30] But when he saw the wind, he was afraid and, beginning to sink, cried out, "Lord, save me!"

[31] Immediately Jesus reached out his hand and caught him. "You of little faith," he said, "why did you doubt?"

And here is the earlier Buddhist parable:[10]

South of Savatthi is a great river, on the banks of which lay a hamlet of five hundred houses. Thinking of the salvation of the people, the World-honored One[11] resolved to go to the village and preach the doctrine. Having come to the riverside he sat down beneath a tree, and the villagers seeing the glory of his appearance approached him with reverence; but when he began to preach, they believed him not.

When the world-honored Buddha had left, Sariputta felt a desire to see the Lord[12] *and to hear him preach. Coming to the river where the water was deep and the current strong, he said to himself: "This stream shall not prevent me. I shall go and see the Blessed One,*[13] *and he stepped on the water which was as firm under his feet as a slab of granite. When he arrived at a place in the middle of the stream where the waves were high, Sariputta's heart gave way, and he began to sink. But rousing his faith and renewing his mental effort, he proceeded as before and reached the other bank.*

The people of the village were astonished to see Sariputta, and they asked how he could cross the stream where there was neither a bridge nor a ferry. Sariputta replied: "I lived in ignorance till I heard the voice of the Buddha. As I was anxious to hear the doctrine of salvation, I crossed the river and I walked over its troubled waters because I had faith. Faith. nothing else, enabled me to do so, and now I am here in the bliss of the Master's presence."

The World-honored One added: "Sariputta, you have spoken well. Faith like yours alone can save the world from the yawning gulf of migration and enable men to walk dry-foot to the other shore." And the Blessed One urged to the villagers the necessity of ever advancing in the conquest of sorrow and of casting off all shackles so as to cross the river of worldliness and attain deliverance from death. Hearing the words of the Tathagatha, the villagers were filled with joy and believing in the doctrines of the Blessed One embraced the five rules and took refuge in his name.

Again, the similarity between the much earlier Buddhist parables and those in the New Testament is striking—particularly the parallel to the version found in Matthew. Indeed, so close is the similarity that it is hard not to see the version in Matthew as a re-write of the Buddhist tale.

Once again, though, the key difference is that Buddhists are generally fully aware that these stories are metaphorical. We are not meant to think that if we follow the Buddha's teaching we will suddenly be able to *actually* walk on water. While people over the millennia have spoken of Jesus walking on water—indeed it has become almost synonymous with his being divine—it is rare that people also note that according to the same story Peter also walked on water. When he felt doubt, he faltered and needed help to stay up on the surface, but he too walked on water. This exactly parallels what the Buddha allegedly said about faith and walking on water in the original Indian story.

Once again, these stories—both the Buddhist originals and those in the New Testament—are intended to be metaphorical: we are not meant to be having a competitive water-walking competition!

That said, if you are minded to believe Christ actually walked on water, then you must surely also accept that Peter also did so. He may have faltered, but it is clear that the story says Peter walked on water, too. Thus, walking on water, according to this story, is something not only the Messiah did, but something one of his ordinary, human disciples did. Whereupon you may ask yourself, can you walk on water? Or is it clear that this was always a metaphorical event, a teaching about faith and trust, and more? I believe it is.

While this has only been a cursory review of the parallels between the earlier Buddhist parables and those in the

Gospels, the parallels are striking. So much so, that it seems certain that Christ was familiar with the Buddhist stories. Indeed, the Buddha and Christ remain the best-known historical religious teachers to use such parables.

---

[1] Whalen Lai, *The Buddhist Prodigal Son: A Story of Misperceptions*. The Journal of the International Association of Buddhist Studies, Vol 4, No 2, 1981, 91-98.

[2]

[3] The Buddhist version is found in several sources: Kumaralata's *Kalpanamanditika*, Asvaghosa's *Sutralamkara*, and the *Jakata* stories that date from as early as 300 B.C.E. It is also referenced as being in the *Dhammapada* and it is referenced by Burouf in his *Introduction á l'histore du Bouddhisme Indien*, Paris 1844 as being a text that predates the time of Christ.

[4] Funk, *The Five Gospels*

[5] In various very early Buddhist writings, including the *Śārdūlakarṇāvadāna*

[6] An honorific title for the Buddha

[7] The Buddha's given birth name

[8] Another honorific title for the Buddha

[9] From the *Jakata*, stories that date from as early as 300 B.C.E.; Fu-*Pen-Hing-tsi-King*, tr. by S. Beal; referenced in Charles Aiken, *The Dhamma of Gotama the Buddha and the Gospel of Jesus the Christ*, Marlier & Co., 1900 as predating the time of Christ.

[10] From the *Jataka*, 190 (vol. ii, 77), referenced in *Transactions of the Royal Society of Literature of The United Kingdom*, Second Series, Vol. XVBIII, Asher, 1897: Chapter *Coincidences* by The Right Hon. Professor Max Muller.

[11] The Buddha

[12] An honorific for The Buddha

[13] Another honorific for The Buddha

9

Buddha-Nature, Christ-Nature

Your Buddha-nature *is* your Christ-nature, and vice versa. How this can be true perhaps needs a little explanation. So, what do these terms really mean? In both Buddhist writings, notably Zen, another way of saying this is your 'true self.' In both Zen and non-dual ('mystical') Christian writings, realizing your true self—who you truly are—is synonymous with awakening (Zen) and becoming one with God (Christian).

You will recall that early in this book I chose to speak of Christ and Buddha rather than Jesus and Siddhartha Gautama (the Buddha's birth name). The distinction is important: I cannot become the historical person of Siddhartha nor can I become the person of Jesus. But Buddhists teach that we are all Buddhas, and Christ's teaching, when carefully reviewed, tells us we are all Christs. That is, we are all what Christ called a *Son of God*.

On the face of it, these two traditions seem diametrically opposed: one is theistic the other atheistic. Christians believe in a God, Buddhists do not.[1] How could two traditions be more different? Let alone, how can we say they are essentially—in a deep sense—the same? Or, rather, how can we say that what Buddha and Christ was teaching were teaching was essentially the same?

Christ's core teaching, what became known as "The Way" to his followers, was deceptively simple and yet is rarely taught from the pulpit in churches. His key message can be summarized thus: practice self-emptying (*kenosis*) by meditating alone in silence, practice *metanoia* (going beyond thinking), thereby go beyond the ego to align your will with God's will, and you will enter the Kingdom of Heaven which is within you and become a Son (or Daughter) of God. By doing this, by entering Heaven within, Christ taught you will achieve eternal life.

In Buddhism, or more specifically in Zen, we learn that through practice (which includes meditation (Zazen) or doing *koan* introspection with a teacher), we realize the goalless-goal of waking up and finding our true selves. And that in this awakening we come realize our true self, our Buddha-nature, is not subject to life and death: who we truly are is eternal. By awakening we enter a realm here, now, where we overcome the cycle of suffering and death (*dukkha*), and this is known as *nirvana* or enlightenment.

These summaries were simplifications, of course, but side by side like this it is easier to see that the two traditions—or "Ways"—have far more in common that most people are led to believe.

Historically, there have been a number of major hurdles to realizing just how similar the teachings are: they include the pedestalization of Christ, the failure of the established church to teach his actual teachings (rather than those of Saul of Tarsus or the early church theologians), and misconceptions surrounding what Buddhism is, what Zen is, and what awakening is. Another roadblock has been the misleading simplification that one Way is theistic, while the other is atheistic as if this makes them irreconcilably different.

Let's refresh our recollections of what is meant by pedestalization and the distinction between what we believe Christ actually taught compared to the later corruptions of his teachings. In their excellent writings such authors as Marcus

Borg and John Dominic Crossan, draw a distinction between the pre-Easter Jesus and the post-Easter Jesus. The pre-Easter Jesus is the human being born (we believe) around 4 B.C.E., who died around 30 C.E. and who is written about in the core parts of the synoptic Gospels before later writers made amendments and additions.

The pre-Easter Jesus, then, while an outstanding teacher is clearly a low-born Jew, just as completely human as you and me, decidedly mortal and finite. He is known as "Jesus of Nazareth," and is a monotheistic Jew who laid no claim to being better than others or being divine. When asked "Are you the Messiah?" He is the Jesus who consistently dodges the question and responds with retorts like "Who do you say I am?" He is referred to at most as a "Son of Man" which is the Jewish term for a regular human being, flesh and blood like all of us.

Yes, "Son of Man" was also a term used in the Old Testament for an anticipated 'Messiah,' but this also goes to the point that the Messiah was always presumed to be a man, a leader, a kind of King to lead the Jewish people. A "Son of Man" to a Jew of the first century (or even earlier) was thus a human (in *contrast* to a deity or Godhead), and it emphasized the frailty and weakness of being human (Job 25:6, Numbers 23:19, Psalms 8:4, Psalms 144:3, Psalms 146:3, Isaiah 51:12, and so on).

Another factor in the Jewish legend of the Messiah is that this human, this savior come to rebuild the Temple—
and was to be from the paternal Davidic line through King David and King Solomon. This is important because it goes to the pedestalization of Jesus and the deliberate additions and amendments to the Gospels to create the post-Easter Jesus.

The post-Easter Jesus is the Jesus now known as Christ and refers to the era from about 30 C.E. onwards. The post-Easter

Jesus is suddenly now not a mere human but a spiritual non-material reality, infinite and eternal. He is now divine. This revised Jesus has become King of Kings, Lord of Lords, the only Son of God, and in real terms "God with a human face."

This reinvention of the human, brilliant teacher, Jesus of Nazareth was woven out of whole cloth soon after he died and perpetuated notably by the likes of Saul of Tarsus (also known as Paul). This creation of a post-Easter Jesus was also brought to us by writers who edited and added to the original synoptic Gospel texts, and led to the writing of new texts such as the Gospel of John which is in large part of post-Easter invention that has little to do with the actual life of Jesus or what he actually did and said.

This is not wild conjecture: the original version of the Gospel of Mark (the oldest of the Gospels) ended with Jesus being crucified. This early version had no mention of Joseph, no birth story, and no clear statement of resurrection or of any post crucifixion visions or sightings. This original version of Mark, much shorter than the other Gospels, was seen by early Christians as deficient. It failed, in their minds, to place Jesus properly in his role as a third of the Trinity, a divine being who died and came back to life.

This bears repeating: this text, the original shorter version of Mark, is the oldest Christian writing we have other than some letters by Paul. So deficient was Mark to the early Christians trying to pedestalize Jesus that they switched the order of the Gospels so that Matthew would come first, rather than have them in chronological order. In the form they had received Matthew, it was far more satisfying with its birth story, resurrection and post crucifixion stories.

Just to be clear, the oldest versions we have of the Gospel of Mark end at Mark 16:8:

16 When the Sabbath was over, Mary Magdalene, Mary
the mother of James, and Salome bought spices so that they
might go to anoint Jesus' body. 2 *Very early on the first day*
of the week, just after sunrise, they were on their way to the
tomb 3 *and they asked each other, "Who will roll the stone*
away from the entrance of the tomb?"
4 *But when they looked up, they saw that the stone,*
which was very large, had been rolled away. 5 *As they entered*
the tomb, they saw a young man dressed in a white
robe sitting on the right side, and they were alarmed.
6 *"Don't be alarmed," he said. "You are looking for Jesus*
the Nazarene, who was crucified. He has risen! He is not
here. See the place where they laid him. 7 *But go, tell his*
disciples and Peter, 'He is going ahead of you into Galilee.
There you will see him, just as he told you.'"
8 *Trembling and bewildered, the women went out and*
fled from the tomb. They said nothing to anyone, because
they were afraid.

That's it: no mention of anyone seeing Jesus after the crucifixion, and note it is a young man—not an angel—who Mary Magdalene meets and who tells her Jesus will see his disciples again in Galilee. But no mention that they ever did so.

The last part of Mark (16:9-19) is thus a complete fiction added much later by those who found the original ending disappointing. This again bears repeating: the most respected Biblical scholars all agree this ending with the resurrection and post-crucifixion appearances, that is so familiar to many, is pure invention not found in any of the early manuscripts:

9 When Jesus rose early on the first day of the week, he
appeared first to Mary Magdalene, out of whom he had
driven seven demons. 10 She went and told those who had
been with him and who were mourning and weeping. 11 When
they heard that Jesus was alive and that she had seen him,
they did not believe it.

12 Afterward Jesus appeared in a different form to two of
them while they were walking in the country. 13 These
returned and reported it to the rest; but they did not believe
them either.

14 Later Jesus appeared to the Eleven as they were eating;
he rebuked them for their lack of faith and their stubborn
refusal to believe those who had seen him after he had risen.

15 He said to them, "Go into all the world and preach the
Gospel to all creation. 16 Whoever believes and is baptized
will be saved, but whoever does not believe will be
condemned. 17 And these signs will accompany those who
believe: In my name they will drive out demons; they will
speak in new tongues; 18 they will pick up snakes with their
hands; and when they drink deadly poison, it will not hurt
them at all; they will place their hands on sick people, and
they will get well."

19 After the Lord Jesus had spoken to them, he was taken
up into Heaven and he sat at the right hand of God. 20 Then
the disciples went out and preached everywhere, and the
Lord worked with them and confirmed his word by the
signs that accompanied it.

The post-Easter accounts and birth stories in Matthew and Luke do not help, since having been written many years later they are even more likely to be later inventions that have no roots in Jesus' actual life, acts or teachings. Dating the various texts in the New Testament is notoriously difficult, and hotly disputed. Our best scholarship as at the time of writing is that the earliest texts are letters written by Paul and that some of those date from about 50-55 C.E.

As far as the Gospels are concerned, Mark is the earliest and the oldest version we have identified so far seems to date from somewhere between 66-70 C.E. The Gospels of Matthew and Luke and Acts then follow, all estimated to have been written around 85-90 C.E. Finally, John was written much later (90-110 C.E.) with Revelation also being somewhere about 95 C.E.

What is often overlooked is the implication of some of Paul's letters as the earliest texts we have. As some say, Paul essentially invented Christianity as many know it today as a set of teachings and theology, much of which has little to nothing to do with what Jesus himself taught. Paul was an early leader of the post-Easter Jesus movement—a movement that sought to pedestalize Jesus and invent a religion based on this elevated, deified version of the actual teacher and his actual teachings.

What is often missed, then, is that by as early as 50 C.E. within around 20 years of Jesus' death there was a full-fledged drive toward creating a version of the church that was at odds with the actual church established by Jesus, run after his death by his Brother James in Jerusalem. These writings, and writers like Paul, undoubtably influenced the editing, amendments and additions to the early Gospel texts. To understand the arc of what transpired, how we went from a pre-Easter Jesus to a post-Easter one, we need to look at the historical context.

Since ancient times, the Jews of the first century had been expecting a Messiah to come as a savior. This person would bring together all the tribes of Israel and unify the Jewish people in a new world order founded on universal peace. This Messianic Age would see the Temple rebuilt and be led by "the anointed one" (what *Messiah* literally means) who would be of the direct Davidic line.

It is also important to note the arc that had occurred in the Jewish people and their belief in God, or Gods. It is a common mistake to equate Judaism with monotheism, as if the Jewish people had always believed in one God, the God of all peoples on earth. This, though, is an entirely Christian concept that came about with Jesus. Considering the prior millennia of the Jewish peoples, we see a transition from an era where they had kings (David and Solomon being well known), to a Priestly era where there were no more kings, only priestly leaders. This culminated in Christ's time in an era when there was no longer a priestly class, only rabbis and rabbinic leaders.

Paralleling this arc of the leadership of the people was a change in the view of deities. It is abundantly clear from the Old Testament (in particular the Pentateuch, or Torah) that the main God who the Jews worshiped was Yahweh, but he was not the only God they worshiped. He is mentioned as being the main God, leading the Counsel of Gods, but certainly not the only God. There was also the popular God Salem, the Canaanite God of dusk, and another was Baal the fertility God often prayed to by farmers hoping for better crops.

It has been argued that at least two of King David's wives worshipped Salem rather than Yahweh. Bethsheba, his 7th and last wife, gave birth to Solomon, who was of course to become King Solomon and was named after the God Salem. Another of King David's wives, Maacah bat Talmai, gave birth to Absalom, also named after the God Salem. There are also numerous mentions in the Old Testament of various "household Gods" that Jewish people worshipped.[2]

By the time of Christ in the first century of the common era, there was still either worship of, or acknowledgement of the existence of, various other Gods besides Yahweh by most Jews. What had changed was that Yahweh had been commonly accepted as *the* God of the Jews. And it is in *this* sense that we say the Jewish people were monotheistic. But it would be a mistake to suggest they believed in only one God, a God who was God of all peoples of the world. Indeed, even today I have met conservative Jews who are puzzled when someone talks of a single common God of the Jews, Christians and Muslims. Many of course refer to these three religions as the People of the Book, or the "Abrahamic Traditions," acknowledging their commonalities.

The arc of the concept of this main God, the one God of the Jews, moved from an Old Testament view of an avenging angry God to a distant God whose very name is so sacred it should not be spoken or written, hence the tetragrammaton (Greek for "four letter word") YHWH, where it is frowned upon to add vowels to the consonants. Yet that is often done, expanding YHWH to Yahweh in English.[3] The other popular anglicization of course is Jehovah, often translated simply as "the LORD". Together with others such as the Hebrew *Adonai* (meaning "My Lord") and translated as *Kyrios* ("Lord") in the Greek texts.

Yet other names for God are El, Eloah, Elohim, Elohai, El Shaddai, Tzevaot, and Jah. And of course, the name for God in Aramaic, the language Jesus spoke, *Elaha* which is also written in Syriac (closely related to Aramaic) as *Alaha*. To this day, Arabic Christians refer to God as Alaha or Allah: it is not the name for God that only Muslims use, which is a common misconception.

All of which is to say that by the time of Christ Jews held

the name of God to be so sacred that the true name could never be uttered, only various variations such as common words meaning "Lord" or adding vowels to YHWH to produce Yahweh. Indeed, Christ's actual name in his language, Aramaic, was *Yeshua*. It was a common name for a man in first century Palestine, and an abbreviation of the also common *Yehoshua* which is everywhere else in the Bible translated as Joshua.

The derivation of Christ's given name is a combination of "yeho" and "shua" which roughly translated means "Yahweh saves." But while everywhere else in the Bible, this name is then translated consistently as "Joshua," only in the case of Christ did the scribes decide to translate the name uniquely as "Jesus." This is another indication of the early pedestalization of Christ, giving him an uncommon variation of an exceptionally common Jewish boy's name, to make Christ "different," or "other" than we mere mortals.

By the time of Christ, then, while God (Yahweh) was sometimes known as "Father" it was a formal name for a distant God. Not an intimate God. The Jews were waiting for a Messiah to liberate them from Roman oppression, to be their savior and usher in a messianic era of global peace. Instead, Christ started teaching his unique brand of Judaism: and make no mistake, it was unique despite being deeply rooted in Jewish tradition.

However, what Christ taught was a substantial departure from Jewish traditional teaching, God as a loving intimate father who in his native Aramaic he referred to as "abba." There has been much confusion over the years as to what "abba" means. Simply, abba was the name for father in Aramaic—there were not several names for various shades of familiarity like the English "father," "papa," "daddy," etc. As far as we can tell, for the familiar as well as for the formal, "abba" was used with presumably the tone of voice conveying the level of familiarity or respect, warmth or formality. To this day Middle Eastern speakers of languages related to Aramaic (e.g. Syriac) use the word "abba" whether they are referring to a formal father (e.g. a title for a priest or abbot), or where in English we might use "papa," "pops" or "daddy" for our own father.

This, though, misses the context of Christ's use of the word "abba." Christ often uses the term in a very familiar way to refer to an intimate God, a God who *is* Love (not merely is lov*ing*), and it would be reasonable to assume his use was both intimate and respectful. Sadly, what this means is that we don't have a good word in English to translate the Aramaic "abba," but it is perhaps best to think of it as a mix of our words "father" and perhaps a less formal but still respectful "papa" (which relates to the word pope, of course, from the Greek *páppas*, originally an affectionate term for father).

In fact, the word *abba* is not used very often in the New Testament and is often paired with the Greek word for father "pater" as in "abba, pater" which in turn has been translated as "abba, father." There is much speculation as to how the scribes came to write this, since it is unlikely this is actually what Christ himself said. One idea is that after his passing it became important to clarify to those being introduced to Christianity that it is for everyone—Jews and Gentiles alike, hence the use of both the Aramaic and Greek words.

The other emphasis of Christ's teaching was on our all being one, all being equal. Thus, he didn't just speak of God as "abba" but pushed the idea that we are all brothers and sisters, not fathers and mothers, sons and daughters, cousins etc. Nowhere is this idea clearer—and, for some theologians, more troubling—than in the passage where someone informs Christ that his mother and brothers are stuck at the outskirts of a large gathering. In Mk 3:31-35:

> [31] *Then Jesus' mother and brothers arrived. Standing outside, they sent someone in to call him.* [32] *A crowd was sitting around him, and they told him, "Your mother and brothers are outside looking for you."*
>
> [33] *"Who are my mother and my brothers?" he asked.*
>
> [34] *Then he looked at those seated in a circle around him and said, "Here are my mother and my brothers!* [35] *Whoever does God's will is my brother and sister and mother."*

And again, in Mt 23:9: [9] *And do not call anyone on earth 'father,' for you have one Father, and he is in Heaven.*

Here is Christ at his more radical. Seen through a modern lens we might wonder if this was a sect of some kind where the sect leader is asking followers to abandon their families. But in context it is clear Christ is using these terms to teach and anyone hearing him would know much of what he is saying is metaphorical.

But here was his radical revisioning of the traditional Jewish teachings: God as loving abba and our only abba. Here Christ teaches that we are all brothers and sisters, all equal in the Kingdom, all sons (and daughters) of God so long as we align our will with God's will.

Indeed, here is some of the clearest teaching we have that the pre-Easter Jesus—the Jesus we come to know in the synoptic Gospels before they were modified to pedestalize him—would never have referred to himself as "the only son of God." This teaching could not be clearer: he refers to everyone, including his Mother and his brothers, as his brothers and sisters. And makes clear that in this theology, this teaching, there is only one abba (God) and if we can just align our wills with God's will then we all become Son of God (or by inference, Daughter of God).

Interestingly, this is one time we can find a nugget of truth buried in the Gospel of John that otherwise completely pedestalizes Jesus. Depending on the translation of Jn 1:12 we either get:

> 12 *But as many as received him, to them gave the power to become the Sons of God, even to them that believe on his name*

Or, in the NIV version:

> 12 *Yet to all who did receive him, to those who believed in his name, he gave the right to become children of God*

As is often the case with Biblical writings, sexism and chauvinism come in. Thus, the Greek original speaking of becoming "children of God" is rendered as "become Sons of God." But in this one instance it is perhaps helpful, even though the translators clearly had significant trouble writing the phrase "daughter of God" even though the text calls for both son and daughter in that the original was "children."

Christ draws a clear distinction in his teaching between all humanity being "children of God" (part of God's creation), and the potential to *become* a "Son of God" (or by clear inference, a "Daughter of God") if a follower would just adopt "The Way."[4] And he went on to make clear that The Way calls for followers to not be attached to material things, but rather to practice *metanoia* and *kenosis* in order to align their individual (ego-based, dualistic) will with God's (universal, non-dualistic) will.

To highlight how radical this teaching was, note how on its face it seems to go directly against the fifth commandment, “Honor your father and your mother.” Now, of course Christ wasn’t asking his followers to abandon any of the Ten Commandments. He made clear he did not come to replace any existing law, but rather to build upon it. Thus, it would have been understood by his followers at the time that he was speaking of a higher truth. And it is the same truth that he spoke of when he said that in order to enter the Kingdom of God (“Heaven within”) you must be born again of the water and spirit. He went on to clarify, “Flesh is born of flesh, but spirit is born of spirit” (Jn 3:5).

Here, then, is the pre-Easter Jesus: a revolutionary, deeply skillful spiritual teacher with a powerful message. Anyone, he teaches, can enter into union with God, become a Son of God (or Daughter of God), if they would just align their will with God’s will. He advocates not being attached to material possessions. He speaks of going beyond thought (*metanoia*), having a spiritual awakening in order to enter this state of being he calls ‘Heaven within’ or ‘the Kingdom of God on earth.’ And speaks of achieving all this with practices such as giving to others and taking time to empty the self (*kenosis*) with silent prayer and meditation.

He speaks of everyone being equal—men, women, poor, rich—and mixes with the outcasts of that society such as tax collectors and prostitutes. His mission is funded primarily by wealthy women, and he speaks of a spiritual transformation anyone can attain; he does not say that he and only he has attained it, and no one else can ever do so. Similarly, the idea of Christ as a miracle worker, which also places him “above” we mere human beings, also served to raise Jesus up to a superhuman level.[5]

Thus, we get the pedestalization of Christ. During his lifetime many of his followers—perhaps all of them—expected him to bring about a new earthly Kingdom, a messianic era. He was meant to be their savior, free them from Roman oppression; he wasn't supposed to die with no obvious 'Kingdom' having been created. But he did die, and his followers who survived him found differing ways of dealing with that fact. Some dealt with his death by putting him on a pedestal.

This pedestalization included elevating Christ to be more than a "mere human." They reasoned that he could not have 'just' been an incredible teacher; it must be that he was indeed the 'only Son of God,' even though he himself never claimed any such thing during his lifetime. On the contrary, he clearly taught that anyone can become a Son (of Daughter) of God if one would just go beyond dualistic thought and align one's will with God's will.

But if Christ is on a pedestal then emulating him is unattainable,[6] so different from us that we can only be amazed by how far above us he is. In other words, Jesus having taken the historic view of God as transcendent and distant, brought God down to the intimate level of Heaven as within you, then gets puts at a distance in the rewritten post-Easter version of himself. A version that bears no resemblance to the pre-Easter Jesus we learn about in the synoptic Gospels when they are stripped of their later additions and amendments.

It's not difficult to see that core of Christ's message is that God *is* Love (again, not just lov*ing*) and that this Love is the kind of love a father has for his only begotten son. As a male-centric society, it would have been natural to liken God's Love as being like that of a father, whereas today perhaps we would more readily liken this selfless love to being like that of any parent for their only child. Couple this teaching about God as Love with his othmmer core teaching of aligning his will with God's will to become the Son of God, and it isn't hard to see how the pedestalizing occurred that lead to the depiction in John and Paul of Jesus as the *only* begotten son of God.

This deification of Christ and the creation of a post-Easter Jesus had various implications. Now Jesus is no mere man, he is God. Or, as they struggle with the theology of their invention, he is fully human and fully divine (which, ironically, Christ would say we *all* are). In deifying Jesus, they needed to have him somehow escape death, since a God cannot die. Hence the contrivance of the resurrection and his coming back to life three days after crucifixion.[7]

The resurrection narratives, essential to the invention of a post-Easter Jesus, not only differ but are terminally vague. As we noted above, Mark originally ended with the discovery of the empty tomb but no appearances of a risen Christ. Nowhere is the moment of resurrection described, and the appearances to various people post-crucifixion are marked by either being witnessed by women (who had no legal standing to say they had witnessed anything), or are described as Jesus not appearing as himself, or by those he appeared to not recognizing him.

In first century Palestine, women had no legal standing. If a woman said she saw or heard something her words could not be used to prove anything, could not be used in court. The writers who amended and added to the Gospels knew this, hence the choice of women to be the witnesses of the alleged risen Christ. The appearances are disparate with no agreement between the Gospels. This is notable given the high degree of consensus on other matters pertaining to Jesus' life and teaching.

In the additions made to Mark many years after the original version of Mark, the writer has an angel appear to Mary Magdalene, Mary the mother of Jesus, and Salome, saying they should tell Peter and his disciples that Jesus will appear to them in Galilee. None of the women tell Peter or any of the disciples, and there is no record of any appearance to Peter or the disciples, in Galilee or anywhere else.

Matthew mentions a single appearance in Galilee, Luke speaks of several appearances in Jerusalem, and John mentions both the appearances in Galilee and Jerusalem. There is the appearance to two followers on the road to Emmaus, but allegedly Jesus took an appearance so that they could not identify him. Then of course, being part of the invention of a post-Easter Jesus, Paul needed to be able to say he had experienced an appearance, too, to make himself the equal of Peter or the other disciples. The issue of course is that Paul never met Jesus and thus could not have known any experience he had was of seeing the physically resurrected person of Jesus.

The deification necessary to create the post-Easter Jesus lead to further additions to the Gospels. Part of the reinvention of Jesus had to include proof that he was indeed the anticipated Messiah, and that he, being divine, was not born of human flesh. This part of the reinvention is particularly ironic given Jesus' own teaching that flesh is born of flesh and spirit is born of spirit which explained what he meant by being born again. At no point in his teachings did he suggest that any human being, or anyone with a human appearance, could never be born of other than a usual human union.

For the deifiers, it thus became necessary to add birth stories to the original Gospels. No such story was added to Mark, of course, which goes right to introducing John the Baptist and the baptism of Jesus, skipping Jesus' birth and life prior to starting to teach at around the age of 33. Matthew, however, the later Gospel written many decades after Jesus' death, starts with a detailed genealogy. It states right up front that Jesus was the Messiah, the Son of David and the Son of Abraham—both of which facts are known preconditions of a person being deemed the Messiah.

There then follows a lengthy genealogy which cannot be historically accurate since by the time of Jesus no one had a record of the family trees of either Abraham or Kind David since they respectively lived two thousand and one thousand years earlier. All such records, if they ever existed given the predominantly oral tradition, had been long lost. But what is most notable, and often not commented on in Biblical commentary, or teachings from the pulpit, is that the list culminates with Joseph, husband of Mary, mother of Jesus.

The obvious observation is that this list is pointless anyway if you then go on to argue that Joseph was not actually the biological father of Jesus. That in fact, God was Jesus' father by a miraculous immaculate conception whereby Mary as a virgin becomes pregnant without knowing a man sexually. This obvious problem was apparently irrelevant to the writer(s) who put a priority and emphasis on elevating Jesus to being a God and to a divinely ordained status of the prophesized Messiah.

A God cannot be born of a human thus, a fiction had to be created that Joseph was not his real biological father—of which there is no mention in the much earlier Gospel of Mark. Presumably this is a rather important point, and if true, you would have expected the writer of Mark to mention it. Indeed, what becomes apparent is the utter absence of Joseph in the Gospels, as if along with the post-Easter additions to the texts there was a deletion of Jesus having a living human father. By the time Jesus is teaching at around age 33, and when he dies on the cross, Joseph is nowhere to be seen. This is convenient if one wishes to promote the idea after the fact that Jesus only had a divine father, not a human, biological one.

The genealogy is missing from the final synoptic Gospel, Luke. Rather Luke starts with foretelling the birth of John the Baptist and foretelling of the birth of Jesus. An angel visits Mary, telling her of the miraculous birth she is about to experience.

Next, the writers amending and adding to the Gospels after Jesus' death faced another challenge: the Messiah foretold in the historic texts in order to be in the line of King David would need to be born in Bethlehem. It had already been well established in the pre-Easter New Testament texts that Jesus was born and raised in Nazareth. The writers amending the Gospels thus had to get around this impediment to proving Jesus was the foretold Messiah.

Thus, we get the unlikely side-story about Joseph and Mary needing to go to Bethlehem for a census and the elaborate, and highly improbable, birth in a stable, with wise men from the East following a star to find the stable. Scholars have researched this and find no evidence that they would have needed to go to Bethlehem for such a purpose, and that the only census that could be referred to happened well before Jesus was supposedly born.[8]

Then the writers added stories from Jesus' childhood that further bolstered the idea that he was the one foretold in texts such as Isaiah. Such stories, again if they were true, are completely missing from the oldest text, Mark, which if any of them were true would presumably been mentioned in Mark.

As I say elsewhere here, even the scene with Pontius Pilate before the crucifixion has tell-tale signs of being partly historical and part metaphorical teaching or legend. According to the canonical Gospels, Jesus is released to Roman custody and the crowd present ("the Jews" or "the multitude") was asked to choose whether Jesus would die or another also scheduled to be crucified that day named Barabbas.

What Pilate actually says to the crowd is, "Do you wish me to release this one known as the Messiah, the Christ, the King of the Jews, or do you wish me to release Barabba(s)?" What is missed in many considerations of this passage is that Barabba(s) literally means "Son" (bar) of the Father (Abba or Abbas). But it is simply not credible that it really happened this way.

Once you realize that the "other" person named is merely "Son of the Father" it becomes clear this telling of events is a teaching, It is a teaching that the Jewish people had a choice—either affirm Jesus as a Messiah, the foretold savior and King of the Jews, or affirm him as the Son of the Father. He also said we are all Sons of the Father (and Daughters) if we would just align our will with God's will. Thus, "the Jews" in the story decided to opt for Jesus as Son of the Father which implies they chose to kill (the idea of) Jesus the Messiah (King of the Jews).

This is not to say that some such a crowed scene happened prior to his execution, it is just not likely that it resembled the scene depicted in the canonical Gospels. Rather, with the passage of time what has been lost is that this story was told to prove a point about accepting Jesus as the Messiah (which he never claimed to be) or as the Son of the Father, which he consistently *said* he was—but he also said we *all* Sons and Daughters of God, not just him.

We have further evidence of the Gospels being amended after Jesus' death and some of the evidence has been staring us in the face, going unnoticed. For instance, in Matthew:

Do not suppose that I have come to bring peace to the earth. I did not come to bring peace, but a sword. [35]For I have come to turn

" 'a man against his father,
a daughter against her mother,
a daughter-in-law against her mother-in-law—
[36]a man's enemies will be the members of his own household.'

[37]"Anyone who loves their father or mother more than me is not worthy of me; anyone who loves their son or daughter more than me is not worthy of me. [38]Whoever does not take up their cross and follow me is not worthy of me. [39]Whoever finds their life will lose it, and whoever loses their life for my sake will find it. (Mt 10:34-39)

For many, this does not sound like the peace-loving Jesus we had come to know through the rest of Christ's teachings. But was this actually said by Jesus? Clearly it was not, and as support of this conclusion look at this section that many have read and heard spoken so many times before:

"take up their **cross** *and follow me"*

However, the cross did not become a Christian symbol until *after* Jesus' death, therefore this passage in Matthew must have been added *after* the crucifixion. For those interested in exploring this further, I write more about it in Appendix 1.

The consequence of the invention of the post-Easter Jesus was that new theology, not taught by Christ, was invented too. Whereas the core teachings of Christ had focused on the here and now, on realizing oneness with God and entering the Kingdom of Heaven within you, now, the new invented theology focused on rewards in the future. Christ's encouragement to go beyond thought and have a spiritual revelation now, here in this life, led to the term "*metanoia*" being deliberately mistranslated as "repent" or "repentance," when it really means to transform hearts and minds.

What emerged in the decades after Jesus' death was a theology of sin, or more precisely original sin: being born with this original sin we need to repent if we are to enter a place named Heaven that is no longer "within"2 (as Christ taught) but a place you may be able to go to after death. The Catholic version of this sin-based theology even invented a waiting room of sorts, Purgatory, where souls would wait to see if they were to go to Heaven or hell—like some cosmic version of the sorting hat in Harry Potter.

As the early organized church grew, being a Christian became about control of people, hierarchy, and money. People would pay to go to church, where the service was in a language foreign to them, Latin. There was no encouragement for the average person to have a direct relationship with God. Rather the Bible was in a language they could not read (even if they could read at all, which many couldn't), and communication with God needed to be through worldly priests, who in turn communicate with Jesus "in Heaven" who then advocates for us with God on our behalf.

The consequence was that the early church could thus control people, keep them in their place, discourage any real attempt to have a direct relationship with God, and even sold "indulgences" which if you paid enough would reduce the amount of suffering you or a loved one would undergo for your or their sins in Purgatory. In the late Middle Ages such indulgences did pay for some good works, such as charities and hospitals. But these indulgences were commonly abused. Yet, despite the protests of Martin Luther and the rise of the

Reformation that sought to do away with indulgences, they continue in Catholicism to this day.

To be clear, there is no support in the New Testament for the existence of a place called Purgatory. Just as there is no evidence for the other early Catholic invention of Jesus' mother Mary's Immaculate Conception. These were creations out of whole cloth by the early church partly to further emphasize the invented deification of a post-Easter Jesus (if Mary was a virgin then her mother, too, must have been a virgin, rendering Mary free of sin from the moment of conception). And attempts to control the masses and generate money for the church.

But the most serious consequence of the invention of the post-Easter Jesus was to turn people's attention away from the pre-Easter Jesus, and thus away from what Christ truly taught.

The followers of Christ at the time of his death and in the coming decades fell mainly into two groups: those who either understood his teachings (or at least had a fundamental grasp of them), and those who did not understand his teachings but got caught up in the "Jesus Movement" built upon the post-Easter Jesus. Among those who failed to grasp what Christ was teaching we must include many of his disciples since as they are depicted in the Gospels, they are often clueless. Indeed, frequently they are used as a narrative foil for Jesus to explain what not to do!

But we know that some of his followers understood his teachings, and we get clues of this from reports that Mary Magdalene was praised as being his star disciple who "got" what he was saying,[9] and his comments that he sometimes spoke in parables for those who did not understand, whereas that was not necessary for some of his followers who did understand. Indeed, we must conclude Christ felt at least some of his disciples "got" what he was teaching, despite his suggesting otherwise. Matthew 13:10-17 speaks to this:

> [10] *The disciples came to him and asked, "Why do you speak to the people in parables?"*
>
> [11] *He replied, "Because the knowledge of the secrets of the Kingdom of Heaven has been given to you, but not to*
> *them.* [12] *Whoever has will be given more, and they will have an abundance. Whoever does not have, even what they have*
> *will be taken from them.* [13] *This is why I speak to them in parables:*
>
> *"Though seeing, they do not see;*
> *though hearing, they do not hear or understand.*
> [14] *In them is fulfilled the prophecy of Isaiah:*
> *"'You will be ever hearing but never understanding;*
> *you will be ever seeing but never perceiving.*
> [15] *For this people's heart has become calloused;*
> *they hardly hear with their ears,*
> *and they have closed their eyes.*
> *Otherwise they might see with their eyes,*
> *hear with their ears,*
> *understand with their hearts*
> *and turn, and I would heal them.'*
>
> [16] *But blessed are your eyes because they see, and your*
> *ears because they hear.* [17] *For truly I tell you, many prophets and righteous people longed to see what you see but did not see it, and to hear what you hear but did not hear it.*

Furthermore, there is a third group of Christ's followers, who grasped some of the basic teachings but misunderstood the core teachings, instead buying into the post-Easter Jesus invention. Key among this group were people like Saul of

Tarsus (also known as Paul). We have only a sketchy record of what took place in the early years of the Christian movement following Jesus' death. But it seems the successful part of the movement—if success is measured in pure numbers of followers—was with the Gentiles. Christianity gained great popularity outside of Palestine in the Gentile world. This part of the movement is solidly based on the post-Easter Jesus invention, and has ultimately formed the foundation of most Christian churches and institutions today.

The other part of the movement, that part which comprised of followers who understood Christ's teachings, was considerably smaller and seemed to have its base at the Church in Jerusalem run by Jesus' brother James.[10] One of our main sources of this early period is the writings of Josephus. Flavius Josephus was a Roman-Jewish historian who published his work *Antiquities of the Jews* around 93-94 C.E. Books 18 and 20 of this work include references to Jesus.[11]

While some parts of Josephus' text were edited later by Christian scribes[12] who changed the depiction of Jesus from a charismatic teacher to being "the Messiah." Other parts that mention Jesus' brother James ("the Just") have been judged entirely authentic. This amendment of what Josephus wrote is further evidence that a movement was in progress by the early second century to promote Jesus as "the Messiah," a movement which was not as prevalent in the late first century when Josephus was writing.

Core Teachings of the Pre-Easter Jesus

It would be timely to review some of Christ's teachings, and how they inform us about concepts of "Christ" and of "Christ-nature." The pre-Easter Jesus was a prophetic, charismatic teacher in the first century Jewish Wisdom

Tradition. He was very much a human being, just like you and me, and he did not claim to be otherwise. At the core of his teaching was the potential for everyone to enter a state of consciousness he called 'Heaven within' by achieving oneness with God. In doing so, he taught, you will achieve eternal life and help bring into being (uncover) the Kingdom of God on earth.

Central to his message was the necessity of transforming yourself if you are to enter the Kingdom (or, rather, to awaken to the fact you are already in the Kingdom). He spoke of the importance of becoming like children in order to enter the Kingdom, Heaven within (Mt 18:3). Indeed, he says if you do not become like children you will never get in.

Here are some of the other elements of transformation required to enter the Kingdom: be born again of water and the Spirit (Jn 3:5); seek the Kingdom (Mt 6:33); have righteousness that exceeds that of the Scribes and Pharisees (Mt 5:20); be poor in spirit (Mt 5:3): don't look elsewhere for it, its right where you are (Lk 17:20-21); receive the Kingdom of God like a child in order to enter it (Mk 10:15); you don't enter the Kingdom just by calling Jesus "Lord" or simply by praising him (Mt 13:1-58).

Jesus also taught the following about getting into the Kingdom, becoming one with God and finding 'Heaven within': you must enter by the narrow gate (Mt 7:13-14); it is easier for a camel to get through the eye of a needle than a rich person to get into Heaven (Mt 19:24); have a spiritual transformation by going beyond thought, for the Kingdom is right where you are (Mt 3:2).

Now, of course, we noted before that the last quotation from Matthew is perhaps the worst mistranslation in the entire New Testament. It is usually wrongly translated as something like "Repent, for the Kingdom of Heaven is at hand." The word they translated as "repent" is *metanoia*, and as we previously discussed there is no reasonable way you can translate this word as "repent." However, those pushing the invented movement of the post-Easter Jesus needed to also propagate the idea that Heaven is a place you go to after you die,[13] and during this life you were born into sin and need to repent of this sin to enter Heaven. That theology is not found in anything Jesus actually taught.

What he taught is the need to free yourself of a dualistic reliance on material things to define who you are. He repeatedly emphasizes that a rich person cannot enter the Kingdom. He also taught that you must become as a child to enter the Kingdom. Taken together, what he was teaching was a need to be in the present moment, perceiving the world in a non-dualistic manner as children do, and unattached to material things or to your ego (the false self).

It is often missed, but it is inherent in Christ's teaching that Heaven within is not something you 'gain' it is a state of being you awaken to by aligning your will with God's will. He called for "Thy will not my will be done" as a central mantra in his movement known as "The Way." Aligning your will with that of God is another way of saying, "Go beyond the ego and discover your true self, which is aligned with God, is God." By doing this, Christ taught, by dropping dualistic perception and seeing everything through a non-dualistic lens, you become a Son (Daughter) of God.

What he meant by this term "becoming a Son of God" was realizing your True Self by going beyond the ego, seeing the world beyond thought (unconstrained by your preconceptions) and this is what he means by aligning your will with God's will.

It is this state of being, a state that is always here merely waiting to be awakened to, that we call your "Christ-nature." Just as for Christ his ego-based human self (with a small 's') was Jesus of Nazareth, so his True Self (with a large 'S'), aligned with God (that is, one with God) is what we mean by the title "Christ." In this sense we are all Christ because we all have Christ-nature awaiting to be realized: always ready to be wakened to. We are at one with God, always have been, we just have to realize that.

What this means is that the Kingdom of Heaven is here: right here, right now. It has always been here and did not need to be created. Christ realized this and taught this, but it was a crucial misunderstanding of those who created and promoted the concept of a post-Easter Jesus that they thought he had died without creating the Kingdom.

Since they mistakenly thought he did not establish the Kingdom as expected, it follows that he must have been talking about some future achievement. His teachings, therefore, in hindsight, they said must have been eschatological,[14] referring to a future time when there would be an end of days, a final reckoning. Hence, the fiction of his coming again "to judge the living and the dead," which has no relation to anything Jesus really taught. It was a concept that arose as part of the creation of the post-Easter Jesus, from a misunderstanding of his teaching, a misunderstanding of what he meant by the 'Kingdom' and by 'Heaven within.'

Those who have delved into Zen will find much of the above discussion of Christ-nature, and finding your true Self, familiar even if sometimes the words are not those you are accustomed to, or comfortable with. Because Zen deals with the human condition, we should not be surprised that there are strong parallels to Christ's "Way" that of course also deals with the human condition.

Because Zen is not a religion in the same sense that we see Christianity as a religion, the two can coexist with perfect ease. One of the beauties of Zen is that it defies simple categorization. Is it a religion? Not in the usual sense. Is it a philosophy? Insofar as philosophies tend to invoke the intellect, then no Zen is decidedly not a philosophy. Like Christ's teachings, Zen recognizes that people easily fall into the trap of thinking that being wealthy and having possessions, power, prestige is what life is ultimately all about and what will bring happiness.

We know, of course, that this is not true. The more you define life in terms of wealth, power, prestige, the more you try to grasp it the more it slips away. With age sometimes comes wisdom, and with that comes the realization that all people are truly equal whether they sit on a throne or on a broken crate below an overpass. Relying on building up your possessions, constantly craving praise from others for your "achievements" is ultimately hollow. There is always someone wealthier, more highly regarded, and so on. Are they happier? More satisfied with their life? Frequently the answer is no.

In Zen we come to realize that if is not just an attachment to material things that blocks our spiritual advancement, but it is the failure of the intellect to grasp deep spiritual truths. A lot of Zen practice is about letting go, not about "gaining" anything. Zen is full of contradictory language, so much so that you might be forgiven for thinking it was invented by someone with a really impish sense of humor.

In Zen we talk of there being nothing to achieve, nothing to gain, there are no goals. Then you may hear someone say that the only goal of Zen is simply to fully awaken in the moment. Thus, we have the goalless goal of being fully awake, going beyond thought. Sound familiar? It should since this exactly what Christ taught too: to enter what he called Heaven within by practicing *metanoia*—going beyond thought. We will talk more about *metanoia* in the following chapter.

In the Buddhist tradition it can feel wrong to say, "I am Buddha," just as in the Christian tradition it can feel blasphemous to say, "I am Christ." Indeed, there has been a degree of pedestalization of both Siddhartha and Jesus such that there is a tendency to think there can only be one (historical) "Buddha" and one "Christ." Holding such views misses the fundamental point that "Christ" was a title, just as "Buddha" was a title. With wisdom we can see that any of us can be a Christ or be a Buddha. Indeed, for each of us that is our true nature.

For such reasons, though, some may be more comfortable with the terms Christ-nature and Buddha-nature. In both cases they invoke "realization" rather than invoking the "I am" language that so strongly associated with the ego, with selfishness (as in "I am Christ" or "I am Buddha"). Both Buddha and Christ taught that this is a key goal of their "Way:" in Zen it is about realizing your true self, waking up, and seeing your Buddha-nature. In Christ's teachings it is about experiencing *metanoia*, going beyond thought (the intellect) to align your will with God's will. This in turn is an emptying of the self (freeing oneself of the illusions of the ego, dualistic thought) and becoming in his terminology a "Son of God." This is realizing your Christ-nature.

To say Buddha-nature and Christ-nature are the same thing is to miss the point. To say they are different is also to miss the point. Put it all down, as Korean Zen Master Seung Sahn said.

---

[1] To be more accurate, the Buddha did not teach whether there is a God or not. Thus, Buddhism makes no statement as to whether there is a God.
[2] Genesis 31:19, Genesis 31:34, Judges 17:1-6, Judges 18:18, 1 Samuel 19:13-16, Ezekiel 21:21, Deuteronomy 7:25-26, Exodus 20:4-6, Deuteronomy 5:8-10, 2 Kings 23:24, Genesis 35:204, Isaiah 44:9-11, Ezekiel 18:5-6, and Zechariah 10:2
[3] This tradition of not speaking the name of God continues to the current day among observant Jews.
[4] For those following the parallels to Zen, being a child of God is the relative (dualistic), being a Son (Daughter) of God is the absolute (non-dualistic). The first being the self with a small s, the second being the True Self, with a capital S.
[5] To be clear, I am not saying I do not believe in miracles—far from it. Working with people as I have all my adult life, especially in recent times as a priest and chaplain, I have witnessed many extraordinary events that I have no explanation for. Rather, the point here is that emphasizing Jesus as performing acts we "mere humans" cannot perform only served to place him on a pedestal and make him unattainable other than via worship as if he were a deity. While Mark emphasizes the miracle work, the other gospel writers switch the emphasis to Jesus as teacher but a teacher who is then pedestalized by being someone who has supernatural powers of rising from the dead, and so on.

[6] There is a meme on the Internet that goes something like this: "*Being just like Christ is easy: First, get yourself born of a virgin, then die and come back to life three days later...*" While blasphemous to some, there is some merit in the observation in that it points out the unattainability of being 'just like Christ.'
[7] Some have pointed out the lack of logic here: if a God cannot die then where did Jesus go for those three days? Legend suggests he used that time to explore the netherworld, which is hard to justify theologically. Others posit a kind of Schrodinger's Jesus: neither dead nor alive for those three days, but definitely not actually dead since a God cannot die. On top of all these inconsistencies are of course the problems that (a) there is no Old Testament prediction of the Messiah dying and coming back to life in three days, and (b) it wasn't three days. From late on the Friday to dawn on the Sunday is only a little over two days. But as I have said elsewhere, such considerations don't further the spiritual path of The Way. Put it all down if you find yourself drawn down these rabbit holes.
[8] The Census of Quirinius that Luke alludes to took place in 6 C.E. and thus cannot be one that had anything to do with the birth of Jesus—thought to be in about 4 B.C.E. Further, Luke has the birth during the reign of Herod the Great, but he died in 4 B.C.E. The only reasonable

conclusion is that the writer of Luke tried to invent a birth story for Jesus but failed by getting his facts completely wrong.

[9] Although a questionable source, the gnostic *Gospel of Mary* (2nd Century C.E.) has Mary Magdalene stating that she was the only disciple of Jesus who fully understood his teachings. See: Bart Ehrman, *Peter, Paul and Mary Magdalene: The Followers of Jesus in History and Legend.* Oxford University Press, 2006

[10] The American Catholic Church (ACC), which the author is ordained in, derives its lineage from James the Just in contrast to the Roman Catholic Church which derives its lineage from the apostle Peter. Peter of course assisted James in the first Church, but James was the head of it. The ACC, through its affiliation with the Philippine Independent Church, is in communion with the Episcopal Church and the worldwide Anglican Communion).

[11] Paul L. Maier, *Josephus, the essential works: a condensation of Jewish antiquities and The Jewish war.* Kregel Academic, December 1995, 284-285

[12] Bart Ehrman, *Jesus Interrupted.* Harper Collins, 2009, 159.

[13] Jesus, like most Jews of the first century C.E., did not believe in life after death or a separate place called Heaven you would go to after you die. Most modern Jews also do not believe this; it has been a consistent belief within Judaism since millennia before Jesus and since.

[14] Adj. relating to death, judgment, and the final destiny of the soul and humankind.

10

Metanoia: Awakening and Eternal Life

I said near the beginning of this book that the often-mistranslated word *metanoia* is a kind of key to unlock the core of Christ's teachings. Still, you may have asked yourself whether Christ himself used this word. *Metanoia* is of course a Greek word, and as we know the New Testament was written in Greek, whereas we believe Christ spoke primarily Aramaic. In fact, it may surprise some to learn that the Hellenistic cultural center of Alexandria in Egypt had a larger Jewish population than Jerusalem in the first century.

Indeed, more Jews in that period spoke Greek than spoke Hebrew.[1] Moreover, many of the Jews in Alexandria spoke mainly Greek and may have had little to no knowledge of Hebrew or Aramaic. So, did Christ speak Greek? New Testament scholars say that he may have: while it is not clear from any specific passage in the Gospels, certainly he appeared not to need a translator when speaking with the Roman authorities—and they would have spoken Greek.[2]

It is thus possible that Christ himself adopted the word *metanoia* in his teaching precisely because no Aramaic or Hebrew word quite captured the meaning he sought of "transformation." Alternatively, perhaps the Aramaic words Christ used were ones that the translators believed were best conveyed in Greek by the term *metanoia*. But if so, then we may never know what exact words Christ himself used since no document exists that records his actual words.

What we do know is that *metanoia* is in many ways unique to the time of Christ, or at least rose in popularity as Christianity took root and grew. In the second and third centuries before the common era the Hebrew Bible was translated into Greek and was known as the Septuagint meaning 70 (often abbreviated as LXX). In the entire Septuagint the word *metanoia* appears only ten times.[3] The two words most used in the Hebrew Bible for regret and repentance are *shuv* and *naham*. There are numerous papers written about which of these terms mean, but ultimately the Greek word used to translate them prior to the common era was consistently *epistrophe* or some variant on the Greek word *strophe* (turn).

Thus prior to the time of Christ the Greek word *epistrophe* was commonly used to represent “repentance” and “regret,” whereas the word *metanoia* was almost never used for that concept. Indeed, according to Guy Nave,[4] there are only 95 instances of the word *metanoia* in all Greek literature prior to the time of Christ. By contrast, Nave found over a thousand uses of the word *metanoia* in texts written from 1 C.E. to 200 C.E. showing the immense popularity the term had suddenly gained as a result of Christ’s teachings.

What this also means is that there is no reasonable possibility that the writers of the synoptic Gospels, writing around 50-90 C.E., decided upon reading words in Aramaic or Hebrew meaning ‘repent’ to suddenly select the (at that time) obscure term *metanoia* rather than the term *epistrophe* (or a term with the *strophe* root) that had been established as the ‘correct’ word for several centuries. While some have tried to argue that the writers of the Gospels merely had such poor Greek that they all used *metanoia* by accident, that is simply not plausible.

It is clear, then, that the writers of the synoptic Gospels used the term *metanoia* specifically and deliberately to translate Christ's teaching about transformation. Further credence for this interpretation is gained from considering how *metanoia* and *epistrophe* are used more broadly in the New Testament. Variations of *metanoia* appear more than 20 times in the synoptic Gospels (Mark, Matthew and Luke) while variations on *epistrophe* only occur six. And whereas variations of *metanoia* appear around 54 times in the entire New Testament, the word does not appear at all in the Gospel of John.

Adam Ellwanger makes another rather interesting observation: while it is commonly thought that both the Gospel of Luke and Acts were by the same author, Luke makes more use of *metanoia* than the other Gospels while rarely using *epistrophe*, whereas Acts would appear to use the two words interchangeably as if indifferent to the term *metanoia*. Perhaps, then, the two books were not by the same author, or they were by the same author but another author later edited Luke to add in the enthusiastic, repeated use of *metanoia*.

Given the influence both Platonism and the works of Philo had on spiritual teaching in first century Palestine, it is worth considering how transformation was understood in Hellenistic philosophy. The philosopher Martin Heidegger[5] suggested that Plato's allegory of the cave offered the most complete description of personal transformation ever written. Here Plato is describing a "turning around" (the *strophe* part of *epistrophe*) not to something new but to something that is already known but had been forgotten. It is possible to simplify the difference between *metanoia* and *epistrophe* as the former being a turning 180 degrees, whereas the latter implies a full 360 degree turning back to where one was originally.

What Plato described, then, was a transformation that was not to something original and different, but by lifting the veil of ignorance of illusion, a turning back to what was hidden but had always been there. Epistrophe is used in the early Christian world to mean "conversion" and yet the word used in the synoptic Gospels seems closer to Plato's use than that of the earlier Christian church—*transformation* rather than *conversion*. Perhaps no surprise, then, that the synoptic Gospels used *metanoia* whereas the early church later used *epistrophe*.

Metanoia connotes a sense of turning away from how things were before, and this aspect of its meaning perhaps lead to the mistranslation of repentance. It is a dropping away of the prior life a follower had, giving up an attachment to material things, living a simpler life, and so on. But the word clearly carried a much deeper meaning in its context: it meant both a 180 degree turn away from the life previously led, and also a 360 degree turn back to the state of your true Self (your state of being a Son of God, your will and God's will in alignment), the state that had always been there.

This also explains why the Gospel of John makes no use of *metanoia*, since it would have been understood as representing the pre-Easter Jesus teaching of awakening and oneness with God. John, by contrast, was the flag bearer for the post-Easter Jesus. This was the newly invented narrative of Jesus as divine, a resurrected pedestalized entity that suddenly was now a teacher of original sin and repentance from sin in order to enter a remote place named Heaven after one dies. Not surprising, then, that *metanoia* as the very core of the pre-Easter Jesus, First Century Wisdom Teacher, whose teachings would be jettisoned by the time John was written.

Philo: the Terms "Son of God," "*Metanoia*," and "*Logos*"

This is an appropriate point to review what we know about the works of Philo of Alexandria (also known as Philo Judaeus, 20 B.C.E.-50 C.E.). A Jewish philosopher and teacher, Philo was a highly respected leader among the Jewish population in Alexandria at the time of Christ. He was also a leading syncretist[6] of that time, seeking to find commonalities between the Hebrew Bible and Hellenistic philosophy. He relied upon the Septuagint (written in Koine Greek) since he does not appear to have been skilled in Hebrew and focused on integrating the Bible (*Tanakh* or Masoretic Text, MT) with Platonic and Stoic ideas.

Before considering what Philo wrote it is worth noting that at the peak of his career he was in his forties and fifties, at the time that Christ would have been in his twenties to early thirties. Philo died in 50 C.E. which means he died before any of the extant Christian texts we know of were first written. The earliest Christian texts appear to be some of Paul's letters written around 50-55 C.E. and the earliest Gospel seems to date from a decade or more after Philo died.

This is important when we come to discuss whether Philo influenced Christianity or the other way around. We can make two significant observations, one with certainty and the other with some confidence: first, since he died in 50 C.E. his writings cannot be drawing upon any Christian texts. Second, given his fame as a thinker and teacher in the period 20-30 C.E., it is quite possible that Christ came to know of his teachings. Indeed, if Christ was familiar with Greek, then he may have read some of Philo's works.

There are numerous points of interest to any student of Christology in Philo's works, but I want to focus on three: he spoke frequently of *metanoia*; he proposed that someone who attains the highest level of self-transformation should be known as the "Son of God" and; he coined the term *logos* for this Son of God, this shadow of God as he termed it.[7] All Christians will find these terms very familiar (although the term *metanoia* has been largely hidden from those attending mainstream churches). What may be shocking is that these terms, these ideas, came out of Alexandria prior to the time when Christ first started teaching.

It probably doesn't need to be mentioned, but while Philo was a very famous teacher of that time, Jesus of Nazareth was only known in a narrow geographic region. We have nothing that suggests that in this early part of the first century C.E. any of Christ's teachings, or even knowledge of Christ's existence, had reached Alexandria. By contrast, it is far more likely that Christ learned of Philo's work and became familiar with it.

We know that prior to the common era (prior to the time of Christ) the Greek word *metanoia* was rarely used. Then, suddenly, Philo starts using this term in the first two to three decades of the common era. We noted above that the majority of uses of *metanoia* in the first 200 years from 1 CE. to 200 C.E. were in Christian texts. The singular exception was Philo's use of the word, and his use comes immediately prior to the first use by Christ and by then by the Gospel writers and Paul.

Indeed, in Philo's work *On the Virtues* he devotes and entire section to *metanoia* (section XXXIII, 175-186)

> *"the brother and closest relation of which is metanoia, which is not indeed ranked in the first and highest class of blessings, but which has the principal in the class next to the first. (177) For absolutely never to do anything wrong at all is a peculiar attribute of God, and perhaps one may also say of a God-like man."* (176-177)

Of this man Philo adds in *On Flight and Finding*:

> *"God being his father, who is also the father of all things, and wisdom being his mother, by means of whom the universe arrived at creation."* (XX, 26).

Here Philo is introducing a recurring theme in his writings: namely, that this state of being—become a "Son" of God—involves the union of God the Father and Sophia (wisdom). Might this be a possible source for Christ's teaching that to achieve *metanoia,* to enter the Kingdom on earth (Heaven within), a follower needs to be born again of the Father and the Spirit? Yes, since Philo is reported to have been heavily influenced by the Essenes and the Therapeutae[8] and since Christ was a Teacher in the Jewish Wisdom Tradition, it does seem likely he drew upon Philo's writings.

Philo introduces that the idea of the highest achievement is to be without fault like God and to become a God-like man. This, of course, is what Christ was talking about when he speaks of aligning your will with God's will. Philo goes on to clarify that *metanoia* (which he makes clear is a transformation of self, not simply regret or repentance of some wrongdoing), leads to this state of perfection whereby one becomes a Son of God. Not just any Son of God, but he terms those who achieve this state as the "eldest Son of God," God's "first-born." And you will notice, too, that Philo's use of the term Father or "Father of the universe" for God. The language is like that used by Christ later, and some of the ideas are identical to those that those who invented the post-Easter Jesus used when they described Christ as the *logos*.

In his work *On the Confusion of Tongues* Philo wrote:

"(63) For the Father of the universe has caused him to spring up as the eldest son ... the firstborn; and he who is thus born, imitating the ways of his father..." (XVI).

Then in section XXVIII he goes on to clarify:

"(145) ... but they who have real knowledge, are properly addressed as the Sons of the one God ... (146) And even if there be not as yet anyone who is worthy to be called a Son of God, nevertheless let him labor earnestly to be adorned according to his first-born word ... for he is called, the authority, and the name of God, and the Logos, and man according to God's image ... (147) ... For even if we are not yet suitable to be called the sons of God, still we may deserve to be called the children of his eternal image, of his most sacred word; for the image of God is his most ancient Logos."

In another of his works (*Who is the Heir of Divine Things)* Philo describes the *Logos* (the "Word" of God) being both the envoy of God to the world, and the advocate on behalf of human beings to mediate with God on their behalf (XLII, 205-206). What emerges, then, is a both that Christ used or was strongly influenced by Philo's writings (*metanoia* and aligning with the will of God to become a "Son" of God), and that Philo's work was also relied on heavily to craft the post-Easter Jesus. A use of Philo's thought is most clearly shown in the Gospel of John which opens by almost directly quoting from Philo (Jn 1:1-5):

"In the beginning was the Logos, and the Logos was with God, and the Logos was God. [2]He was with God in the

> *beginning. [3]Through him all things were made; without him nothing was made that has been made. [4]In him was life, and that life was the light of all mankind. [5]The light shines in the darkness, and the darkness has not overcome it."*

The writer of John, and others creating the post-Easter Jesus as a pedestalized divine version of Jesus the Wisdom Teacher, relied heavily on Philo's writings and ideas:

> *"In the same manner God, being his own light, is perceived by himself alone, nothing and no other being co-operating with or assisting him, a being at all able to contribute to pure comprehension of his existence; But these men have arrived at the real truth, who form their ideas of God from God, of light from light"* (Philo, *On Rewards and Punishments*, 45-46).

For Philo, the *Logos* is eternally begotten of the Father, which is how he refers to the Supreme Being, and this *Logos* is the mediator between human beings and God (*Concerning Noah's Work as a Planter*, 9-10). He also wrote that to human beings the divine appears as a triad—the Father, the *Logos* and God's actions in the world. Thus, Paul, along with the writer of the Gospel of John, and various other early writers, drew heavily on Philo to create the post-Easter Jesus fiction, identifying Jesus as the *Logos* Philo had written about. From Philo's works Paul and the writer of John merged the ideas into this newly invented "Christianity" of a Trinity (Father, Son and Holy Spirit) that Philo had written about, along with the specific ideas that the Son is eternally begotten of the father (Nicene Creed), Light from Light, true God from true God, and that the Son is the mediator between humanity and God.

However, for Philo the *Logos* was not a person, not an individual like Jesus, the *Logos* is an aspect of God, God's shadow or twin. In Philo's philosophy, then, the *Logos* is accessible to anyone who achieves unity with the Father, and thereby becomes a 'first-born Son' or 'eternally begotten Son' as Philo described *all* those who achieve enlightenment. Thus, what Philo described as a universal cosmic aspect of God, the aspect humans can merge with, Paul, the writer of John, and others converted this universal idea into a narrow idea that only referred to a single person, a 'Messiah.' But let us return now more specifically to the topic of *metanoia* and its uniqueness to Christ's first century Wisdom Teaching.

What this pattern of use of *metanoia* suggests, then, is that it was a specific term deliberately selected by the writers of the synoptic Gospels as either the specific word used by Jesus or the Greek word most closely fitting the Aramaic terms used by Christ for the complete transformation needed to enter the Kingdom. The term was unique and chosen deliberately to convey a difficult new concept: the awakening to the True Self, oneness with God. It is the first century Palestine equivalent of the Buddhist term enlightenment, or better, awakening.[9] This would be an appropriate moment to have a brief review of Zen.

What is Zen?

Zen is a form of Buddhism which first arose in India around 500 B.C.E. It has its origins with Siddhattha Gotama (or Siddhartha Gautama) who was a spiritual teacher and religious leader whose teaching was based on the realization of suffering (known as *duhka*) and the end of duhka by entering a state of consciousness known as *Nirvana*. The title he received—*Buddha*—simply means "Awakened One." According to the stories about him, having tried many methods of meditation and other spiritual practices, he decided to sit under a tree (known as the "Bodhi tree") until he realized the fundamental Truth he sought.

This Truth was essentially the answer to the question "Who am I?" and his moment of awakening was by all reports his going beyond thought to realization. Thus, Buddhism, like Christ's teachings, speaks of having a *metanoia* moment where you realize who you truly are. We call this awakening to your Buddha-nature, the realization that you are Buddha.

It is common knowledge that by around 100 B.C.E. Buddhism had formed into two main branches: The Southern Indian school known as *Hinayana* (the small vehicle) and the Northern Indian school known as *Mahayana* (the great vehicle). The Mahayana school was the path of the Bodhisattva, to become one who seeks complete enlightenment in order to benefit all beings. Bodhisattvas are those who sacrifices themselves for others, those who having awoken commit themselves to the benefit of all beings: Jesus was thus a quintessential Bodhisattva.

The Mahayana version of Buddhism arose during the time of Christ—we place its beginnings in the period 100 B.C.E. to 100 C.E. And it is this version of Buddhism that arrived in China in about 527 C.E., brought there by a sage known as Bodhidharma. According to some legends, he was a red headed, bearded man with striking blue eyes. Thus, while some texts refer to him as "Indian," these tales of his appearance suggest he is more likely to be of Middle Eastern or European decent. Indeed, some have speculated that he was one of the Greek Buddhists who by this time were travelling East and spreading Buddhism to China.

According to stories about Bodhidharma he brought with him teachings he referred to as "the Way." Interestingly, as

Buddhism evolves into Zen it becomes more and more usual to talk of "the Buddha Way." Could there be a historic connection between Jesus referring to his teachings as "the Way" and this branch of Buddhism—Chan/Zen—also referring to its teachings as "the Way"? Possibly. We may never know, but the parallels are striking.

Having been assimilated in China, this branch of Buddhism blended with traditional Chinese thought, in particular it merged with Taoism, the national philosophy of that era. Central to this branch of Buddhism was the use of meditation and the word associated with this is *Dhyana* which roughly translates in English as "contemplation." This term was translated into Chinese as *Ch'an* (or simply *Chan)*. Anyone familiar with Taoism will immediately see how the resulting Chan Buddhism is a blend of Indian and Chinese thought. Indeed, reading Taoist texts such as the *Tao Te Ching* can feel very much like reading a Chan (Zen) text. "The Tao that can be spoken is not the eternal Tao." For instance, the Tao is equivalent to the Buddhist *sunyata*.[10] By the way, "Tao" is pronounced "dow" and you may see it written as Dao or Daoism.

From China, Chan Buddhism first spread to Vietnam (as Thien Buddhism) and Korea (as Seon Buddhism). Then around 1191, the Japanese Buddhist priest Eisai is credited with bringing *Rinzai* (Chinese *Linji*) Buddhism to Japan from China. And then around 1227 the Japanese Buddhist priest Dogen brought *Soto* (Chinese *Caodong*) Buddhism to Japan. These two branches of Japanese Buddhism, both introduced to Japan from the Chinese Chan tradition, became known as "Zen" which is the Japanese transliteration of the Chinese word Chan.

Broadly speaking, Rinzai Zen has a focus on working with *koans*, which appear to be word puzzles and pithy statements to wrap your mind around[11]—having some parallels to Christ's parables and sayings. By contrast, Soto Zen has a focus on meditation: its Japanese founder Dogen is famous for having promoted *shikantaza* which means "just sitting" and reflects the Chinese Caodong school of Buddhism's focus on "Silent Illumination."[12] This also has parallels with Christ's "Way" and his focus on *kenosis* or "self-emptying" as a method of entering into oneness with God by sitting in silence.

Whether practicing meditation (known in Zen as Zazen) or practicing *koan* introspection (the practice of working with a teacher on the pithy texts known as *koans*). The "goal' of Zen practice is the same: to wake up. This "waking up" is also known as "entering Nirvana," or misleadingly as "becoming enlightened." I say misleadingly since in Zen we learn that you achieve nothing, there is nothing to be gained or lost. Rather, we are already awake, already Buddha, so there is no "enlightenment" to be gained or achieved. Rather it is a *realization*, hence an awakening.

Zen literature is replete with stories of people suddenly realizing their true nature, becoming awake, or (while an inaccurate term) becoming enlightened. This sudden enlightenment or waking up is also known as *satori* in the Japanese tradition. And there are numerous accounts of people experiencing what one might call "glimpses" or insights into *satori*, which in Japanese Zen are known as *kensho* (literally means "seeing into the nature or essence").

In Christian terms, this may be likened to having a mystical experience where you have a sense of oneness with everything, a merging with God, a moment when time seems to stand still and you experience a deep sense of peace. Many

Christian mystics and saints have reported having such experiences, and we can see that Christ was trying to encourage his followers to find the path to such an experience. This is what he meant by the need for *metanoia*: he went so far as to say you cannot enter Heaven within, the Kingdom of God, unless you have such a spiritual "ah ha!" moment.

That said, this is circular logic: for most having the "ah ha!" moment of realization of your true self, your Christ-nature, *is* your entry into (or at least a glimpse of) the Kingdom of God that Christ was referring to as Heaven within. For some this experience may be a lifting of the veil, a glimpse (or *kensho* as the Japanese say), for others it can be an extremely life-transforming experience where the veil remains lifted. Indeed, for many even getting a brief glimpse can be life changing for years after the experience.

It is the nature of *metanoia*, of *kensho*, that the experience is highly individual and almost always difficult to put into words. Accounts of such experiences are often similar whether coming from a Christian mystical source, or Zen. People often speak of a sudden experience of merging with everything—of feeling at one with all, and a deep sense of peace, a "peace that passes all understanding."[13] Some speak of colors and sounds being enhanced, more vivid. Another common report is that time seems to either stand still or what perhaps only lasted a few seconds feeling as if it lasted much longer.

The path to a *metanoia, kensho*, or *satori* (an awakening experience) is as unique as the experiences themselves are when they happen. The path to this non-dualistic state of being, realization of who you truly are, sounds simple on the face of it. All you need to do is "wake up," or "align your will with God's will," or "become as a little child," and so on. The fact is, as Christ pointed out, the gate is narrow and rarely found: *"small is the gate and narrow the way that leads to life, and only a few find it."*[14]

Why is it that something so fundamental, true (indeed, Truth with a capital T), is so difficult to realize? Clearly it is difficult, since if it were easy for a teacher to convey how to realize this state of being, then Christ would have helped numerous of his followers. Similarly, if it were easy, the many Zen Masters would have had a long list of students who became "enlightened." The fact seems to be that aside perhaps from Mary Magdalene, few of Christ's followers truly got what he was teaching, and Zen Masters over the centuries have related a few students here and there.

When a Zen Master's students awake and realize their true selves, indeed stories of when Zen Masters themselves awoke, the story may seem incredibly ordinary. If not ordinary stories, then the other extreme of bizarre or weird stories. A Zen Master might have a student who believes they have achieved something significant and have totally understood their master's teaching. Then the teacher says something seemingly innocuous like, "Did you wash your bowl after breakfast?" and with this question the student had a sudden realization.

This recalls a famous story of awakening involving the Buddha, known as the Flower Sermon. In one lesson with his students, the Buddha simply held up a flower. On seeing the flower, it is said that his disciple Mahakasyapa was instantly enlightened. This story in particular goes to a Zen tradition of wordless transmission: the direct transmission of a truth that focuses on experience rather than dogma or intellectual analysis.

Then we have strange stories like the one about a Zen Master Gutei who was known to raise his finger whenever he was asked a question about Zen. A boy attendant started to imitate Gutei so whenever anyone asked the boy what the Master had preached about he would just hold up one finger. Gutei heard about this mischief, grabbed the boy and cut off his finger. As the boy cried and started to run away, Gutei stopped him, and as the boy turned around Gutei held up his finger. Instantly the boy was enlightened. Having said that, do not make the mistake of thinking it is all right to cut off appendages to help someone achieve oneness with God, or 'enlightenment'! Many Zen stories need to be read beyond the literal words, and this is one of those.

It has been said that not being aware of your True Self, not being aware that you are already one with God or awake (and always have been), is because both what we perceive and the manner we perceive it is an illusion. In popular literature, especially that devoted to non-dual spirituality and mindfulness, you will see endless references to how you need to destroy your ego. This is at best a naïve, and at worse a dangerous suggestion.

Insofar as what we mean by "ego" is the illusionary self (with a small 's') that we believe is a "me" separate from others, there is merit in practices that help you to realize this and become more non-dual in your view or the world, more selfless in your dealings with others. The danger comes when you if you get the idea you are meant to become some kind of superior 'spirit only' being who has no 'self'—some kind of spiritual zombie or comic book superhero.

Realizing there are dualistic and non-dualistic ways to perceive does not mean the dualistic ways are 'bad.' When a truck is hurtling toward you as you cross the street, having the non-dualistic view that its all an illusion will end badly for you compared with your dualistic view that has concepts of "truck," "mass," "speed," and concepts about what would happen if you don't get out of the way!

In Zen this is addressed by helping students to realize the absolute and the relative views are equally true, equally valid. One way teachers approach this is to introduce the *koan* Mu. In the book of *koans* known as the *Mumonkan*, the first "case" is known as Joshu's dog:

> *A monk asked Joshu, "Has the dog the Buddha nature?" Joshu replied, "Mu"*

The word *Koan* means "public case," and from that we get the numbering of Case 1, Case 2, etc. Chao-Chou Ts'ung-shen (ZhaoZhou, Japanese, Joshu) was a major Chinese Chan/Zen Master of high repute. Anyone in the Zen tradition is aware that the Buddha taught that all sentient beings have Buddha-nature. In Christian terms, this is similar to saying all beings have Christ-nature. So, Joshu should have responded to the monk's question with a simple "yes."

However, in the original Chinese, he responds with the word "wu" ("mu" in Japanese), which means "not" or "no." Zen masters are often-known to have a wry sense of humor, so its possible Joshu chose "wu" as a word play on the sound a dog makes when it barks (which of course gets lost when translated to the Japanese "mu"). The student of Zen is asked questions about this: "What color is Mu?" "How tall is Mu?" and so on. Depending on how the student answers (and often the answer sought is non-verbal), the teacher can gauge the degree to which students get what is being taught about their true selves, about their Buddha-nature.

To take one example, if asked "How tall is Mu?" the relative answer would be the student's height (for example

"Five feet eleven") and the absolute response would be "Infinite" or "no height at all." This may sound like *koans* can be dealt with using a simple cheat sheet or answer book. On the contrary, a Zen teacher has numerous "checking questions" she or he can ask to determine whether you have just read what an acceptable answer could be, compared to you actually "getting" what is being asked. But hopefully this glimpse into such *koan* introspection can help one appreciate that this path is not simply about killing the ego (whatever that means) or about becoming a hyper-spiritual 'being' merged with universe, viewing everything in an exclusively non-dualistic manner.

The illusion that you are not your True Self, that you are not one with God to use Christian terms, has some similarity to well-known visual illusions such as the staircase illusion:

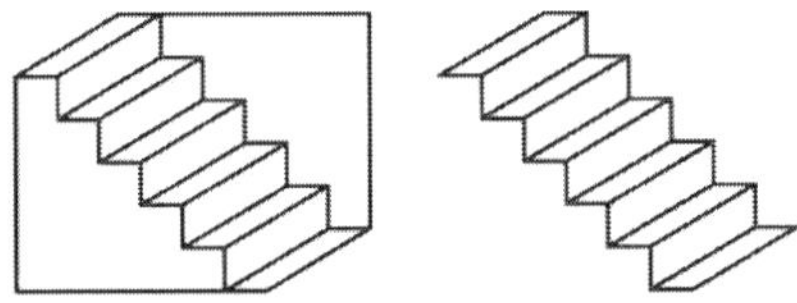

Are the stairs in the above image right way up or upside down? For most people, you can either see that they are stairs right way up, or by concentrating you can see they are now stairs are upside down (as if you are underneath them and they're coming down from above). But usually you cannot see both at the same time. There are some people who can only see one version of the image: perhaps they can see it as right side up, but no matter how hard they try they can't see the alternate view.

This simplistic example has some merit to it: seeing the world as a collection of "things" in which you are also a thing (a separate person, ego) is so ingrained in our core programming that it is as if we can only see the stairs as upright and going down from left to right. Perceiving the world exactly as it is, free of such dualistic concepts, is rather like being able once in a while to see that the steps are also upside-down. A very few people can see both versions of the steps at once, and this has a parallel with the spiritual path: being able to perceive the absolute and the relative at the same time.

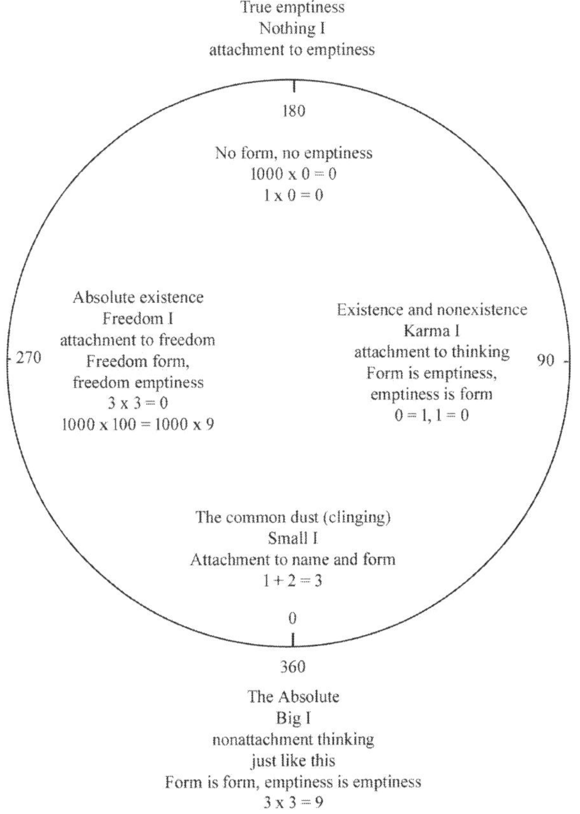

As Zen teachers would say: there is first attachment to name and form; then the realization form is emptiness; then no form, no emptiness; then attachment to freedom, freedom form, freedom emptiness; then form is form, emptiness is emptiness—The Absolute, "just like this" thinking. Korean Zen Master Seung Sahn depicted this as a circle that he called *The Compass of Zen*, revealing how the path is ultimately back home to where you started, everything is revealed, everything is the same, everything is transformed.

The beauty of this diagram is how simply it portrays the spiritual journey from dualism, to non-dualism, to the integration of everything, both dual and non-dual. We start in the world of delusion and illusion that Buddhists (and Hindus) call *samsāra*. This is a Sanskrit word that means world or wandering and conveys the idea of a constant cycle of change. Born innocent and without the numerous veils of constructs and beliefs, we swiftly lose our initial innocence of infancy.

As we grow, we acquire countless concepts and constructs, which frankly as humans we must do if we are to function in the world. If you don't acquire the idea that a shape that is getting larger and larger is in fact a truck hurtling toward you on the road, then you would not get out of the way and probably die. If you don't acquire the knowledge that stove burners are hot, you would repeatedly touch them and get badly burned. Acquiring these constructs and concepts that neatly divide the world up into "things" with each thing being separate from another, is entirely normal and to a large extent necessary.

We are so good at making these concepts and constructs that we convince ourselves that we are separate beings, and that we are a consistent 'thing' that goes about *thinging* alongside other things. We become associated with this thing we call "me" which is a complete illusion—the ego, the self (with a small s). This is all a delusion of course, since as Thich Nhat Hanh termed it, in truth we *inter-are*.[15] Without a cloud there can be no rain, without rain trees can't grow, trees enable us to make paper. If there is no cloud there cannot be a sheet of paper on which to read this (printed version) book.

We make the error of thinking we are some separate person, a being that is constant and that I call "me." We only have to look at photographs of ourselves as children to appreciate that what I call "me" changes all the time. Day to day the changes can seem imperceptible, but they are real and constant. Every cell in our body, with the exception of some cells in our brain and brain stem, completely renew over time. Cells in our intestine and stomach are totally renewed every two days or so. Our skin cells are entirely replaced every ten to thirty days, our red blood cells renew every four months, fat cells every eight years, and our skeleton renews about ten percent a year.

Quite literally, the "me" you view in the mirror today is physically not the same "me" that you saw in the mirror the day before. Here at the bottom of the compass—the zero degrees point—we are deep in the illusion that the world is made up of separate things of which we are also things interacting with other things. At the 90 degree point we gain some awareness of both the dual and the non-dual: we gain some appreciation that there is form and nothingness much as we discussed above. This is an intellectual stage where you grasp that being a thing, being separate, is an illusion but you become attached to thinking.

Some get stuck at this point: they "get it" that they are both separate and not separate as an intellectual concept. They appreciate what people mean when they say everything is one, everything is interconnected, but it isn't their direct moment-to-moment experience of life. They see what the mystics meant when they say they are both mortal, human, and also divine because God is not separate. Intellectually they grasp to some degree that they are both human and divine, but it isn't their lived experience.

At 180 degrees travelers on the Way have perhaps had a *kensho* or *metanoia* experience and may believe they have had a full awakening—that they are now "enlightened." Indeed, many spiritual paths, including mystical Christianity and branches of Zen, speak as if this is the end point. Once one perceives one's True Self as nothingness (some may interpret it as "pure spirit") whether consciously or unconsciously they give themselves a pat on the back: "I've made it, I'm enlightened, I'm one with God."

In Zen we talk of this as being seduced by *śūnyatā* (emptiness). This is the non-self, the seduction of realization that your True Self is this emptiness, this non-dual nature, this experience of being one with everything and not bound by this physical body or the ego. A surprisingly large number of people stop at this point in their journey feeling they have "made it." Many go on to become self-proclaimed teachers, Zen masters, and gurus. One glimpse of awakening and they believe they are fully home. Job done.

But next on the path, for those who are not taken in by the seeming finality of their *kensho* or *metanoia* experience, is the highly seductive—one might say dangerous—point at 270 degrees. Here the traveler realizes what some might call God-like powers having awakened more deeply to the reality that there is a deep and seductive freedom in perceiving everything you thought you "knew" was just socially acceptable constructs. That you can make up your own so-called 'reality' that is just as valid as any constructed by human society. Be careful! Do not play chess with Zen students at this level—they will use their opening pawn's move to take your king and declare "Game over!"

But true awakening, true aligning of your will with God's will, is the arrival at 360 degrees: exactly back where you started. Here you become fully awake to the Absolute, to the fact you are both fully human and fully divine—awake to the fact you are both fully you as self (with a small s) and fully you as Self (with a large S). Form is form, emptiness is emptiness as the Zen teachers say. Your true nature (your Buddha-nature, your Christ-nature) is exactly who you have always been. There never was anything to 'attain.'

Christ's Forty Days in the Desert

One of the beauties of the New Testament scriptures for me is that some absolute gems have been passed down to us unscathed by editing, largely I suspect because the writers did not understand them. One of these is the passages in the Gospels about how after his awakening (as a result of the baptism by John), Christ then retreated to the desert for forty days and there we're told he was tempted by the devil.

This could hardly be a better description of Christ going through the 270 degrees stage of his awakening:

> [1] *Then Jesus was led by the Spirit into the wilderness to*
> *be tempted by the devil.* [2] *After fasting forty days and forty*
> *nights, he was hungry.* [3] *The tempter came to him and said,*
> *"If you are the Son of God, tell these stones to become*
> *bread."*
>
> [4] *Jesus answered, "It is written: 'Man shall not live on*
> *bread alone, but on every word that comes from the mouth*
> *of God.'"*
>
> [5] *Then the devil took him to the holy city and had him*
> *stand on the highest point of the temple.* [6] *"If you are the Son*
> *of God," he said, "throw yourself down. For it is written:*

"'He will command his angels concerning you,
and they will lift you up in their hands,
so that you will not strike your foot against a stone.'"

[7] *Jesus answered him, "It is also written: 'Do not put the Lord your God to the test.'"*

[8] *Again, the devil took him to a very high mountain and showed him all the Kingdoms of the world and their*
splendor. [9] *"All this I will give you," he said, "if you will bow*
down and worship me."

[10] *Jesus said to him, "Away from me, Satan! For it is written: 'Worship the Lord your God, and serve him only.'"*

[11] *Then the devil left him, and angels came and attended him.* (Mt 4:1-11)

The version in Mark is far shorter:

[12] *At once the Spirit brought him into the desert,* [13] *where*
he was tempted by Satan for 40 days. He was there with the wild animals, and the angels took care of him. (Mk 1:12-13)

For once, the version in Mark seems incomplete although we have no way to know how much of what Matthew added was his fancy or contrivance. The Matthew version brings up many issues and ideas: the question of what Satan meant to first century Jews could fill an entire other book on its own.

First, it seems fitting that following his awakening, Christ then went on a retreat to process what had happened to him. It was undoubtedly a life transforming experience to realize his oneness with God, and it reveals something about his spiritual journey and the guidance of his teachers that he retreated to the desert. Whether it was indeed actually for 40 days is hard to say: Moses is recorded as fasting twice for 40 days each

(Deuteronomy 9, Exodus 32) and of course the number 40 arises over and again in the history of the Jews. The twelve spies were a group from each of the twelve Israelite tribes whom Moses sent to scout the land of Canaan for 40 days. When the spies show lack of faith, God has the entire Jewish nation wander in the desert for 40 years.

So, we know that the number 40 had great historical and religious significance. Perhaps it had acquired such significance that by the first century C.E. those following a spiritual path as Christ was had become accustomed to 40-day fasts. With the caveat that we cannot be sure it was an actual 40 days (rather than a symbolic period of days), we're told that Christ retreated to the desert to fast and practice *kenosis* (self-emptying).

Perhaps Christ learned this ascetic practice from John the Baptist, or perhaps from other teachers he studied with. Regardless, it makes sense that he would have taken this time to reflect on what had happened to him. What is interesting is this depiction of the 270 point in the Compass: the descriptions of Satan tempting Christ are a near perfect metaphorical representation of what it can be like for someone at 270 to be tempted by the attachment to freedom—the feeling of power that can come from self-realization as the ego makes one last dying attempt to dominate.

Of course, Satan here is not a real person or entity, but the Jewish personification of 'evil.' Here the personification of temptation as Christ is in danger of being lulled into a sense of being all-powerful, having realized his true nature. Satan written backwards is *natas* (Latin for "be born") with the implication that evil is the opposite of life. Indeed, "evil" is simply 'live' written backwards, just as "devil" is "lived" written backwards.

Evil, then, is the very opposite of your will being aligned with God's will. It is your will out of alignment, your focus on dualistic *thinking* rather than non-dual *being*.

This spiritual journey depicted in the Compass is also what Christ was speaking of, using of course the theistic language of the Jewish faith, and the first century Wisdom Tradition framework. Although, sadly, the detail of the steps he taught in his "the Way" have been lost to us. We can only surmise what it might have entailed. There will be more about that below in the final chapter.

Waking up, aligning your will with God's will, achieving *metanoia* or an "Ah ha!" moment, is like the person who can only see the stairs as going in one direction. The difference is that the teacher can only give general guidelines as to how to break the illusion—you must take that step yourself. What we have in both Christian and Zen traditions are a series of practices which have a track record of success over the millennia. Still, there is no guaranteed method or practice that can be provided that assures the recipient will have the realization that Christ spoke of, or that Buddha spoke of. Hence Christ's warning that the gate is narrow, and few find the way through.

In both traditions we have a collection of 'tools' that can be tried: Christ's practices included his teachings (the parables and sayings in particular), his teaching of *kenosis* (self-emptying through meditation and silent solitary prayer), the scriptures (so-called Old and New Testaments, the Torah and other writings, ancient and modern) and seeking what he called Heaven within through *metanoia* (going beyond thought). There are strong parallels in the Zen tradition: meditation (Zazen), general teachings and scripture (the dharma, precepts, sutras) and *koan* work. In both traditions, having a teacher or mentor is strongly recommended.

Christ's Awakening

Notably, neither the Gospel of Mark nor of Matthew tell us anything about Christ's life as a boy or as a man prior to his becoming around 30 years of age when he commences his teaching. Mark starts with a passage about John the Baptist, and notably when you peel away the text that was clearly added at a later date, Matthew too starts with an account of John the Baptist (at Mt 3:1). This is not a coincidence: there is a reason John the Baptist is central to the telling of Christ's story.

A sizable part of Matthew is the same as Mark, thus since Mark is the earlier work it is tempting to conclude Matthew is based on Mark with elaborations, additions, and a change of focus. For instance, whereas Mark focuses on Jesus as a miracle worker, Matthew focuses on Jesus as teacher. The opening sections of Matthew are a clear later addition, supplementing the original account in Mark with stories of Jesus' genealogy and his birth.

The later additions to the opening of Matthew were clearly written retroactively (that is, as revisionist history) to establish Jesus as fulfillment of prophecy and to reinforce the post-Easter Jesus narrative.[16]

Most notably, though, John the Baptist is mentioned in all four Gospels. Like Jesus, John was an itinerant Jewish teacher. Both the New Testament and various early historians such as Josephus[17] as well as modern authors have hailed John as a major religious figure of the time.[18] He is depicted as being a herald who came to tell the world of the coming of Jesus, whom he called one who is a greater teacher than himself: he heralded Jesus' coming as the Christ, the Messiah.

Some have suggested that John was part of an Essene sect, a Judaic group that practiced asceticism and purportedly spoke of a Messianic figure who would have baptism as central to their teaching.[19] John is depicted as dressed in a camel's hair garment, with a simple leather belt, and who was known to eat just locusts and wild honey (Mk 1:6, Mt 3:4).[20] This description suggests he was an ascetic, but what is under emphasized is that given the central place of John in the texts it is most likely John was one of Jesus' teachers.

But the key reason John has such a central place in the writings is because he was instrumental in Jesus realizing his true self as Christ. For anyone who has had an awakening experience, or a glimpse/*kensho* moment, it is not hard to imagine that moment of having been thrust under the water in a full body baptism, then suddenly rising up to breathe again. That could quite easily have been the jolt Jesus needed to enable him to go into a state of before thought. It would be particularly possible because it was almost certainly the first time he had experienced a baptism. Perhaps it was a particularly bright, clear day with no clouds in the sky, as he emerged from the water, the sun in his eyes. We will never know, but the image is compelling.

For reasons we have discussed, I will tend to go with Mark's record of what happened as Jesus emerged from the river that day:

> [10] *Just as Jesus was coming up out of the water, he saw Heaven being torn open and the Spirit descending on him like a dove.* (Mk 1:10)

Mark uses an unusual word for the Heavens being opened which means literally a 'tearing' or 'ripping apart' (Greek: σχίζω, *schizō*). This is where it ends in Mark, the earliest record of what took place. As we have found before, both Matthew and Luke then build on Mark by adding wording that has God saying either to Jesus (Luke) or to the assembled crowd (Matthew) that this is his son whom he loves and with whom he is well pleased.

Thus, once again the simple telling of what certainly appears to have been Jesus' moment of awakening is embellished in Matthew and Luke to elevate Jesus to the level of being the Messiah and God's son (with the implication no one else is God's son). But the wording that survived to us through Mark of "*and the Spirit descend[ed] on him like a dove*" nearly perfectly conveys the awakening experience, the *kensho* or, more likely here, *satori* (sudden enlightenment) moment. What is consistently mentioned is that this is the watershed moment: it is the moment Christ then starts teaching and begins his active ministry.

It is also interesting to see which aspects of John's teaching Christ decided to take on, and which he did not. John was an ascetic who appears to have lived very simply, wearing rough clothing and eating very simply to the point of depriving himself of good sustenance. There is no evidence that Christ followed any of these aspects of John's teaching (other than taking the time to fast in the desert), on the contrary what we see is Christ adopting a "middle way" between extremes much as Buddha did. Christ adopted the encouragement towards simplicity and not becoming attached to material things, prestige, and a life that boosts ego rather than encouraging selfless love.

Christ didn't recommend the wearing of rough clothing or near starving yourself on a routine basis as part of a spiritual practice. And what is the—perhaps surprising—aspect of John's ministry that Jesus also did not adopt? Baptism. I say this is surprising given the central place of baptism in the modern Christian Church. But the simple fact is that there is no record in the synoptic Gospels (Mark, Matthew and Luke) that Christ ever baptized anyone with water as John the Baptist did. Even in the Gospel of John, which we know to be a highly unreliable source of what Jesus actually said or did:

> 4 *Now Jesus learned that the Pharisees had heard that he was gaining and baptizing more disciples than John—* 2 *although in fact it was not Jesus who baptized, but his disciples.* 3 *So he left Judea and went back once more to Galilee.* (4:1-3)

Even in John, then, the writer goes out of his way to clarify that it was not Christ that baptized anyone. Both Mark and John have John the Baptist saying that although he baptizes with water, another more powerful that he will come and baptize with the Holy Spirit:

> *"After me comes the one more powerful than I, the straps of whose sandals I am not worthy to stoop down and untie.* 8 *I baptize you with water, but he will baptize you with the Holy Spirit."* (Mk 1:7-8)

And now the Matthew version:

> 11 *"I baptize you with water for repentance. But after me comes one who is more powerful than I, whose sandals I am*

not worthy to carry. He will baptize you with the Holy Spirit and fire. (3:11)

Once again, we have Matthew basing his text on Mark but embellishing it with the addition of the idea of baptizing with fire. Needless to say, Matthew's addition of the idea of baptizing with fire has led to countless speculations as to what that might mean although flame has long been associated with the Holy Spirit. The closest we get in what the New Testament claims Christ himself said:

> [4] *On one occasion, while he was eating with them, he gave them this command: "Do not leave Jerusalem, but wait for the gift my Father promised, which you have heard me speak about.* [5] *For John baptized with water, but in a few days you will be baptized with the Holy Spirit."* (Acts 1:4-5)

The problem of course is that neither Luke nor Acts are a reliable source of what Christ actually said. And it does seem rather convenient to have these words put into Christ's mouth words that so perfectly echo what Mark (whom Luke was copying) had reported John the Baptist saying. A more pertinent quotation comes from the Gospel of John: while not the most accurate source of what Christ said, this teaching rings true with what we know about Christ's core teachings:

> [3] *Jesus replied, "Very truly I tell you, no one can see the Kingdom of God unless they are born again."*
>
> [4] *"How can someone be born when they are old?" Nicodemus asked. "Surely they cannot enter a second time into their mother's womb to be born!"*

> 5 *Jesus answered, "Very truly I tell you, no one can enter the Kingdom of God unless they are born of water and the Spirit.* (Jn 3:3-5)

What we can say with a high degree of certainty is that when Christ talks of being born again of water, he is not talking about baptism which he did not practice. Indeed, in this excerpt from John, Nicodemus would have had no concept of baptism so that cannot be what Christ was referring to. It is thus somewhat ironic that baptism with water came to be inextricably associated with Christianity when that cannot be what Christ meant.

In particular, since there was only adult baptism by water (by John the Baptist, notably), there is no evidence of baptizing babies with water. That practice was an invention of the early church which has persisted and become as much part of modern Christianity as the Christmas Tree (devised by medieval Germans and popularized by Queen Victoria in 1840).

Now let's pull together these various threads: John the Baptist had a ministry of baptizing by full body emersion in a river. Jesus undergoes this experience and has his moment of awakening to who he truly is (his true self) as he emerges from the water. And in this moment, he also has the realization that baptism by water is not what he is called to teach and practice. Rather, for him baptism becomes the symbol of experiencing what he perceived as a rebirth as his True Self (with a large S), breaking through the veil of delusion that was his self (with a small s)—the self of the ego. He had died to the dual and been reborn in the non-dual, and he knew this was to be his core teaching for others, not baptizing others as John had done.

So, what is this water and spirit of which Christ taught we should be reborn? This goes to the very heart of Christ's teaching: you are first born of your biological parents (mother/father). Then to reach the state of consciousness he called Heaven within (the Kingdom of God) you need to be born again of your spiritual mother (Holy Spirit/Sophia/ wisdom) and spiritual father (God). Water here is the age-old symbol of life and creation, which is God. And of course, this dovetails perfectly with Christ's teaching that once you have experienced *metanoia*, once you awaken to who you truly are, with your will aligned with God's will, you then become a Son (or Daughter) of God.

Christ's terminology can be confusing, but what he is saying is that you are born a *child* of God but when you awaken you then become a *Son* or *Daughter* of God. One state is the dualistic state you entered as you grew up once out of the innocence of your childhood then entered the era of delusion where you falsely believed yourself to be separate from the rest of creation. The other state, of being a "Son" (or "Daughter"), is awareness of your True Self as being both human and divine. The dual (human) and the nondual (divine) co-existing—one, not two, and yet not one (Zen Buddhists simply say "not one, not two"). While we do not know the full details of Christ's "The Way" teachings, at this point they get as pithy as any teaching by a Zen master.

Eternal Life

Perhaps one of the most misunderstood promises Christ made was that if one followed him, followed his "Way," you would realize eternal life (Jn 3:16, 10:28-30). This is also referenced more tangentially in Matthew:

> [13] *"Enter through the narrow gate. For wide is the gate and broad is the road that leads to destruction, and many enter through it.* [14] *But small is the gate and narrow the road that leads to life, and only a few find it.* (7:13-14)

Here Jesus is at his most "Zen," much as he was when he said to those who have nothing even that will be taken away. The parallel to the Zen "gateless gate" also comes to mind, and here is Jesus using first century Jewish Wisdom language to express what Zen Masters have taught, too.

The wide gate with the broad road is the road most of us travel on much of our lives: it is the road of the ego, of the illusion of me/you, us/them, here/there, the illusion of dualism and the condition of being under the thumb of our concepts and preconceptions. It is the easy road because all we have to do is focus on ourselves, our own needs not those of others. The narrow gate is the gate of self-emptying (meditation, silent prayer, *kenosis*), the gate of not being attached to material things, the gate of being freed of conceptions and preconceptions. The gate of aligning our will with the will of God as Christ put it.

But like the parallel in Zen teaching of the gateless gate, the narrow gate Christ spoke of is in fact wide open, infinitely wide in fact. It leads to life because once you discover your true self, your Christ-nature, you immediately see that your true self is not subject to life and death. Your true self, your Christ-nature, is infinite. It is also "How may I help you?" And it is the deepest experience of Love—or compassion in Buddhist terms—since your true self *is* Love, *is* compassion. This naturally arises from perceiving there is no separation between "you" and the universe you perceive. No separation between "you" and God.

---

[1] Joseph Meleze Modrzejewski, *The Jews of Egypt: From Rames II to Emperor Hadrian*. The Jewish Publication Society, 1995.
[2] I am grateful to Bill Countryman for this observation.
[3] Adam Ellwanger, *Metanoia: Rhetoric, Authenticity, and the transformation of the self*, The Pennsylvania State University Press, 2020.
[4] Guy D. Nave, *The Role and Function of Repentance in Luke-Acts*. Academia Biblica (Society of Biblical Literature), 2002.
[5] Martin Heidegger, *The Essence of Truth: On Plato's Cave Allegory and Theatetus*, Bloomsbury Academic, 1st edn.,2013
[6] A syncretist is someone who blends together two or more different traditions.
[7] A term clearly related to the term syzygy (twin) used by the Gnostics. And of course, the parallel of being a "shadow" to that of being a "twin."
[8] The Therapeutae were a contemplative sect that Philo observed near Alexandria.
[9] Enlightenment is not the best term and is not found in the early Buddhist literature. The original word in Buddhism is *boudi* which means to awaken, and this is a far better term. The term enlightenment came about in the 19th century and got associated with Buddhism through the translations of people like Max Muller. But the term enlightenment is problematic since it connotes something to be attained rather than merely awakened to.
[10] *Śūnyatā* (shoon-ya-ta) is variously translated as voidness or emptiness, and ultimate reality. It can also mean the recognition of non-self (*anattā*) or absence of self apart from the five *skandas* (mental and physical elements of existence).
[11] That is *not* what they are, only what they appear to be to the casual observer.
[12] The schism between those who favored strongly 'just sitting' and those who favored other methods such as *koans* dates back to the early days of Chan in China. Ironically, Dogen who was the most fervent advocate for "just sitting" titled his key work *Shōbōgenzō* ("Treasury of the True Dharma Eye") which is the same title that the rival Chinese teacher in the Linji tradition, Dahui Zonggao, named his major work many years earlier: Dahui was famous for stating his strong opposition to "just sitting." Dogen was well aware of Dahui's work, studying it while he was in China, so Dogen's choice to use the same title for his work was a conscious one.
[13] Phil. 4:7
[14] Mt 7:14
[15] Thich Nhat Hanh, *Interbeing* (1987) Parallax Press: Berkeley
[16] A more in-depth discussion of this can be found in Appendix 1

[17] Flavius Josephus, *Antiquities of the Jews* 18.5.2.
[18] Robert W. Funk, & The Jesus Seminar, *The Acts of Jesus: The Search for the Authentic Deeds of Jesus.* Harper, "John the Baptist" cameo, 1988, 268.
[19] Stephen L. Harris, *Understanding the Bible.* Mayfield, 1985,.382. and Marshall, I.H., Millard, A.R, Packer, J.I., eds. "John the Baptist". *New Bible Dictionary* (Third ed.). IVP reference collection, 1988.
[20] This suggests John was not an Essene as they were well known for wearing pure white robes.

11

Kenosis: Zazen and Centering Prayer

"He made himself nothing." (Phil. 2:7). Here Paul used the Greek word *kenoō* (to make empty) from which we get the term *kenosis* as an expression of Christ's practice of self-emptying. The little said about Christ's view on prayer and meditation reveals he had strong views about it:

> [5] *"And when you pray, do not be like the hypocrites, for they love to pray standing in the synagogues and on the street corners to be seen by others. Truly I tell you, they have received their reward in full.* [6] *But when you pray, go into your room, close the door and pray to your Father, who is unseen. Then your Father, who sees what is done in secret, will reward you.* [7] *And when you pray, do not keep on babbling like pagans, for they think they will be heard because of their many words.* [8] *Do not be like them, for your Father knows what you need before you ask him.* Mt (6:5-8)

Thankfully, we also have some idea of Christ's own practice of prayer and meditation:

[16] *But Jesus often withdrew to lonely places and prayed.* (Lk 5:16)

Some translations say that he withdrew into the wilderness to pray (KJV, NASB), and others say he withdrew to deserted places (ISV). In Mark we have further support for this practice of prayer and meditation:

> [35] *Very early in the morning, while it was still dark, Jesus got up, left the house and went off to a solitary place, where he prayed.* (Mk 1:35)

> And in Mark 6:46: [46] *After leaving them, he went up on a mountainside to pray.*

> And in Luke (6:12): [12] *One of those days Jesus went out to a mountainside to pray, and spent the night praying to God.*

> And Matthew 14:23: [23] *After he had dismissed them, he went up on a mountainside by himself to pray. Later that night, he was there alone*

What Christ did when he withdrew to these solitary places is not recorded, but we have a clear idea that it was likely silent contemplation and prayer. Going to this secluded place was not to be alone, since after his awakening he knew there is no such thing as being alone. Alone, after all, is simply the concatenation of the words "all" and "one" (al-one).

He taught others how to pray with what has become to be known as the "Lord's Prayer" (Mt 6:9, Luke 11:2), although this is not present in the older Gospel of Mark. Although the prayer may be familiar to readers, it is worth reading it again as if for the first time.

It starts with "Our Father"—note, not "*My* Father," but "*Our* Father." This affirms a repeated theme in Christ's teaching of The Way: namely, that the journey of The Way is from being a child of God (a being in creation, ego-centered, dualistic, the self with a small "s"), to becoming a Son (or Daughter) of God (that is, a state of consciousness where you are aware of your oneness with God, the non-dual state that is characterized by "How may I help you?" and is the Self with a large "S").

One can almost see Christ teaching his followers that they are all children of God and can all become a Son (or Daughter) of God. Possibly some responded, "But aren't you the *only* son of the Father?" whereupon Christ perhaps rolled his eyes and said, "Once again, God is *our* Father, not just *my* Father." Even though this clear statement of absolute equality is enshrined in the prayer he taught, still the drive to pedestalize the man Jesus as a divine figure, standing above and apart from we mere mortals, leads many to overlook the very start of the prayer he taught.

It continues "Our Father *in Heaven*" We have learned of course that this 'Heaven' of which Christ spoke is not some distant place that one goes to when you die, but rather it is *within you* (Lk 17:21, particularly the King James version[1]). It is a state of consciousness, divine consciousness, that we may all awaken to.

Then in this prayer Christ identified the next key teaching of The Way, namely "Your Kingdom come." This was the much misunderstood part of his teaching that evoked for many at the time that Christ was saying he was the Messiah that had been prophesized from time immemorial who would be a leader for the Jews and bring about a new Jewish state. The prophesized Messiah would be a leader of men, a king bringing about an earthly Kingdom for the Jews. And remember by this time the Jews had jettisoned kings many years before, and had even jettisoned the priestly class, as well.

This was not what Christ was teaching. He never said he had come to be the prophesized Messiah who would be a leader of men, establishing a new earthly Kingdom for the Jews. Rather he was improvising on scripture and re-envisioning the Messianic age as being not a new age for the Jewish peoples, but a new age for all humanity, an age that would be characterized by the emergence of a Kingdom of God, not a Kingdom of man. Clarified thus, it becomes readily apparent Christ wasn't saying he was the head of this new Kingdom (as the anticipated Messiah would be), but rather it is a Kingdom of God with "Our Father" as the King or Lord, not a human like Jesus the Christ.

But as often happened with Christ's teachings, this aspect of what he was saying was misunderstood. It is a pity that there is not a better word for "Kingdom" since it evokes such a masculine concept that echoes for us oppressive regimes by tyrants and despots. Perhaps "Realm" is similar but more neutral. To complicate matters, as was his usual practice Christ was talking in metaphor. Indeed, metaphor on top of metaphor, since he clearly didn't mean a Kingdom as such (in the earthly human sense), and he didn't mean king nor did he mean father in the exclusive sense implying men to be superior to women.

What he was referring to by this realm is a state of being in oneness with God, awake to your True Self: non-dual awareness, rather than being stuck in the dualism of "me" and "you," "us" and "them." Just as Zen teaches us that there is nothing to realize, nothing to gain, since we are already awake, already Buddha, just so in Christ's The Way teaching we are all in this Heavenly Realm already: we just have to awaken to that fact.

"Your Kingdom come," then, might better be translated as *"Your Realm is here, now, may it be realized."* And of course, what follows in the prayer is a very central part of his The Way teaching: *"Your will be done, on earth as it is in Heaven."* It is amazing that each day people around the world say these words without stopping to ponder what they mean.

This is the core teaching he repeated over and again: in order to enter the state of consciousness he called Heaven within you need to align your will with God's will. To do this you must experience *metanoia.* That is, you need to have a mystical experience, go beyond (*meta*) thought (*noia*). As you will recall, this is the term grossly mistranslated as "repent" in many Bibles as part of an invention of a sin-based theology, quite probably the biggest translation error in the entire New Testament.

To mix the Zen and theistic terms, what he is asking people to pray for is to align the *absolute* (divine) with the *relative* (temporal, human earthly realm of "things"). Achieving this, he taught, is becoming one with your ground of being, one with God, realizing your Buddha nature. When you do this, your will aligns with God's will. In Zen terms, awaken to your Buddha-nature, become fully aware of the absolute and the relative (the 360 point in the prior circle diagram), and right action, right conduct and right speech will naturally follow. Sounds easy doesn't it? But the gate is narrow, remember, and few can pass through.

The first four lines of the prayer thus summarize key points of Christ's The Way teachings—the spiritual or theological portion of the prayer. What follows is the practical portion that deals with the everyday reality of being human. To ask for bread to eat—for basic sustenance—to forgive us as we forgive others, help us not fall into temptation and help us to avoid "evil" ("live" written backwards remember: that is, wrong thought, wrong conduct, wrong action).[2]

There we have it, around 20-30 seconds of word-based prayer. What then? And do we sincerely believe this is what Christ himself prayed when he went alone to those secluded places to pray in secret? Perhaps, but regardless, this word-based part of the instruction to prayer is over in a matter of seconds. But in his teachings, accompanying this request to say just one prayer, is an admonishment not to pray like the others do—selfishly asking for things, for personal benefit rather than that of others, and so on. Your Father knows what you want or need better than you, so you do not need to tell him. And most certainly not to do it out loud in public as Christ saw others doing.

We need to review the scripture well known to Christ and his followers to more fully appreciate the context here of the instruction to pray in secret and not to speak out loud. Praying out loud was common in the ancient world, and indeed was clearly still common in Christ's day, too. But it would have been well known to at least his Jewish followers that there is a famous reference in the Hebrew Bible (Old Testament) to silent prayer:

> [12] *As she kept on praying to the LORD, Eli observed her mouth.* [13] *Hannah was praying in her heart, and her lips were moving but her voice was not heard. Eli thought she was drunk* (1 Sam 1:12-13)

It is probably mere coincidence, but scholars believe the Book of Samuel was written around 630-540 B.C.E., which would put it within a hundred years or so of the birth and life of the Buddha (c. 400 B.C.E.-480 B.C.E.). As an emphasis arose in the East to sit in silent meditation, so the phenomenon of praying silently arose in the Middle East, too. But regardless, the special place of silent prayer or meditation was deeply appreciated by the time of Christ.

This would be an appropriate moment to clarify that what Eastern traditions call meditation tends to be known as contemplation in the Christian tradition, and vice versa. Thus, while mediation is usually thought of in Zen and other Eastern traditions as the act of sitting silently, in Christianity it has been more usual to term this (silent) contemplation. By contrast, Christians have tended to talk of mediation as something that is done on a subject or topic, hence, we talk of meditating *on* a passage from the Bible or meditating *on* love.

That clarified, there were at least four key forces influencing Christ's view of silent prayer and contemplation: they are the Jewish tradition that included Hannah's prayer; Christ's obvious awareness of Mahayana Buddhist traditions and practice (as shown by his use of Buddhist parables); Christ's familiarity through John the Baptist and others of the first century Gnostic, Essene and other ascetic practices; and, finally, the ever pervasive presence of Hellenist thought including the fledgling beginnings of what would come to be known as Neoplatonism.

Of course, as we have seen earlier, these are not distinct influences but rather interconnected ways of thought and practice, and each probably influenced the other. Gnosticism arose in the first century C.E. as Christianity was being birthed and as Mahayana Buddhism was spreading throughout the Middle East. Some have suggested that Gnosticism has its roots partly in Buddhism and perhaps Hinduism; others argue for the influence of Platonism.[3] Certainly, the Gnostic emphasis on illusion and enlightenment evokes parallels with both Buddhism and Platonism (and as we have discussed, it is probable that Platonism, and particularly Neoplatonism, itself was influenced by Buddhism). During this period a high degree of syncretism is very likely during this period.

The Essenes are also a likely influence on Christ since much of what they espoused and taught matches Christ's teachings closely. We have some historic knowledge of the Essenes and know they grew in popularity from around a hundred years or so before Christ on in to the first century C.E. Once again, their emergence roughly tracks the emergence of Mahayana Buddhism in this same period.

Jospehus, the Jewish historian, writes that the Essenes flourished in Roman Judea at the time of Christ. Certainly, while they were not as numerous as either the Sadduces or the Pharisees, they numbered in the thousands. Pliny the Elder first recorded detailed information about the Essenes, reporting that they lived simply in communities, that their leaders were known as contemplatives, favored having no money or possessions. He said they ritually immersed themselves in water each morning and emphasized benevolence and charity.[4]

Indeed, Bratton[5] notes that one early leader of the Essenes ("The Teacher of Righteousness") sounds a lot like Christ:

> *The Teacher of Righteousness of the Scrolls would seem to be a prototype of Jesus, for both spoke of the New Covenant; they preached a similar Gospel; each was regarded as a Savior or Redeemer; and each was condemned and put to death by reactionary factions...We do not know whether Jesus was an Essene, but some scholars feel that he*

was at least influenced by them."

Of course, it would be natural to ask the question whether John the Baptist was an Essene. After all, like the Essenes he emphasized baptism and asceticism. We cannot know with any certainty, but it seems likely he was not since Essenes appear to have kept themselves separate from general society and would not have been out and about preaching as we are told John was. That said, it is entirely possible that John was influenced by the Essenes and borrowed some of their basic practices (notably immersion in water) and teachings to spread as a lone hermit rather than as part of an established community.

What all these first century Jewish groups had in common, though, aside from asceticism and eschewing personal possessions, was a focus on contemplation, silence and a spiritual practice that involved withdrawal from society to contemplate. Surprisingly, little detail of precisely what these groups practiced exists in the texts, but we can triangulate their approach to prayer from what we do know. They were referred to as "contemplatives:" they emphasized hermit like living and solitary practice, and nowhere is it written that they prayed out loud to themselves (as if chanting, or etc.).

From all this, we can conclude with some reasonable certainty that there was a general focus on silent prayer or contemplation in these communities and the practices they encouraged in their members. Such contemplative practices were also associated with Platonists and the Hellenistic Stoics. Both these Greek groups spoke of a God within that one should commune with. And as Pieter W van der Horst wrote in his article titled *Silent Prayer in Antiquity*:[6]

"Communing with a God who is within you can be accomplished without words, say the Stoics."

What is also compelling is that practices that had their beginnings around the time of Christ went on to teach the practice of silent prayer and contemplation specifically. Particularly, for instance, they taught the emerging practice of *via negativa* which had its roots in ascetic practices and was later characterized by such seminal works as the 14th century *The Cloud of Unknowing*. Evelyn Underhill tells us that *The Cloud* was based on the mystical writings of Pseudo-Dionysius the Areopagite, specifically and on Christian Neoplatonism generally.

Pseudo-Dionysius was an anonymous Christian philosopher active around late 600 to early 700 C.E. known for a set of works, the *Corpus Dionysiacum*. He took his name from the Athenian convert "Dionysius" who Paul mentioned in Acts 17:34—hence he added the term "pseudo" since he was not alleging that the author of the works was that actual person mentioned in Acts. The basic ideas espoused in *The Cloud* can also be traced back to the *Confessions of St. Augustine* written between 397 and 400 C.E.

Thus, while we cannot trace the arc exactly for a tradition of silent prayer and contemplation from the time before Christ through to Christ's teachings, we can trace a solid history of the practice in the Middle East from ancient Jewish tradition, through the practices of first century ascetics, on to the later traditions of silent prayer and contemplation in the various Christian monastic traditions. These contemplative traditions culminate in Father Thomas Keating's Centering Prayer[7] and the revitalization of kenotic practice in this book[8] as the confluence of the silent prayer taught in *The Cloud of*

Unknowing and Zen meditation.

The *via negativa*, also known as apophatic theology, is often associated with mysticism and mystical experience. It is a way that realizes that ultimate truth cannot be described in words. Hence, this approach is associated with reports of experiences of oneness with God, or oneness with everything (to use non-theological language) rather than intellectual description or speculation about the nature of God or oneness with God. The use of words, and in particular, the converse *kataphatic* theology (or *cataphatic*, "positive way"), seeks to describe the ultimate reality using positive attributes such as "God is love," or "God is good."

In the writings of Pseudo-Dionysius, he emphasized the importance of both ways of approaching understanding or appreciation of the divine. He saw the *kataphatic* approach as an affirmative way of understanding transcendence using positive attributes, and the apophatic way as stressing God's absolute transcendence and unknowability. Why this is of interest to us here is that what he wrote has parallels with Zen: just as he wrote that it is ultimately important to "understand" God as both *imminent* (known, named) and *transcendent* (unknowable), in Zen we have the parallel of the *relative* (the named; dualism) and the *absolute* (beyond naming or before thought; non-dualism).

Closely aligned with *via negativa* as a parallel "way" to approach the ultimate is *agnosticism*. In modern parlance, agnosticism may invoke the idea of "atheist-lite" or even "believer-lite." Indeed, many even confuse agnosticism with atheism, merging both into the category of "nonbeliever." Agnosticism conjures up the image of someone who is not quite sure about God: "Maybe I believe in God; maybe I don't. I not sure." But that isn't technically what agnosticism means and did not mean that when the discipline or movement started millennia ago.

Strictly speaking, agnosticism is the view that God, the ground of being, or the ultimate nature of reality (whatever term works best for you), is essentially unknowable. Hence the agnostic seeker in the first century use of the term has much in common with the apophatic seeker who also considers God or the ultimate reality to be unknowable and not capable of being described in words. This has a direct parallel in Zen to what we refer to as “don’t know mind,” or “beginners mind”—the state of being before thought (or beyond thought; we are back again to Jesus’ *metanoia*).

These practices, or “ways,” of *via negativa* and *agnosis* were not rare or fringe views. On the contrary some of the better-known theologians, monks, sages, saints, and mystics of the past two thousand years have followed one of these paths. And of course, they formed the basis of both the works of Pseudo-Dionysius and the author of the classic text *The Cloud of Unknowing*.

While the basic ideas behind apophatic thought substantially predate the time of Christ, what is of particular interest is that some scholars such as Diedre Carabine[9] argue that as a practice, it really got underway with Philo of Alexandria who lived from around 20 B.C.E. to about 50 C.E. He was a Hellenistic Jewish philosopher who was based in Alexandria which at that time was in the Roman province of Egypt.

Why this is especially interesting is that this is also precisely when Buddhism was flourishing in Alexandria, and of course apophatic views, like the emergence of Mahayana Buddhism, overlapped exactly with the life of Christ. Moreover, both these movements—the growing Mahayana

Buddhist movement and the apophatic one—were spreading throughout Palestine at the exact time when Christ was absorbing every religious way and philosophy he could as he sought revelation and thereafter prepared to teach.

This is doubly important since Philo is known for synthesizing Jewish scripture and Greek Stoic philosophy, and the *Logos* as an aspect of God which of course found its way into the Gospel of John was his idea. While some dispute it, Philo seems to have had a sizable influence over early Christianity since the *Logos*, God's shadow, God's firstborn son, the demiurge of the world, next only to God himself, is Philo's concept, one which the writer of John drew heavily on.

But such rumination can be a distraction from a more important point: namely that Philo was integrating Jewish scripture and stoicism. For many, stoicism brings to mind an ethical system encouraging someone to live a good life free of moral corruption. But what is less often emphasized is that Stoics believed in practicing spiritual exercises including self-dialogue, contemplation of one's mortality, and—most important—training the mind to be fully present in the moment. This Stoic contemplation practice, as later described by writers such as Marcus Aurelius, sounds a lot like Buddhist mindfulness meditation.[10]

Thus we have the philosophical thought arising in the Hellenistic world of the nature of the One, starting with Plato, being developed by the likes of Philo, and leading to the seminal works of Proclus[11] in the fifth century where Neoplatonic views start to have greater and greater influence on Early Christianity. But during the time of Christ, there was this emergence of the pre-Neoplatonic era where many of the ideas later developed by Pseudo Dionysius and others had their beginnings.

It is this school of thought espoused by Philo and others, that emphasized the idea of *God within* and of silent meditation to focus the mind on the present moment: focus the mind on being at one with God, meditating in silence. With this view of the divine came the idea that there is The One, and that it is the ultimate goal of a spiritual path to become one with The One.

As I mentioned before, Pieter van der Horst said in his *Silent Prayer in Antiquity*, *"Communing with a God who is within you can be accomplished without words, say the Stoics."*[12] Thus, while we lack written evidence of the exact practice of prayer and meditation Christ used when he withdrew to one of his solitary places, we do know that he was influenced by Buddhism, the Jewish Wisdom tradition (including the ways of the ascetics) along with the Hellenistic thought of the Stoics and the early stages of what came to be known as Neoplatonism (or, specifically, Christian Neoplatonism). And each of these ways or philosophies urged the use of silent meditation or focusing of the mind on the present moment in order to seek spiritual revelation or oneness.

Regarding silent prayer and meditation, we have an arc we can draw from the time before Christ with Platonic ideas and the Stoics, through the works of Philo and the emergence in parallel at this time of Mahayana Buddhism in Alexandria (where Philo was also based), through the Jewish Wisdom tradition of the first century, through practices such as Hesychasm, and on through the Neoplatonist tradition in the centuries that followed, on through to the writing of *The Cloud of Unknowing*. *The Cloud* was the ultimate guide to contemplative prayer of medieval times, which was merged with Zen to create modern day Centering Prayer practice and led to the current revival of kenotic practices as are presented later in this book.

Hesychasm is a contemplative prayer practice established within the Eastern Orthodox Church. The term means to keep stillness and has its roots in the synoptic Gospels where Christ advises going to a room and praying to your Father in secret (Mt 6:6). The origins of the practice date back to the writings of the Christian monk and mystic, Evagrius Ponticus (345-399 C.E.), and Maximus the Confessor (580-662 C.E.). Others using the term in the early church include St. John Chrysostom and the Cappadocians, and it is mentioned in the *Sayings of the Desert Fathers* (approx. 5th century).

The goal of this form of mystical contemplation is to attain union with God (*Theosis*). The three phases of the practice include *Katharsis* (purification), *Theoria* (illumination) and then finally *Theosis* (union with God). Key to this practice is the use of the Jesus Prayer: *"Lord Jesus Christ, son of God, have mercy on me, a sinner."* Repetition of this phrase is used to move the contemplative through the stages until, at *Theosis,* there is oneness with God that is spoken of in terms of God as light, so-called "uncreated light," which they also identify with the Holy Spirit. Very often, Hesychasts (as practitioners are known) live a life of hermits and devote themselves completely to this mystical path.

The Cloud of Unknowing is a good early source of guidance on how to engage in contemplation. The *Cloud* espouses a mystical approach to Christianity that sees God as beyond knowing and encourages the follower to abandon the ego to a state of consciousness best described as "unknowing." If this route is followed, the author suggests, then one may gain a glimpse of the true nature of God, become one with God.

Clearly, *The Cloud* draws heavily on the *via negativa* school, and has much in common with the earlier apophatic tradition that came about in the time of Christ. Thus, here is a tradition from the 14th century that has its roots in the writings of St, Augustine and Pseudo Dionysius, who influenced the likes of St John of the Cross, Nicholas of Cusa and Teilhard de Chardin.

We don't know who wrote *The Cloud*. It seems fitting that it drew in large part on the works of Pseudo-Dionysius who also remained anonymous. It is open to speculation, but perhaps in both cases the writers feared retribution for writing what some might call heretical works. *The Cloud* encourages abandoning thought so as to reach a state of unknowing in which one may commune with the divine. This "*cloud of unknowing,*" as the writer calls it, is referred to as a darkness that is between you and God stopping you from seeing the divine clearly and directly.

The work recommends focusing on a single word as a way to entering into stillness and full contemplation:

> *"We must pray, then, with all the intensity of our being in its height and depth and length and breadth. And not with many words but in a little word of one syllable."*[13]

He goes on to clarify which words he recommends be used and settles on "God" and "sin." He elaborates that no two other words so succinctly sum up the totality of being, the essentially good and the essentially bad. Moreover, he advises that having chosen a word you should repeat it with "intensity" which evokes a kind of mantra practice where a phrase or word is repeated over and again. However, he makes clear that this repetition is of a contemplative nature, not the fast-paced repetition sometimes used in Hindu or Muslim chanting.

Elsewhere the author of *The Cloud* says:

> *"Contemplatives rarely pray in words, but if they do, their words are few. The fewer the better, as a matter of fact; yes, a word of one syllable is more suited to the spiritual nature of this work than longer ones."* (95)

Here he likens sin to being a 'lump' and describes the demeanor of one who is in contemplation as seeming completely relaxed and peaceful:

> *"For I believe that a dark generalized awareness of sin (intending only yourself but in an undefined way, like a lump) should incite you to the fury of a caged wild animal. Anyone looking at you, however, would not notice any change in your expression, and suppose that you are quite calm and composed. Sitting, walking, lying down, resting, standing, or kneeling, you would appear completely relaxed and peaceful."* (94-95)

The writer also recommends moderation and adopting contemplation as central to one's way of life:

> *"That by having no moderation in contemplation a man will arrive at perfect moderation in everything else."* (p 101, header to chapter 42) *"That a man must lose the radical self-centered awareness of his own being if he will reach the heights of contemplation in this life."* (102, header to chapter 43)

Then continuing in chapter 43 he introduces what he calls the "*cloud of forgetting*:"

"Be careful to empty your mind and heart of everything except God during the time of this work. Reject the knowledge and experience of anything less than God, treading it all down beneath the cloud of forgetting." ... "And now also you must learn to forget not only every creature and its deeds but yourself as well, along with whatever you may have accomplished in God's service. For a true lover not only cherishes his beloved more than himself but in a certain sense he becomes oblivious of himself on account of the one he loves."

And then he introduces the idea of "naked knowing" and the goal of destroying the self (ego) as being a state of pure love:

"Long after you have successful forgotten every creature and its works, you will find that a naked knowing and feeling of your own being still remains between you and your God. And believe me, you will not be perfect in love until this, too, is destroyed."

And then chapter 44, he gives a description of how the self (ego) is to be "destroyed" by freedom from knowing, but without self (bodily) harm:

"And yet, in all this, never does he desire to not-be, for this is the devil's madness and blasphemy against Got. In fact, he rejoices that he is and from the fullness of a grateful heart he gives thanks to God for the gift and the goodness of his existence. At the same time, however, he desires unceasingly to be freed from the knowing and the feeling of his being."

Two other notable authors we should consider are Meister Eckhart and more recently still the writings of Angelus Silesius. Meister Eckhart was a Catholic German mystic and theologian who lived from 1260-1328 C.E. His writings are truly remarkable, and I heartily recommend you explore them. Importantly, what he wrote speaks to this topic of discovering God within, and the importance of stillness, quiet and contemplation as the path to God within.

Perusing quotes from his works shows how pertinent they are to this discussion: *"A quiet mind is one which nothing weighs on, nothing worries, which, free from ties and from all self-seeking, is wholly merged into the will of God and dead to its own [will]."*

And a further selection:

> *"Unmovable disinterest brings man into likeness of God ... To be full of things is to be empty of God, to be empty of things is to be full of God." "All that the Eternal Father teaches and reveals is His being, His nature, and His Godhead, which he manifests to us in His Son, and teaches us that we are also His Son."*

Not surprisingly, then, Eckhart favored silent contemplation as a way to seek unity with God. And as you can see, like Christ he emphasized the need to align one's will with God's will and said that we are [God's] Son just as Christ is. It is a revolutionary theological position to take in the Middle Ages. A similar writer worthy of exploration on this topic is Angelus Silesius. He also was a Catholic mystic, and lived from 1624-1677 C.E. Here is a sampling of his poetry:

True prayer requires no word, no chant
no gesture, no sound.
It is communion, calm and still
with our own Godly Ground

God far exceeds all words that we can here express
In silence He is heard, in silence worshiped best

Even before I was me, I was God in God;
And I can be once again, as soon as I am dead to myself

Time is eternity and eternity is time, just as long as you yourself don't make them different

Two eyes our souls possess:
While one is turned on time,
The other seeth things
Eternal and sublime

Thus, we find the arc extending from centuries before Christ, through the Middle Ages to the Renaissance and beyond, with a repeated focus on the importance of silence in the pursuit of unity with God, and constant theme of self-emptying. Continuing this line through to the present day, we have the work of Father Thomas Keating and the advent of Centering Prayer, and through this book, the revived practice of Kenotic Contemplation/Meditation.

Centering Prayer has its roots in the work of Thomas Keating when he was the abbot of St. Joseph's Abbey in Spencer, Massachusetts from 1961-1981. During the latter period of his tenure as abbot he and his fellow monks invited a Zen master to introduce them to the idea of a "sesshin" (week-long intensive retreat) and from this, coupled with reviving the ideas in *The Cloud of Unknowing*, Buddhist Zen meditation evolved into Centering Prayer.

While we shall explore it in more depth in the next chapter, it is tempting to liken the kind of meditation that Christ himself practiced to Zazen. While we can never know precisely how he practiced, as we have discussed he favored retreating to a secluded place and sitting in silence. His repeated invitation to align your will with God's will, and the need to achieve *metanoia* in order to enter Heaven within, and his general admonition not to pray out loud, is all suggestive of a silent form of prayerful meditation. In the next chapter we shall explore this and tease out the difference between Centering Prayer and Kenotic Meditation as practices to follow in replicating Christ's "The Way."

---

[1] *"Neither shall they say, Lo here! or, lo there! for, behold, the Kingdom of God is within you."* (Luke 17:21, KSV)

[2] It is arguable it is all spiritual since "bread" could also refer to Christ's teaching, and atonement together with forgiveness are key parts of a spiritual practice. Christ clearly played with the symbolism of bread as manna from Heaven, here for him in the form of teachings, the word of God: "Man shall not live on bread alone, but on every word that comes from the mouth of God." Mt. 4:4

[3] For instance, see Pagels, Elaine (1989). *The Gnostic Gospels* New York: Random House.

[4] Pliny the Elder. *Historia Naturalis.* V 17 or 29.

[5] Fred Gladstone Bratton, *A History of the Bible*. Boston: Beacon Press, 1967, 79-80

[6] Pieter W van der Horst. *Silent Prayer in Antiquity* in the journal *Numen*, Vol 41 No 1 Jan 1994, pp 1-25.

[7] Thomas Keating, *Intimacy with God* New York: Crossroads Publishing, 1994

[8] See the final chapter of this book.

[9] Deidre Carabine, *The Unknown God: Negative Theology in the Platonic Tradition*, Wipf and Stock Publishers, 2015.

[10] *Meditations*, a series of writings by Marcus Aurelius, a Roman Emperor from 161 to 180 C.E.
[11] Carobine, *ibid.*
[12] Horst, *Silent Prayer*
[13] William Johnston, (Ed.) *The Cloud of Unknowing* Doubleday. 1973, Ch 37, 97.

12

Christ and The Way: Practicing the Teachings in Everyday Life

There are two ways you can explore "The Way" in your daily life, one as a lay follower, and the other as a more serious student of The Way. For the latter you would need to work with a teacher. While we cannot know in detail exactly what The Way was comprised of for Christ's followers, we can recreate a good model or facsimile, one that is rooted in first century teaching and tradition but updated for our time.

Regardless of how seriously you wish to explore The Way, there are going to be common elements: reading teachings in their various forms (ancient and modern), practicing *kenosis* (self-emptying) by establishing a routine of daily contemplation, and becoming a member of a group that is also following The Way. And, again, if you wish to pursue The Way more seriously then identifying a teacher or mentor to work with will be essential.

Daily Contemplation Practice

While the Gospels do not detail the frequency with which Christ prayed, or how he suggested his followers pray, he was a Jew and at that time praying three times a day was standard. Whether you are looking to be a casual follower of the The Way or dig far deeper into the teaching, you will want to try to establish a discipline of daily contemplation. This practice should ideally include a morning session, a midday session, and an evening session.

Many of us live busy lives, and it may seem difficult to establish a routine that includes meditating three times a day. But if you can do so, the benefits can be disproportionately great compared with the time expended. If three sessions in a day does not fit with your schedule, then I highly recommend you at least aim for a daily routine of a morning and an evening session. That said, bear in mind that your midday session could literally be 1-5 minutes long. You may be surprised what benefits can come from even such a brief daily session and how it can immensely help cope with what the day may bring us.

However, this is not a competition to see who can meditate the longest or the most frequently. Nor does meditating several times a day, every day, make you a "better" person than those who do not. I can assure you, however, that there are significant benefits to establishing a consistent meditation practice. Thus, even if the times you set aside for contemplation are short, it is more important that you be consistent than that you find extended periods of time for your practice.

You'll see that in the above I alternated between using different words like prayer, meditation and contemplation. This is deliberate: in The Way there must be recognition that each of us may have baggage associated with one or more of these terms, and thus in a sense some terms need to be interchangeable. You need to use the term you are most comfortable with. For some the word 'prayer' may have negative connotations of a male-centered theology, of petitionary prayer where you are asking God for things you want, so a different term like contemplation or meditation may be more palatable.

Yet others may be triggered by terms like meditation or contemplation. We have discussed before how the Eastern traditions refer to sessions of sitting in silence as 'meditation' whereas in the West, that has often been called 'contemplation' with meditation being reserved for the act of meditating *on* something. Again, whichever terms works best for you. These are ultimately all only words, signifiers that are essentially empty. That said, we need to be aware that certain words carry baggage or can trigger people, and I hope my using these terms interchangeably is acceptable.

As to how long to set aside for your daily practice, that will be up to you to determine what is comfortable: what works for you. As a bare minimum, your morning and evening sessions should be at least around fifteen to twenty minutes, and the midday session at least five to ten minutes. If you are able and feel called to it, then a more serious practice would involve forty-minute sessions morning and evening, and a thirty-minute session in the middle of the day.

Kenosis or Centering Prayer?

Centering Prayer draws on the practice recommended in *The Cloud of Unknowing* combined with elements drawn from Buddhist meditation practices. However, we have no evidence that Christ himself had a practice that involved using such words; rather aside from the specific prayer he taught, the suggestion is that he 'prayed' in complete (internal and external) silence. This version of the practice we call *kenosis*: silent, wordless meditation/contemplation. Whether you opt for one or the other, or for a practice that mixes the two forms, is entirely up to you—the two practices are very similar.

Centering Prayer

Centering prayer is associated with Fr. Thomas Keating, a Cistercian monk and former abbot of St Joseph's Abbey in Spencer, Massachusetts. In his book *Intimacy with God*, Keating acknowledges the source of the practice is in *The Cloud of Unknowing* combined with techniques he learned when doing sitting meditation with Zen Buddhists. He recounts how the abbey entertained a Zen master who introduced the monks to the idea of a 'sesshin'—a week-long intensive retreat. To use Fr. Keating's language, he sees Centering Prayer as choosing a word that "represents our intention to consent to God's presence and action within us." For some this language may work well, for others more non-dualistic language that affirms an aspiration to recognize (awaken to) unity might work better.

He summarizes the key elements of Centering Prayer thus:[1]

1. Choose a sacred word as a symbol of your intention to consent to God's presence and action within.
2. Sitting comfortably and with eyes closed, settle briefly and silently introduce the sacred word.
3. When you become aware of your thoughts, ever-so-gently return to the sacred word.
4. At the end of the prayer period, remain in silence with your eyes closed for a couple of minutes.

The sacred words he suggests include "God," "abba," "Jesus," and "peace." It is important, of course, that you select a word that does not trigger you or cause you to start thinking. Afterall, the purpose of the chosen word is to settle the mind, not agitate it or provoke more thoughts. I am also aware that readers of this book may include non-Christians or those who may style themselves as "spiritual but not religious" (one of the fastest growing demographics in the U.S. and Britain, as well as elsewhere worldwide) for whom the language used may be an issue.

You may thus find that words such as "now," "here," or "silence" may be better choices for you. Some have found that a variation of Psalm 46:10 works well for them—either as what they say as their sacred 'word' or what they say in preparation for sitting Centering Prayer, especially when sitting as a group:

Be still, and know I am God
Be still, and know I am
Be still, and know
Be still
Be

Indeed, some of my students have found this works well for their midday practice: to sit quietly for a moment, then slowly say this series of words (silently or quietly out loud), and then sit for a couple minutes longer. It is quick, usually no more than five minutes in all, and yet can be a very effective dipping into the deep, refreshing well of silence within.

Practical advice on practice

Establishing a routine that you can adhere to is very important. For this reason, I do not recommend pushing yourself beyond what you are comfortable doing, since doing less on a regular basis is more important than doing more but sporadically. So, first determine how long you intend to sit for and how many times a day. And I say "intend" deliberately here, since setting intentions is a core part of The Way.

Second, establish a place you will do your practice: at home, if you can, set aside an area where you can be in quiet and not disturbed. By all means, do whatever you feel comfortable doing to make this area a 'sacred space.' What that means is entirely up to you: for some it is having a comfortable chair, for others a cushion on the floor. For some, it is creating a kind of altar or a table with some calming items on it such as a small flower arrangement, some item that invokes peaceful thoughts in you, perhaps a candle.

On a practical note, you will want to identify a way to time your sessions. For most of us these days this involves using the timer on our smart phone, or an app that can both time a session and have gentle sounds such as bells or bowls to mark the start and end of the period.[2] Wearing relaxing clothing can also be useful and you may wish to explore the variety of meditation and yoga clothing on sale to see if something in particular works for you.

Of course, your middle of the day session, if that is part of your daily routine, may be at work or somewhere else you have less control over where you can meditate. If possible, try to still find somewhere quiet away from others. But just go with what is possible—I have had students who are nurses or doctors and who do their midday session at their computer stations on the ward or in their breakroom. Others can leave their place of work and go to a nearby park, or some other place more conducive to sitting in silence. Whatever works for you.

Kenosis (Kenotic Meditation/Contemplation)

This book introduces an alternative to Centering Prayer, one that I believe is closer to the practice Christ himself used: I call it simply *kenosis* or Kenotic Meditation. This alternative practice is the kind I recommend for my students who wish to delve deeper into The Way. Centering Prayer can help with relaxation and, to a degree, communing with the ground of your being, but it is less likely than *kenosis* in my experience to help you realize a *metanoia* moment.[3]

Kenosis involves a focus on self-emptying, and on being fully present to God in the moment. A single word can fill your being and completely distract you from this moment, from union with the ground of being. For this reason, we do not use words while practicing *kenosis*. The other aspect that differentiates *kenosis* from Centering Prayer is the goal of being fully awake in God in the moment, and for this reason we employ all the senses and do not close our eyes. The other reason we do not close our eyes is that this leads to a greater tendency to doze off, have a waking dream, or to just drift.

That said, we do not keep our eyes wide open either. Rather, you should have your eyes about half open, look roughly forty-five degrees down, and hold a soft gaze. This soft gaze is slightly unfocused, rather than focusing sharply on a spot on the floor or whatever is in front of you, since the idea is not to be concentrating on an object or a specific spot but rather to be fully open to all the senses.

How you sit is important, even more important for *kenosis* as you will usually be sitting for longer periods than in Centering Prayer sessions. The overriding consideration is that you sit comfortably in a way that, for you, remains comfortable for extended periods of time. You should also sit so as to promote being full awake, and for this reason you will need to sit upright, spine straight but comfortably so (don't sit such that you are straining to keep your back straight).

Your shoulders should be relaxed, and your head upright but tilted forward slightly (chin in) so that your gaze can naturally fall about forty-five degrees down. It may help to imagine a string attached to the center of the top of your head as if someone is pulling very gently on it to keep your head upright without straining to do so.

Next, we come to what you sit on, in what posture, and how you hold your hands. Because of the influence of Eastern practices, you may associate sitting for meditation as being crossed legged, on a cushion on the floor. In the East, sitting on the floor crossed legged is a cultural norm in most societies. In the West this is less common since many of us are used to sitting on a chair. There is nothing inherently more "spiritual" or closer to God about sitting on a cushion on the floor, so if sitting in a chair is what works for you, that's absolutely fine. There are a number of postures that can work well:

If you are sitting crossed legged on a cushion, then there are some scientific reasons why if you're able to cross your legs fully that can help you sit longer without back pain. You may have heard this being called "full lotus" (the first image on the left above). It does have the advantage of creating a more perfect stable triangle to help your posture during a longer period of contemplation. Second best is to cross one leg over the other (so called "half lotus"), and next best is to tuck the legs in with each other as in the upper right image (so called "Burmese" posture).

Others find kneeling to be the best for them. You can kneel on your legs but be aware this can lead to your legs "going to sleep" because you're cutting off their circulation to them. It is better to either sit on a small stool (see the lower left image above) or perhaps on a cushion that is placed on its side (lower middle image). This of course is the position in which many in the West feel most comfortable, sitting in a chair.

If you are sitting on a cushion, then you should sit on the edge of it so that you're using a forty-five-degree angle of the cushion edge to create a more natural arch to your lower back. This also helps keep your chest open, and generally helps you feel more relaxed. As I mentioned above, your shoulders should be relaxed, drawn slightly back and down. Your chin should be tucked in a little—as with other aspects of your posture, you may wish to experiment with what works best for you. Your jaw should be free of tension so check that you are not clenching your teeth. Your tongue should be gently resting on the roof of your mouth, tip touching the back of the upper teeth. Finally, if sitting in a chair then your feet should be shoulder width apart, legs at a right angle to the floor, feet flat on the floor.

Returning to the question of your gaze for a moment: ideally for *kenosis* you should have your eyes about half open, looking with a soft gaze about forty-five-degrees down. But if you find that, at least at first, you can relax better with your eyes closed then do so. Ideally, in time, if you do start with your eyes closed then I would invite you to switch to opening them halfway and experiment with what difference this makes to your contemplation sessions. Again, our goal with *kenosis* is to become fully awake in God, in unity, in the moment, embodying "don't know mind."

The *Kenosis* Session

You can of course do *kenosis* on your own or in a group. Indeed, I strongly recommend finding a group to meet with on a regular basis (weekly if possible). If you are unable to find a group offering *kenosis* or Centering Prayer, then you may seek out a Zen meditation group as being the most similar. Zen meditation (also known as Zazen) is also silent, and so a Zen session can be a good fit for someone practicing *kenosis*.

For your regular daily practice, you have hopefully set aside an area of your house to be able to sit quietly without distraction. As we discussed above, you have also hopefully done something to make this area a "sacred" space in some sense of that term to you. Enter this space, or the gathering room if this is a group session, reverently as if treading on holy ground. Since, in a real sense, that is what you are doing.

Facing your chair of cushion, put your hands together as if in prayer, chest level, and make a slight bow of reverence to your chair or cushion.

Then turn round with your back to the chair or cushion, retaining your praying hand position, and make a slight bow again. On your own this is to the room (or to the universe); in a group this is to the other sitting in contemplation with you. Now, gently sit and make yourself comfortable. At this point when sitting on your own you will be setting the timer for your session. In a group someone can be been assigned this task.

Having settled into a comfortable position, take a moment to run a mental check of all the points above regarding your posture, how you are sitting, relax your shoulders, make sure your tongue is gently in the roof of your mouth, tip resting lightly on the back of your top front teeth. Now take a few deep breaths: breath slowly and deeply from your belly area, not shallow breaths from your chest. It may help to count slowly to five as you breath in, then hold your breath for five, and breath out for five ("one one-thousand, two one-thousand ... etc. to ... five one thousand"). During the session, though, you should be careful to breath naturally—this is not a "yoga style" practice that involves deep breathing or controlled breathing techniques.

As you sit, the goal can be summed up by "Let go and let God." In a real sense, you are aiming to get yourself (the "self" with a small "s") out of the way and become a non-judgmental presence, becoming fully awake to the moment just as it is. As the joke goes, "*God, I prayed to you every day, all day long, and you never answered me!*" to which God responds, "*That's because I couldn't get a word in edge-wise!*"

As Meister Eckhart put it:

> "*There is a huge silence inside each of us that beckons us into itself, and the recovery of our own silence can begin to teach us the language of Heaven.*"

Our goal with *kenosis* isn't to stop our thoughts, but as thoughts come up just observe them like clouds and let them float by. As Shunryu Suzuki wisely said: "*[When meditating] leave your front door and your back door open. Let thoughts come and go. Just don't serve them tea."* The same goes for feelings and emotions: if they arise, just watch them and try not to be triggered by them or let them start your thinking processes.

Now, if you are like most people, letting your thoughts just float by is far easier said than done. For many, thoughts rampage through us constantly, moving from one thought to another at a quick pace. Or we have a pattern of thoughts that we keep going round and round on, in a vicious circle that seems hard to break. "*Did I remember to turn the stove off*?" "*I wonder if I have time to go to the gas station on the way to my next meeting?" "What if I hadn't said that thing to him, maybe he would still be speaking to me..."* And so on. We call this *monkey mind*.

Whereas in Centering Prayer we seek to calm our thoughts by repeating a word to ourselves, in *kenosis* we focus on non-verbal means that do not use words that could trigger further thoughts. For instance, a standard method to rein in monkey mind is to count breaths. What I suggest is to start counting your breaths with a count of one for a complete cycle of in-breath and out-breath, then continue to count to ten. When you get to ten, I recommend starting at one again rather than counting on up to higher numbers. Then, when your thoughts have quietened down a little, try returning to not counting and just breathing naturally.[4]

Just like learning a new physical exercise routine, *kenosis* can take time to accustomed to, but you will improve significantly with experience. By establishing a regular daily routine and practicing consistently, you will be able to get to a point where counting breaths is no longer necessary.

Indeed, one of the major benefits to *kenosis* over Centering Prayer is that by focusing on open-eyed, wordless silent contemplation we can more easily transfer this practice into our every-day life. Ultimately, it becomes possible to practice *kenosis* not just for limited periods in a special space but also to remain in mindful unity with God in all that you do throughout each day. This is a practice not dissimilar to that advocated by the seventeenth century French monk, Brother Lawrence, in his work *The Practice of the Presence of God*.[5]

You might wish to start your meditation session with something that you say—either out loud (particularly if you are in a group) or silently to yourself. This may be a prayer or words that you find helpful to center you ready for a contemplative session. For instance, you may wish to use the variation based on Psalm 46 above. Or, as Christ instructed, you may wish to say what is known as "The Lord's Prayer." I am aware, though, that for some people this prayer runs the gamut from being a central part of their faith to something that they may have issues with due to the male-centered wording.

The Lord's Prayer is not in the Gospel of Mark, but versions of it appear in both Matthew and Luke. This has led scholars to speculate that its origins are in the speculated missing source text "Q" which is thought to mainly be a collection of Christ's sayings. It does not, however, appear in any other text such as the Gospel of Thomas which is otherwise thought to resemble "Q." And Thomas does consistently refer to God, or the supreme being, as "Father."

For some, referring to God as he, or indeed as Father, is problematic for various reasons. God is beyond labels, beyond male and female, and thus is not a "he." In more recent times others have pointed out that for some who have a negative view of a father—perhaps those abused by their fathers, or their fathers left them—it may be difficult to have one's ground of being or higher power referred to as "father," or even as male.

Despite Paul having not met Jesus, and thus not getting his teachings firsthand or quite accurate, there are some "gems" within his letters. For instance, in Galatians Paul says that God does not use a mediator because "God is one," (3:20), and that in Christ[6] "*there is neither Jew nor Gentile...nor is there male and female*" (3:28). And of course, we have Christ himself teaching that everyone is everyone else's brother and sister so long as their will is aligned with God's will (by which they enter the Kingdom of Heaven and become a Son of God/Daughter of God).

While it is understandable that there has been a growing pushback against the use of male terms for God, on the other hand there is poetry in Christ's metaphor of the need to be born again of water/God (the spiritual Father) and Spirit (the feminine aspect of God, God as Mother, Sophia/Wisdom). One contemporary approach—used by many progressive churches—is to convert all male references to God to neutral language, but while it has merit this can lose a key part of Christ's message.

For this reason, to retain the metaphor so central to Christ's teachings, I would advise using both Father and Mother rather than going gender neutral in all our spiritual language. That said, it is equally important to bear in mind that God is beyond sex, beyond gender and thus in instances where it does not make sense to add both Father and Mother (*Abba* and *Amma* in Aramaic) it will be more appropriate to use neutral language stripped of any suggestion God is male. In short, use the wording that works best for you, but bear in mind that words can be powerful—both in their impact on you and on others—so use them mindfully with an eye on the consequence of their use.

That said, I'd draw your attention back to a key teaching of The Way to fully awaken—and that includes fully awakening to both the absolute and the relative. Absolute views of God include God is infinite, God is everywhere, God is everything, God is nothing ("no-thing"), everyone and everything is God, God is Love, and so on. Relative language includes God as Father, God as Mother, God as anything (that is, any language that implies a dualistic view of God as separate from you, separate from any*thing* or any*one*), and so on. In following this path of The Way, you will be fully exploring all of this. The intellect is a useful tool, but it can also be a seductive, deceitful enemy on the path to Truth.

A few more comments here on the language of God: first century Middle Eastern culture was male dominated. Thus, it would have been natural to talk of God as being Love (not as being lov*ing*) and that this Love—*agápe* not *éros*—is like the exceptionally unselfish love a father has for his only begotten son. In more recent times, especially in the West, it might have become more usual to liken this absolute unselfish "Love" as being like that of a mother for her only child.

But even this can be seen as a feature of a male-dominated society that relegates women's role of to that of child-bearer, mother, housewife and so on. In our more enlightened current age we can now understand this extreme unselfish love is like that of any parent for their only child, be those parents male and female, both male, both female, or whatever other gender or sexual identification or orientation the parent(s) may be.

When all else is stripped away—our ego-based view of the world, the world of dualism, and we fully integrate the absolute and the relative—what remains is Love. In Buddhist terms what is left is compassion since most Buddhists prefer the term "compassion" to a concept of unselfish love. This Love—this pure compassion—is who you truly are. It is your True Self, your Christ-nature, your Buddha-nature.

Following the path of The Way

While silent time in your secluded place is central to your practice in this Way, the full teaching has several stages on your journey to Unity. Studying the core teachings, stripped of the post-Easter Jesus language that was added at a later date, should also be central to your path. And as I have mentioned before, this part of your path is best pursued with a teacher or mentor.

The Seven Stations of The Way (or the Seven 'Demons')

If you have spent any length of time studying first century Wisdom Tradition texts and Jewish teachings of that era, you will have noticed how important certain numbers are. In particular the numbers three and seven. Thus, when we read that Mary Magdalene was someone Christ had helped overcome seven demons, we know there is something symbolic in this statement because of the use of the number seven.

In Jewish culture of the first century, three was the number of holiness and love. Hence, twelve was seen as the number for union of the people with God as the product of three and four (it was not coincidental that Christ was said to have twelve disciples). And seven, as the sum of three and four, was the symbol most often associated with all aspects of God—acts of atonement and purification always involved seven sprinklings of water. Most pertinent here, seven was the divine number of completion. Hence to rid someone of seven demons meant to complete something divine with that person, here almost certainly completing a course of teachings, achieving unity.

In various texts we have repeated mention that Mary Magdalene was Christ's most favored disciple, and that she deeply grasped his teachings in a way the other disciples did not. In ancient teachings that substantially pre-date the time of Jesus, a spiritual journey was said to have seven stages (also known as "stations"): these are intention, self-examination, atonement, initial awakening (*metanoia*), oneness (the heart of the secret), the station of freedom (attachment to freedom), and finally The Truth, the Absolute, nonattachment thinking, "this just as it is".

In the context of first century Palestinian culture it is entirely possible that these stations are what was referred to as the demons that Mary Magdalene was relieved of. Each station is like a demon, in that archaic sense of the term: something one needs to expunge. But in reality nothing is gained, nothing is expunged. Eyes are made one, and opened wide, veils are lifted (but there never were veils).

Station 1: Intention

This initial stage is just as simple as it sounds, it is just a matter of setting the intention to follow the path of The Way fully and completely. There is a strong element of discernment in this first phase: is this the right path for you? Is it a good fit for you? During this first phase one will be identifying a teacher or mentor to work with.

Circle of The Way

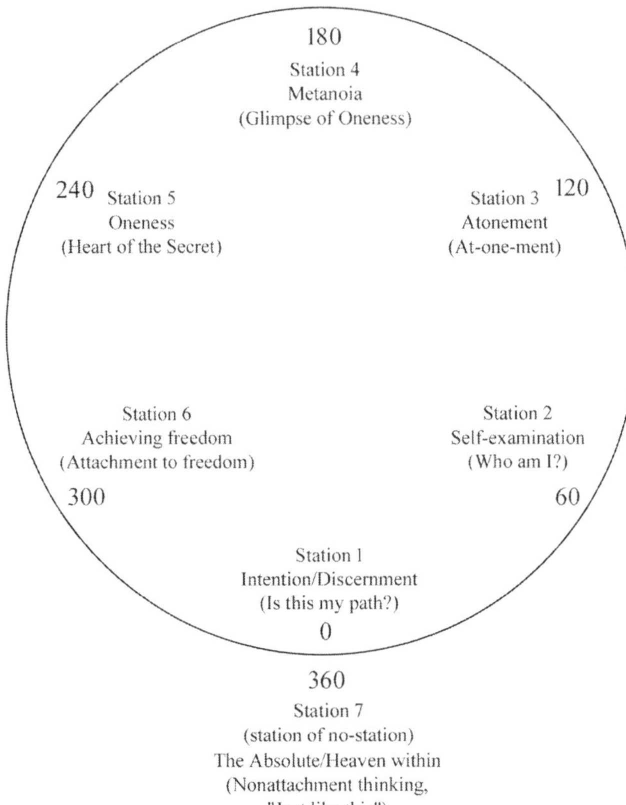

An essential part of this first phase is also setting the clear intention to have helping others be central to your life. If one does not already have some way in which one is helping others as part of one's everyday life, then seek a way to start doing so—either by volunteering your time or by a change of profession. The core of who you truly are is "How may I help you?" and from this first phase onwards you will be seeking ways to uncover this truth in your life.

Station 2: Self-Examination

This phase is a deep dive into the question "Who am I?" in all its meanings and consequences. It is also a reflection on what the word "God" means to you, or what higher power, ground of being, palpable presence, means to you. These questions are related, of course, since the question "Who am I?" includes who do you perceive your 'self' to be (with a small "s") and your "Self" (with a large "S"), your true self? What do these terms mean to you? Again, having a teacher or mentor can be invaluable.

To truly know yourself is to know God: how this counter-intuitive phrase make senses is part of what The Way is all about. Thus, discerning perfectly who you are in this phase is not the goal. Rather it is to take this deep dive and see how far you get. Like many aspects of a spiritual path, this exploration of "Who am I?" will remain a core part of your practice on an ongoing basis, as will cultivating a state of *metanoia*.

The more fully you explore your "self" in this phase the more you will benefit from the practice going forward. Be aware, though, that our intellects and egos are remarkably good at placing blinders on our eyes. We see what we want to see, and what we imagine others see when they look at us. So, start with absolute basics: How tall are you? How old are you? What is your gender? How would you describe yourself and how do you believe others would describe you? What would you say are your main qualities and strengths? What are your least attractive qualities and your weaknesses?

If you haven't done so, consider finding out what your enneagram type is, and if you can take a personality test such as the Myers-Briggs. Ask yourself, "Do you agree with the results? If not, why not? Would you describe yourself as a caring person? If not, why do you think that might be? What would you consider your major sins to be, both past and present?" And here I use the term "sin" in its broadest sense—go beyond what you believe you have been taught the word "sin" to mean. Consider sin to be anything other than your will being aligned with God's will.

This can be murky water, down in the mud and weeds, for most of us. So be gentle with yourself. The idea of this phase isn't to itemize all that is bad about yourself and then beat yourself up about it. Focus equally on your good qualities as much as you are tempted to focus on your "bad" ones. Above all, focus on what you really find to be true, right here right now, in this moment. Not on what you have been told is true, or the image or your "self" that has been constructed by others or by society. That said, ask those closest to you to give a candid summary of how they see you, your strengths and weaknesses. Consider this a fact-finding tour: you are not trying to give yourself a home brewed psychotherapy session: this is about dispassionately, objectively itemizing everything you can respond to the question "Who am I?"

Station 3: Atonement (At-one-ment)

To the casual observer looking at Christianity from outside, it may appear to be a generally pleasant religion that promotes a standard of good conduct coupled with an overarching call for people to love one another. Pervasive Christian love is nothing too deep or terribly spiritual, just an ideal model for how to live a good life. The reason this exterior simplified view of Christianity so widely believed is the post-Easter Jesus fabrication of the sin-based theology that Christ himself did not teach.

Stated most simply, this fabricated version of Christianity

says that if you don't repent of your sins then you won't go to a place called "Heaven" after you die. But if you do repent of your sins then your entry to this afterlife is assured. And in many cases the concept of "original sin" gets added, ensuring that you get off to a bad start in life by being born a sinner because of what Adam and Eve did. Saint Augustine has a lot to answer for in this aspect of the post-Easter Jesus invention.

I've discussed elsewhere that this sin-based theology is derived partly from an appalling error in translating the Greek word *metanoia* as "repent:" this precipitated a failure to grasp what Christ was teaching when he spoke of "Heaven within." This is not to say that Christ didn't teach that to sin was wrong or that you shouldn't repent your sins. However, what constitutes "sin" in Christ's teachings? At one extreme, the answer is anything you do that is your will rather than God's will. This is an accurate statement, but hardly helpful for most people since aligning your will with God's will is, as Christ taught, the narrow door through which few pass.

On a more granular level, it is not obeying the ten commandments, or not obeying the new commandment to love God and to "Love your neighbor as yourself" (Matt 12:31). This second part of Christ's new commandment is actually the same as his teaching to align your will with God's will. There is a tendency to add in words that are not there in Christ's teaching: to read it as if it says "Love your neighbor as you would love yourself" or "Love your neighbor as you would have them love you"—which is not what it says.

Rather, it is a commandment that is really a deep teaching of interdependence. A teaching of non-duality that says the other is you, and you are the other. It is a call to love others being aware that they *are* your "self." Your true self is not separate from lots of other selves, but rather is a unity. And this is the "Love" that he teaches that God "is"—hence to love another recognizing that they are your self is to align your will with God's will and become a Son/Daughter of God.

But this takes us full circle, since to say that sin is failure to align your will with God's will is no more useful than to say that sin is a failure to appreciate the non-duality inherent in loving all others with the recognition that they are you. When asked most people would say that their concept of "sin" goes beyond failing to adhere to the ten commandments or failing to adhere to the commandment to love their neighbor.

Yet, Christ's teachings do not give much further granularity as to what constitutes right action, right conduct, right speech, right thought, and so on. Instead, the Church has tended to guide people toward priests to tell them what is or is not a sin, thus keeping mainstream church and the priesthood in control of the definition of "sin." This is not helpful to followers of The Way since by our nature we are not drawn to formalized religion with strict hierarchies where clerics tell us what to do and what not to do, where male-based language dominates, or where the purpose of the hierarchy is, or appears to be, to control church members or to be driven by financial gain.

The following vows or commitments assist in our clarifying the ethical guidelines we adhere to as followers of The Way. Some bear a resemblance to the Ten Commandments, but with added nuance and subtlety:[7]

I vow to not kill, but rather to encourage and cultivate life.

I vow not to take what is not freely given to me, but rather to cultivate and encourage generosity.

I vow not to misuse sexuality and instead to remain faithful in relationships.

I vow not to lie or speak dishonestly, but rather to promote truthful communication.

I vow not to become intoxicated but rather to polish clarity and dispel delusions.

I vow not to slander others, but rather to encourage respectful speech.

I vow not to praise myself above others, rather to promote modesty and lift others up where appropriate.

I vow not to be greedy, either with wealth and material things, but also with understanding and teachings.

I vow not to harbor ill-will or anger, but rather promote equanimity, harmony and selfless kindness.

I vow to be conscious of what I consume, the way in which it was produced, and what harm might result from my consuming it. I vow to bring awareness.

This of course isn't an attempt at an exhaustive list of vows one might consider adhering to. But it is a good core to carry with one as a key part of your walking on The Way. In this phase we do a deep dive into our ethical behavior and an honest introspection of our less than perfect behavior. This process does not work, though, unless you are entirely honest with yourself.

Having identified areas of your life that could use some improvement (remember Suzuki "*You are perfect as you are, but you could use some improvements*"), the next step is atonement. This word, often equated with "repentance," literally translates to "at-one-ment" which is important to us on The Way, since this is precisely our goal. It has at least two meanings: to be at one with this whole big mess we call our lives, and to be at one with God in the sense of constantly vowing to bring our will into line with God's will. Helping us on this journey is a short verse of atonement that we shall be using:

> *All evil thoughts and actions by me since of old,*
> *because of my beginningless greed, anger, and ignorance,*
> *born of my body, mouth and thought,*
> *now I atone for it all.*

Now you will note some unusual language here. The use of "since of old" and "beginningless ..." this is because as we follow this path of The Way we come to realize that we are all connected. We "inter-are" as Thich Nhat Hanh says.[8] A crucial part of this station is the appreciation that you are not an island, you are not a separate "thing" in a world of separate "things." In assessing your own issues, you come to find that they are both yours and not yours. That what others do is what you do since there is no "you" and "them"—that is dualistic thinking conning you into a false belief that you are separate and distinct from the universe, from God.

Thus, we bring forward into this phase what we developed in the first phase: the "by me" in the first line above should constantly have you harking back to "Who am I?" or in this case "What does me mean here?" And this greed, anger, ignorance, is it "mine" or is it shared with all sentient beings? All 'children of God' (to borrow Christ's phrase)? If my brother or sister (and here we recall who Christ says your brother and sister are) act badly or speak badly, there is no "they" who are wrong and no "I" who is right. Certainly, there are actions, words, thoughts that I am in direct control of, but we are not separate from others. What any one of us does, thinks, says, is what we all do, think, say.

Station 4: *Metanoia*

In this phase you will double-down on cultivating a "beginner's mind" or "don't know mind:" a state of perceiving, acting and being arising from before thought. This is God's mind, complete beginner's mind, not the "I know it all" mind of the typical human being. This is also known as *shoshin* in the Japanese Zen tradition; it refers to having an attitude of eagerness, openness, and a lack of preconceptions. As simple as this might sound, it can be remarkably difficult to cultivate this beginner's mind, this "don't know mind."

In this phase one will be focused on meditation (Centering Prayer or *Kenosis*, or what other practice works for you). One will also be focused on reading deeply but selectively, and at all times asking yourself "What is this?" and then immediately answering to yourself "Don't know." You will also continue to ask yourself "Who am I?" since this reflection will never be exhausted while you follow this path of The Way.

This phase concludes when you have experienced at least one instance of *metanoia* (the "Ah ha!" moment or glimpse of awakening), or when your teacher or mentor believes you are ready.

Station 5: Oneness

You've had a moment of awakening to oneness, and whether by direct ongoing experience or by intellect, you now grasp that you are one with everything, one with God. Your true self, the Self with a capital S, is infinite and not subject to life and death. The true you, having glimpsed Heaven within, knows you have been around since beginningless time. Everyone who has ever existed, everyone who will ever exist, are all present in this moment.

It is a deep, profound realization, but one that can be seductive and deceptive. It is not unusual for those who experience this astounding awareness of oneness to believe "That's it! I've done it! I've overcome the ego and become one with God!" Or more simply, "I've experienced oneness, so that's the end of this spiritual path. I'm home." Of course, nothing could be further from the truth.

Rather, this is the station where you real work begins. This station is also known as the *Heart of the Secret* because in a sense it is the heart of what we seek in discovering Heaven within and entering what Christ called "The Kingdom." So, here you are, born again of water and the Spirit (God the Father and God the Mother, your spiritual parents). Now is the time to learn what it is to live this new life, reincarnated as you are, in your spiritual rebirth, in the body of a human being.

If you think you overcame the ego, destroyed the ego, fully entered non-dual perception and overcome all dualistic perception, then you have indeed deluded yourself. What then do you find as you explore this new "you" (which is absolutely no different from the old you), this spiritually reborn "you?" The danger here is becoming addicted to this oneness, addicted to the idea of "being pure spirit."

One thing you may discover in this phase is what we call Freedom. But this isn't freedom as you usually think of it, it is a more dangerous, very seductive freedom. A freedom that feels God-like: "There's nothing I can't do now that I am spiritually reborn, awake in God."

Station 6: The Seduction of Freedom

This is the phase that Christ experienced in the desert for 40 days following his awakening at his baptism by John the Baptist. The description of what Christ allegedly experienced in that time in the desert is an almost perfect example of what Zen Master Seung Sahn called "270" on his compass, and what we call "300" on our Circle of The Way.

Here you have broken through your addiction to oneness, to the idea of no form (just being spirit) and realize the deep sense of freedom that will come from this breakthrough. The ego already jumped in during station 5: "You're so great! Very few people have a true *metanoia* experience! You've achieved spiritual greatness!" Now, the ego enters even more assiduously, one last gasp, one final attempt to regain control of your mind, your being.

In the Gospels, the so-called temptation of Christ is the narrative in all three synoptic Gospels detailing his experience in the desert of 40-days after his baptism by John. The language used is that of Satan (remember, that is *natas*, life, backwards) tempting him while Christ was fasting and meditating on the experience of awakening he had had—his major *metanoia* moment as he rose from the water.

In these temptations Christ is encouraged to use his new powers to turn stones into bread. Then he is encouraged to jump from the highest point of the temple and show that he will land below unhurt. Next, he is taken to the highest nearby mountain and told that all this that you can see will be yours if you would just worship "me" (Satan) and not God.

These are a near perfect description of the kind of experiences someone will experience in this station 6. Replace the word "Satan" with "ego" and it becomes somewhat clearer what is happening here. Although we talk of this station as being associated with freedom, another word for it is power. And power is seductive: power corrupts, and absolute power corrupts absolutely, as the saying goes. And there is no power greater than that of the divine ground of your being.

In this phase people have reported experiencing what they can only describe as 'powers' such as the ability to foresee the future, the ability to heal others, and other supernatural abilities. Still others have reported a sense of having extraordinary power, but not of experiencing any actual evidence of it. The sensation of it is sometimes all it takes for the ego to convince you that you are some kind of God. As your realization of your True Self, your Christ-nature, is coming close the ego tries all it can in one last desperate attempt to prevent that.

This can be particularly true if you appear to others as what they describe as "charismatic," the kind of personality that having experienced *metanoia* then finds people are very drawn to them. And that people having been drawn to them tend to do whatever the 'master' (teacher, guru, etc.) suggests they do. That can be a very seductive sensation to have that degree of power over others.

Station 7: the station of no station, The Absolute, Unity

This is home, and it is exactly where you started: appropriately depicted as 360 on the circle, exactly where zero is and the point of your departure on this path of The Way. Here is the mature and full integration of the infinite (the absolute) and the finite (the relative). The final answer to the question "Who am I?" in all its nuances and levels of truth.

This is where you rest in the mind of God, living the reality of, "Thy will not my will be done." This is the station of "just like this" nothing is other than just as it is. Here is the awareness of being fully human and fully divine, of what it means to be both a Son of Man (the term the Jews used for a human being) and a Son of God (of Daughter of Man/Daughter of God). This is the realm of nonattachment thinking, this is the realm of non-dualism with full and deep awareness of dualism, too.

It is also the phase of which even this commentary is already too much said since it is the realm best conveyed in silence. But it is not a station you have arrived at. It is not a final phase you have "achieved." You are exactly where you have always been, one with God. Fully human and fully divine. Home.

Some final thoughts on putting it all into practice in everyday life...

Find a Teacher or Mentor

Find a teacher or mentor to walk this journey with you, one who fully understands this path of The Way described in this book. Also seek out a local group if you possibly can where you can regularly practice either Centering Prayer or *Kenosis* and become part of a like-minded community of seekers on The Way. Visit the website for this book (www.christwaybuddhaway.org or christbuddha.org) for help in this.

Seek Liminal Space(s)

In the literature the term *liminal space* is used in various ways, but here I am talking about the hard to describe sense that there are places or circumstances where the veils between us and unity with God are thinner. For some this can be when we walk in the woods, spend time in nature, or perhaps when they climb a mountain. I don't think it is a coincidence that there is repeated reference to Christ retreating to his solitary place, or ascending a nearby mountain to pray.

I invite you to find your liminal space: that place where you feel the spiritual air is rarified, the veils are thinner or fewer, a place where there is a greater sense of a palpable presence.

---

[1] Keating, Thomas (1994) *Intimacy with God*. Crossroad Publishing: NY. p 64

[2] There are many such apps, but one I have found good is *Insight Timer*.

[3] But a note of caution here: what will bring about a *metanoia* experience for someone is unpredictable. Some may follow a strict practice for many years and then it is an off-hand comment by a co-worker, or an inane tagline for a product advertisement, something random, that triggers the "ah ha!" that is *metanoia*. Teachers, including Christ, can only suggest a series of practices, The Way, that have been shown to be more likely than not to help someone experience *metanoia*.

[4] Counting breaths uses words. Don't get hung up on this, since to count breaths is the training wheels of this practice. After a while you will not need to do this.

[5] Brother Lawrence, *The Practice of the Presence of God: with Christian Meditation Practice Guide by Tim Langdell*. StillCenter Publications: Pasadena (1692; 2020, updated, modern language version).

[6] Paul uses this term "in Christ" 170 times in his letters, although he never clarifies what he means by it. Just as he uses the term "Christ Jesus" whereas the Gospel writers tend to use "Jesus Christ."

[7] These vows draw on various religious groups and Zen centers, all of which are hereby acknowledged, with gratitude.

[8] Thich Nhat Hanh, *Interbeing, 4th Edition: The 14 Mindfulness Trainings of Engaged Buddhism* (reprint edition) Parallax Press, 2020.

Appendix 1

What Jesus Actually Said and Did

It is difficult to determine precisely who Jesus was, what he did and exactly what he did or did not say. Biblical writers have passed down to us a mishmash of "fact," rumor, story, myth and logical (and illogical) extrapolation and interpolation—and the word *fact* is in quotes to indicate that little of what he said and did can be definitively stated as fact in the modern sense of the term. This problem was exacerbated by those compiling the canonical version of the New Testament using arbitrary reasons for what was included, what excluded, and what order texts should be in.

Many understandably assume that the New Testament is in chronological order. But that is not the case: it is in a theological order—the order those who put it together thought made the best sense theologically. For instance, this is why the Gospel of Matthew comes first whereas it was not the earliest of the Gospels.

The earliest Gospel to be written is Mark dating from around 65-75 C.E. Next chronologically comes the Gospels of Matthew and Luke some decades later, both probably written around 80-90 C.E. (although some scholars place both of these Gospels potentially as late as 110 C.E.). Finally, the Gospel written last was that of John, most likely written around 100 C.E., or possibly later.

The reason the Gospel of Mark is not placed first in the New Testament is because those who invented the canon found Mark to be dissatisfying both as a historical record of

Jesus, and from a theological perspective. Mark lacks any record of the Virgin Birth and doesn't mention the resurrection or subsequent appearances of the risen Christ to various people. For this reason, they placed Matthew first as being a more satisfying rendition of the Christ story.

However, there is a sizable problem with this: when we compare the Gospels of Matthew and Luke to Mark, we find that both of them were clearly partly copied from Mark, frequently almost word for word. From this we can infer that the tradition of the earliest Christian church from Jesus' death around 30 C.E. to around 65 C.E. when Mark is written was not based on a theology of Christ being born of a virgin or that he rose bodily and was seen by various people post-Crucifixion before being taken up "into Heaven."

This bears repeating: given the average life expectancy of someone living in first century Palestine was around 38 years, this means that for essentially one entire generation after Jesus' death the early Christian church did not believe he was born of a virgin or that Jesus rose bodily or was seen by various people after rising from the dead. This is all, then, a fiction created some time later toward the end of the first century C.E. and added into the canonical texts as late as the second century or early third century.

It is unfortunate that so many over the centuries have considered Mark to be deficient or unsatisfying. On the contrary, as the oldest of the Gospels, it is the one we need to rely on the most for details about Christ and his teachings. The reason many find Mark so unsatisfactory is because they have accepted so thoroughly the later added fictions about Jesus' birth and resurrection, that they have trouble accepting the more authentic Gospel, simply because it lacks all this invented theology.

Part of the dissatisfaction with Mark is that some say it lacks a 'proper' beginning or ending. However, it does have a perfectly good start and finish, it just isn't the start and finish followers of the later version of Christianity wanted to see. The writer of Mark starts by talking about John the Baptist, who as we have seen in this book is crucial to Christ's spiritual awakening. John the Baptist is thus the appropriate and ideal place for the Gospel to commence. The ending is strange to some, but it really isn't that odd when seen in the context of Markian theology.

Scholars generally agree that the ending of Mark that has made its way into the accepted canon for most branches of Christianity, that is Mark 16:9-20, is a complete fiction added at a later date. While there is no consensus as to when this extended ended was written, it is widely believed to have been created in the early second century and added to Mark some time toward the end of the second century.

In all the earliest copies of the Gospel of Mark, the Gospel ends at chapter 16 verse 8. The original ending that so many find puzzling or unsatisfying is thus this:

> [4] *But when they looked up, they saw that the stone,*
> *which was very large, had been rolled away.* [5] *As they*
> *entered the tomb, they saw a young man dressed in a white*
> *robe sitting on the right side, and they were alarmed.*
>
> [6] *"Don't be alarmed," he said. "You are looking for Jesus*
> *the Nazarene, who was crucified. He has [been raised]! He is*
> *not here. See the place where they laid him.* [7] *But go, tell his*
> *disciples and Peter, 'He is going ahead of you into Galilee.*
> *There you will see him, just as he told you.'"*

> [8] *Trembling and bewildered, the women went out and fled from the tomb. They said nothing to anyone, because they were afraid.*

I have altered the wording slightly from the NIV translation, for good reason: the NIV got it wrong here. The word passive verb form *ēgerthē* used by Mark translates as "he was raised" rather than "he is risen."

This wording in the final chapter of Mark is foreshadowed in the fourteenth chapter (14:27):

> [27] *"You will all fall away," Jesus told them, "for it is written:*
> *"'I will strike the shepherd,*
> *and the sheep will be scattered.'*
> [28] *But after I have [been raised], I will go ahead of you into Galilee."*
> [29] *Peter declared, "Even if all fall away, I will not."*
> [30] *"Truly I tell you," Jesus answered, "today—yes, tonight—before the rooster crows twice you yourself will disown me three times."*
> [31] *But Peter insisted emphatically, "Even if I have to die with you, I will never disown you." And all the others said the same.*

Two parts of this section jump out: first, Mark foreshadows that after he is killed Jesus will be "raised up" and will "go ahead of [the disciples] into Galilee." Noting this, the original conclusion of Mark is simply book-ending this point. He has Mary Magdalene and Salome getting confirmation from the stranger (a young man, note, not an angel) that Jesus has been "raised up" and gone ahead of the disciples into Galilee.

The other point worth noting in the chapter 14 section is that it has Peter saying he won't abandon Jesus *"even if I have to die with you"* (Mt 26:35). These are not the words of someone who thinks what he was just told is that after being killed Jesus was saying he would rise bodily, come back to life, and meet Peter in Galilee. If you believe you have just been told your teacher says he will come back to life if he is killed, then you don't say you'll be happy to die with him.

We get another clue about the Markian theology regarding death and resurrection from the twelfth chapter (12:18-27) where the Sadducees are grilling Jesus on which of a woman's several husbands she would be married to after the resurrection. Essentially, the writer of Mark has Jesus respond that the Sadducees are wrong if they think there is bodily resurrection. Rather, Jesus says, when the dead are raised they are more like angels in Heaven (not bodily on earth).

Mark then has Jesus chide the Sadducees by saying that all this nonsense about the dead rising goes against Old Testament teaching. He ends by saying to them essentially they need to stop talking about the dead or the dead rising, and rather focus on the fact God is the God of the living. If you think people are bodily resurrected, then "*You are badly mistaken!*" Jesus concludes.

Again, while the Sadducees believed in bodily resurrection, core Jewish tradition did not then (as it generally does not now) hold that there is an afterlife, a Heaven you go to after you die. For Jesus, according to Mark, this raising up is in the here and now with Heaven (where God resides) being in the here and now, too.

Then we have the brain-teaser at the end of the original Mark text where the scribe reports that after this young man in white robes told them Jesus had been "raised up" and tells

Mary and Salome to go tell Peter and the disciples to meet up with Jesus in Galilee, the scribe then tells us they didn't do as instructed. Instead they told no one. Obviously, if Mary and Salome told no one what happened at the tomb that morning, then no one could know about it not even the writer of Mark.

This literary device of stating "*they said nothing to anyone*" is a common one of that time when a scribe wishes to convey his own interpretation of what took place—*his* interpretation, *his* theology. To Mark—and as far as we can tell from this earliest testimony of what was said, to Jesus—the concept of someone rising bodily from the dead was an aberration of the Jewish teachings believed only by the likes of the Sadducees.

For Mark, and we must assume for Jesus too, after death there is a merging with God, a raising up into Heaven which is here and now ("Heaven within"). We shall never know precisely what the writer of Mark meant when he both had Jesus prophesize that he after being "raised up" (into Heaven) by God, would go out into Galilee ahead of the disciples and then have the young man in the tomb say it, too. Most likely, the writer of Mark is referring to Christ's teachings being spread into Galilee ahead of the disciples returning there after Passover. Christ as the eternal Word, *Logos*.

We have some support for this since a number of scholars believe the scribe of Mark was writing for an audience in Galilee. If so, then the reference to Galilee in both chapter 14 and the ending in chapter 16 make sense, whether the Christ, raised up in Heaven in the here and now, went out into Galilee ahead of the disciples, or whether it was a metaphorical reference to Christ's teachings being out in Galilee ahead of the disciples returning to teach there.

And remember in this teaching everyone who has ever lived is still here in this moment: not bodily, but Christ's true self, which is the same as your true self, is eternal and not subject to life and death. To come back to life bodily thus made no sense in Christ's teachings; similarly, Christ *was* still there in Galilee, *is* still there (here), now.

What is also notably missing in Mark is any clear statement that Jesus was the Messiah. In fact, it is a theme of Mark that whenever Jesus is asked if he is the Messiah he responds with a phrase like "*Who do you say I am?*" (Mark 8:29) thus dodging the question. In 1901, William Wrede named this the "Messianic secret," referring to Jesus' secrecy about whether or not he was the Messiah. That said, naming it the Messianic secret stems from the assumption that he *was* the Messiah. Another interpretation was that Jesus in this earliest record was denying that this was the correct title for him.

We have further evidence of the Gospels being amended after Jesus' death and some of the evidence has been staring us in the face, going unnoticed. For instance, in Matthew:

> *Do not suppose that I have come to bring peace to the earth. I did not come to bring peace, but a sword. 35For I have come to turn*
>
> *" 'a man against his father,*
> *a daughter against her mother,*
> *a daughter-in-law against her mother-in-law—*
> *36a man's enemies will be the members of his own household.'*
>
> *37"Anyone who loves their father or mother more than me is not worthy of me; anyone who loves their son or daughter more than me is not worthy of me. 38Whoever does not take up their cross and follow me is not worthy of*

me. [39]Whoever finds their life will lose it, and whoever loses their life for my sake will find it. (Mt 10:34-39)

For many, this does not sound like the peace-loving Jesus we had come to know through the rest of Christ's teachings. But was this actually said by Jesus? Clearly it was not. Look at this section that many have read and heard spoken so many times, but perhaps have not noticed the obvious problem:

"take up their ***cross*** *and follow me"*

The cross did not become a Christian symbol until *after* Jesus' death, therefore this passage in Matthew must have been added after the crucifixion and could not have been said by Jesus. The cross became a symbol when those writing after Jesus' death conveyed the scene of Christ carrying his cross to the place of crucifixion. Over the years, this passage in Matthew has received relatively little coverage, partly because it sounds so unlike the rest of Christ's teachings, partly because it is a difficult teaching to understand, and partly because scholars and clergy alike have struggled with how to explain the mention of a cross.

Some have tried over the centuries to explain the mention of the cross by saying it was perhaps well known as a symbol of death and oppression under Roman rule. Still others have suggested that part of the story is missing and that when Christ said this someone present asked him what he meant by taking up his or her cross, and he explained it to them. Still others have argued that this came shortly after Jesus foretold of his pending death, but then hastily add there is no evidence he mentioned the cross as the method.

In fact, none of these explanations work since even if they

were true, they still wouldn't make sense of Jesus' use of the word cross when its symbolism wasn't established until after his death. The cross being a method of killing criminals under Roman rule did not make it a symbol that could be used in the sense Jesus is purported to have used it here. It would rather like someone now saying "take up their lethal injection and follow me" or "take up their noose and follow me" when no symbolism in the context of a spiritual teaching had been set up for a lethal injection or a noose. Employing Occam's razor (where there are competing explanations, the simpler should be preferred), the mention of the cross means this was added after Jesus' death and therefore this was not said by Christ.

Was any part of it said by Christ? I believe it was—another difficult teaching by Christ was where his mother and brothers were stuck at the edge of the crowd trying to get to him. Once again, Christ taught that everyone is his mother, brother, and sister. It was a teaching on the absolute equality in the Realm of Heaven. The root of this passage in Matthew is thus probably a variation on the same teaching. But whoever rewrote this teaching did so from the perspective of the post-Easter reinterpretation of Christ's message. They added more violent language, and more extreme statements about needing to give up family to follow him, perhaps attempting to make sense of a difficult teaching on equality. However, the author rewriting the passage got it wrong since its simply not credible that these words could have been spoken by Jesus.

Jesus was a real historical person

Of course, we can be certain that Jesus was a real historical figure. I say this since there have been those who have tried to argue that he was a fiction, one based partly on other historical figures such as the Buddha or certain Greek mythological figures. But we have several written confirmations of both Jesus and of his brother James. For instance, we have the Roman historians Tacitus and Josephus who both wrote about Jesus. In his *Antiquities*, Josephus writes about the death of James and clearly labels him as "the brother of Jesus who was called Christ." Now, the last part of that—where Jesus is confirmed to be Christ—is suspected to have been added at a later date by a Christian writer. But even if we omit these last few words, there is clear confirmation that both James and Jesus were real historical figures (since no one has suggested this part of what Josephus wrote was not genuine).

Josephus was a Roman Jewish historian who wrote in the last first century (he lived from about 37-100 C.E.). Tacitus lived from around 56-120 C.E. and was a Roman historian. He records the plight of a group of people known as Christians and mentions they take their name from one known as "the Christ" who lived during the reign of Tiberius and was executed by the Procurator Pontius Pilate. In addition, we have other early Church writings that confirm Jesus and James were actual historical figures, and we have some evidence that various disciples were real (including Thomas who is recorded as a disseminator of Christianity in India).

As we have also seen in this book, many of the descriptions of the post-Easter Jesus are drawn from the writings of Philo and other sources in the Middle East so as to pedestalize Jesus. But this isn't evidence of Jesus as fictional, rather it points to the fact that the Jesus his followers knew—the pre-Easter Jesus—was pedestalized after his death. Thus, the fact fantastical attributes became associated with him is understandable and does not mean that he himself was a fictional figure. Indeed, it seems certain he was a wise sage and teacher, in the first century Jewish Wisdom Tradition.

This all having been said, we should focus primarily on Christ's teachings, the ones that we can be reasonably certain he actually taught.

If you are interested in exploring this topic further then I commend to you the writings of the *Jesus Seminar* such as Robert Funk's *The Five Gospels* and the books written by Marcus Borg and John Dominic Crossan, among others.

Appendix 2

The Historical Jesus and Siddhartha Gautama

There are a number of parallels between the life of Siddhartha Gautama, known as Buddha, and Jesus of Nazareth, known as Christ:

Buddha	Christ
Miraculous pregnancy	Miraculous pregnancy*
Mother named Maya	Mother named Mary
Said to be a child prodigy	Said to be a child prodigy
Fasted for forty days	Fasted for forty days
Tempted by but overcame evil	Tempted by but overcame evil
Began his ministry at 30-35	Began his ministry at 30-33
Known for having disciples	Known for having disciples
Taught using parables	Taught using parables **
Performed miracles	Performed miracles ***
Cured blindness	Cured blindness
Walked on water	Walked on water
Rebelled against establishment	Rebelled against establishment
Dispatched disciples shortly before death	Dispatched disciples shortly before death

* As for Buddha, it is written that his mother Maya dreamed that four archangels carried her to a mountain where she was bathed and dressed by royalty. The Great Being entered her body from her side to impregnate her. Mary, mother of Christ,

was said to have been a virgin impregnated by God after being visited by an angel.

** Not only did Christ teach in parables, but many of his parables and sayings are either identical to or similar to those attributed to Buddha five hundred years earlier.

*** Many of the miracles Christ is reported to have performed were the same as those Buddha reportedly did, too (including curing blindness, bring the dead back to life and walking on water).

~*~

Of course, we should exercise caution in reading any list like this. Certainly, we shouldn't jump to the conclusion that because of the similarities Jesus was not a real historical figure, but rather one invented based on the life of Buddha and other figures. Indeed, we have good evidence from historical texts that he did live in Palestine at the time in question, did have a brother named James who ran the Church in Jerusalem after Jesus died, and who was referred to as "the Christ." Rather, what we are seeing is undoubtedly the common tendency for great teachers to be pedestalized after their death.

It's as if those who write about such great teachers cannot accept that in a real sense they were just ordinary people, like us. Instead, they need to have been special in some way that is beyond the reach of ordinary human beings. So, with Buddha not only do we have the stories about his birth, etc., but also a healthy debate surrounding whether he was a prince, born to a king and queen. Many argue that while it would appear he was born into a fairly wealthy family highly placed in the Shakya clan, perhaps his father was even the head of a clan, there is little evidence his parents were in the aristocracy as legend suggests, or a king and queen, at least not in the Western sense.

ABOUT THE AUTHOR

Born in Oxford, England, Tim Langdell is both a Zen Priest and Master Zen Teacher in the Korean and Vietnamese traditions and has over 40 years of practice in the Soto Zen tradition. Tim is also an ordained Christian Priest in the Independent Catholic Church (in communion with the Episcopal Church) and member of a Thomasine Order. He became passionate about Zen and Mystical Christianity at age 19, when he had what he would now describe as a mystical experience, or *kensho*. He became a life-professed member of the Anglican *Third Order of St. Francis* around that time, too.

Tim has lived in Pasadena, California since around 1990, while spending time in his beloved Oxford whenever he can. Tim gained his MDiv at Claremont School of Theology where he also studied at Bloy House Episcopal Seminary. He also holds a PhD in clinical psychology from University College, London, an MA in Educational and Clinical Child Psychology from Nottingham University, and a BS (known in the UK as a BSc) in Physics and Psychology from Leicester University.

Tim is the Abbot and Guiding Teacher at the Pasadena Zen Center (known as StillCenter), and he is Rector of The Church of the Beloved Disciple, too. He is ordained and trained as a Zen teacher in the *Five Mountain Zen Order*, where his ordinations are in the Korean and Vietnamese Zen traditions. His teacher in FMZO is the Venerable Wonji Dharma (Paul Lynch). Tim has over 40 years of practice in the Japanese Soto Zen tradition, mainly through association with the Zen Center of Los Angeles where he trained under Taizan Maezumi,

Bernie Glassman and Egyoku Nakao. Tim received Japanese Soto Zen Priest training from Sensei Gyokei Yokoyama. He was also trained as a Buddhist Chaplain at Upaya Zen Center, under Roshi Joan Halifax, with training by Bernie Glassman, Alan Senauke, Kaz Tanahashi, Frank Ostaseski, and others. Tim is a Board-Certified Chaplain, having gained certification with the Association for Professional Chaplains. He is ordained in the independent Catholic movement, originally through the American Catholic Church (established 1915), and his lineage there includes ordination with the Philippine Independent Church which is in full communion with the Episcopal Church. He is a fully ordained Priest in the Ecumenical Catholic Church which is the only independent Catholic group to be a member of the National Council of Churches.

Tim is by training and by passion, a chaplain, a psychologist, an astrophysicist, a computer scientist, an author, and a musician (blues guitar and Middle Eastern oud). He currently serves as the staff chaplain at a hospice in the Los Angeles area of Southern California. He is an author of books on various topics from how to design and code computer games, to dealing with Alzheimer's, to coping with vision loss, as well as books on Zen, Christian meditation and other spiritual topics. He has also written a fantasy novel in the style of Douglas Adams and intends to write more fiction.

He is married to his wife Cheri, an English Professor, has two children, several grandchildren, two cats and a parrot. He and his wife live in Pasadena, California.

www.timlangdell.com
www.stillcenter.org
www.christbuddha.org
www.christwaybuddhaway.com
www.oxbridgepublications.com
and Tim's non-profit, www.kids-rights.org

Printed in Great Britain
by Amazon

67673166R00183